THE MACMILLAN GOVERNMENT AND EUROPE

The Macmillan Government and Europe

A Study in the Process of Policy Development

Jacqueline Tratt

First published in Great Britain 1996 by
MACMILLAN PRESS LTD
Houndmills, Basingstoke, Hampshire RG21 6XS
and London
Companies and representatives
throughout the world

A catalogue record for this book is available
from the British Library.

ISBN 0–333–66238–5

First published in the United States of America 1996 by
ST. MARTIN'S PRESS, INC.,
Scholarly and Reference Division,
175 Fifth Avenue,
New York, N.Y. 10010

ISBN 0–312–16369–X

Library of Congress Cataloging-in-Publication Data
Tratt, Jacqueline, 1946–
The Macmillan government and Europe : a study in the process of
policy development / Jacqueline Tratt.
p.   cm.
Includes bibliographical references and index.
ISBN 0–312–16369–X (cloth)
1. Macmillan, Harold, 1894–1986.   2. Great Britain—Politics and
government—1945–1964.   3. Great Britain—Foreign relations—Europe.
4. Europe—Foreign relations—Great Britain.   5. Great Britain-
-Foreign relations—1945–   I. Title.
DA566.9.M33T73   1996
327.4104—dc20   96–23688
                                                                                    CIP

10   9   8   7   6   5   4   3   2   1
05   04   03   02   01   00   99   98   97   96

Printed in Great Britain by
The Ipswich Book Company Ltd
Ipswich, Suffolk

In politics, all situations are exceptional situations; those who write about them at the time rarely understand their complexity; those who handle them are, because human, fallible and, because political animals, neither free nor unfettered in their choice of action.

(L.C.B. Seaman, *Victorian England*, 1973)

Contents

Preface

At a time when the political process in Britain has come under critical scrutiny, it is tempting to hark back to an age of political rectitude and stability – when policies were formulated through recourse to the proper machinery of government; when ideas were thrashed out in cabinet and when the power of decision rested, ultimately, with the people. There never was such a time, and if there was, the Macmillan premiership was not it.

This is a study of democratic government under pressure. Then, as now, it was the issue of Britain's relationship with Europe that provided a major source of frustration, disillusion, conflict and compromise. Then, as now, a Conservative government was confronted with a challenge that had the potential for splitting not only the cabinet but also the party itself.

Although there have been several studies relating to how the Macmillan government handled the European issue, none has addressed the question from the perspective of the key players themselves. Because this work relies heavily upon recently released documents, together with interviews with some of the officials involved, it offers a new way of looking at the machinery of government as well as pointing up some inevitable flaws of an essentially unplanned democratic system.

This work adds to our knowledge in two important ways. First, it highlights the tendency for error among able officials and politicians faced with an apparently imponderable dilemma. Secondly, it illustrates their proneness to machination and dissimulation, which arises, it transpires, not out of an innate tendency to perfidy or dishonesty but out of the intractable contradiction between the democratic process and the obligation on democratic governments to work towards (their interpretation of) the long-term national good – even while incurring short-term political and economic costs.

The work differs from previous studies in respect of both sources and method. With regard to *sources*, the wealth of new material, recently made available to readers at the Public Record Office, provides valuable insight. It is only through careful scrutiny of government papers that the significance of the role of officials in the development of policy can be properly assessed. This resource is supplemented by interviews with (retired) government officials. With regard to method, my concern throughout is not with *why* the change of direction came about, but with *how* it was brought to fruition.

The British initiative announced by Harold Macmillan on 31 July 1961 sprang overwhelmingly from relationships and interactions in the external international environment. But that is not to say that the development of policy was not based firmly upon domestic considerations. It is important to make the distinction here between the development of policy as a response to domestic *demand* and the development of policy judged to be in the national *interest*. In the former, policy decisions are coloured by the nature of the demand – and reflect the influence of corporatist, pressure group and party activity – whereas in the latter, the government itself determines, within the constraints of external forces and domestic political considerations, what is and what is not in keeping with the national interest. This fine, but important, distinction is at the heart of this research because once it is established that government ministers and officials were acting, for the most part, independently of the domestic constituency, questions arise with regard to how policy was developed and how this policy development was presented to parliament and the people.

I opted for a chronological account partly because the events are bewildering enough in their own right without attempting to describe them through complicated theoretical constructs. More importantly, though, because I have relied heavily upon day-to-day documentation, the work shows policy *as it evolved*. In this respect it shows how ideas were developed or discarded by politicians and officials who were working largely in the dark, without the benefit of hindsight, which allows historians to assess their actions in the light of later developments.

Acknowledgements

Thanks are due to the staff of the PRO at Kew who provided (even with 'the builders in') an environment of tranquillity and comfort which made my work there a pleasure. I am also grateful to the staff of Sussex University Library, to the Keeper of Western Manuscripts at the Bodleian Library, Oxford, and to Henry Gillet at the Bank of England Archive for their kindness and assistance. I would like to acknowledge the prompt assistance of the Cabinet Office (Historical and Records Section) and the FO Historical Branch (Library and Records Department), who furnished me with information that was not available to readers at the PRO.

Particular thanks must go to those who allowed me to interview them. They all showed the utmost patience in dealing with my questions and were, without exception, courteous, hospitable and helpful. It remains a matter of great regret that I was unable to obtain an interview with Sir Edward Heath or Sir Frederick Bishop. For their part, the official documentation together with the recollections of their colleagues will have to suffice.

I am grateful to Dick Roberts whose constructive criticism resulted in some important additions to the text. My special thanks go to Professor Keith Middlemas, whose comments and suggestions have been invaluable. Finally, I am indebted to my husband and daughters for their support and encouragement, to my mother for her boundless confidence and to Melissa KilBride for making time – sometimes at an unspeakable hour – for proof-reading. Any omissions or errors are, of course, my own.

List of Abbreviations

BOT   Board of Trade
CO   Colonial Office
CRE   Commercial Relations and Exports
             Department (Board of Trade)
CRO   Commonwealth Relations Office
ECSC   European Coal and Steel Community
EDC   European Defence Community
EEC   European Economic Community
EFTA   European Free Trade Association
EMA   European Monetary Agreement
EPU   European Payments Union
EQ   Economic Questions
FBI   Federation of British Industry
FO   Foreign Office
FTA   Free Trade Area
GATT   General Agreement on Tariffs and Trade
MAG   Ministry of Agriculture, Fisheries and Food
mfn   Most favoured nation
NATO   North Atlantic Treaty Organization
NFU   National Farmers Union
OEEC   Organization for European Economic
             Co-operation
TUC   Trades Union Congress
WEU   Western European Union
WO   Western Organizations Department (Foreign
             Office)

Introduction

This work is concerned with the process of decision-making during a period that marked the final painful stages of what was widely perceived as Britain's transition from a world power to a European nation. What, in the end, proved to be the deciding factor with regard to Britain's first application to join the EEC has always been keenly debated. Coral Bell in *Europe Without Britain* (1963) argues that it was all about strategy or, more correctly, 'diplomacy'. This view is supported by Alan Sked and Chris Cook in *Post-War Britain* (1984). They assert that the economic argument was used to 'camouflage' the underlying political motives. And Edward Heath maintains in *Old World, New Horizons: Britain the Common Market and the Atlantic Alliance* (1970) that the reason why Britain sought membership of the EEC in 1961 was political 'in its widest sense'. (Many may argue that he, of all people, should know.)

Notwithstanding these views, evidence now available indicates that the underlying reasons behind the change of Britain's European policy were not quite as clear-cut as they might have seemed from the pronouncements of government ministers. In this regard, the distinction between *political* and what I shall call *strategic* concerns as sources of policy – and their respective legitimacy – has often been overlooked. While fears about the consequences for Britain of being left outside an integrating and influential European bloc may be regarded as *political* in nature, fears for the strength of the Western Alliance arising out of a disunited Europe – much emphasized in the spring and summer of 1961 – should be regarded as being of *strategic* interest.

In all this, one thing at least is clear: British membership of the EEC was not seriously considered by the British government until after the Stockholm Convention was signed in November 1959. If the reasons for the British application were mainly political – or strategic – the question that must be asked is what changed in Britain's political outlook and in the position of the Western Alliance between November

1

1959 and July 1961? The answer to this question is more likely to be found in the *process* of decision-making than in any discernible change in Britain's political standing – or any decay in the Western Alliance – during these crucial years.

In order to ensure an accurate explanation, I have found it helpful to approach this work from the same point as that of the government when it was first faced with the 'European issue', that is, from the perspective of European trade. For it was in the problem of trade and trade discrimination against Britain that the development of a new European policy began and, whatever other considerations came, or were brought, into play, I believe that it was the likely upshot of trade discrimination for the British economy that remained at the heart of the issue throughout. To address the issue in the context of *political* or *strategic* exigencies, then, would be to start from where the policy ended rather than from where it began and would rule out proper examination of when and how the political and strategic arguments were developed.

My concern, then, is to establish *how* the change of policy came about. In this respect my interest coincides with that of Douglas Evans and the later work of Uwe Kitzinger. Although in his polemical work *While Britain Slept: the Selling of the Common Market* (1975) Evans concentrates upon the later stages of the European debate, he raises (or, more accurately, harnesses to his cause) doubts about the functioning of democracy and the decision-making process when it was faced with such an exceptional challenge. Kitzinger, too, in *Diplomacy and Persuasion* concentrates mainly on the later stages of Britain's attempt to gain admission to the EEC. He looks at how the issue was handled between 1970 and 1972 and considers the ramifications for the British political system of the way policy was developed. In this regard, I believe that the way the *initial* decision was reached, and implemented, is perhaps even more worthy of attention.

The historic change of direction, undertaken by Macmillan's government (which has never, despite controversy and dissension, been reversed), proved a unique challenge to the aspirations, perceptions, assumptions and traditions – economic as well as political – of the British people. A nation that clung to the ideals (if no longer to the practice) of free trade and to notions of world power status – which had no little foundation, it has to be said, in its ongoing obligations and world-wide responsibilities – was poised on the brink of entering a tight-knit customs union, itself under-pinned with institutions that had the potential, if not the immediate capability, for undermining national sovereignty.

In the event, the dramatic change of British policy to-wards Europe (which was not, in fact, to come to its final fruition for another decade and more) was accomplished with a minimum of internal turmoil. But it need not have been so – nations have been torn apart over less conten-tious issues. How, then, was this comparatively smooth tran-sition achieved? Was it a victory for common sense or a defeat for democracy – or, worryingly, was it both? What factors informed the way that policy was developed, and could it have been done better? Who were the key players and how was cabinet unity achieved? Which government depart-ment was the first to press for a new policy – was it, as commonly supposed, the Foreign Office or were Treasury officials 'ahead of the game'? When did Macmillan become convinced that British membership of the EEC was the only viable option – when he came to power in 1957 or after the failure of the 1960 Summit, over Christmas 1960 or even later? Why did the government enter into the EFTA agree-ment? – a move which ultimately added to the problems. Did the rationale behind a British application to join the EEC change over time and if so, why? These questions are fundamental to this work, which sets out to establish how internal demands were reconciled to external pressure and whether this was accomplished in keeping with or in spite of the principles of democratic government.

There is no doubt that it was external pressure arising out of the anarchic nature of the international state system that instigated a review of existing policy.[1] In this context, the dynamic system of capitalist development and the ideo-logical and strategic challenge of the bipolar international system were of particular significance. With regard to the former, attempts to mitigate the effects of change that arose out of the economic laws of supply and demand and com-parative advantage resulted in the continuous adjustment

of commercial relations. With regard to the latter, the necessity
for the 'West' of maintaining political unity between economic competitors amounted to a peculiarly delicate challenge. Both of these 'systemic' forces played a material role
in the development of British policy with regard to Europe,
although I will argue that while the economic forces presented a real and irresistible challenge, the notion of political
– or strategic – exigency constituted more of an opportunity
than a challenge for government ministers in the promotion
of their European policy.

Towards the end of the 1950s and during the early years
of the 1960s, it was a Conservative government (and its civil
service secretariat) that was charged with handling the European issue. Typically, the British government was peopled
by men[2] of varying perspectives, insight, temper, preferences
and attitudes. A key variable, which was to be of great long-
term consequence for Conservative Party policy on Europe,
was defined by Macmillan in characteristically nineteenth-
century terms. Although his comments arose as a result of
ministerial dissension over the National Economic Development Council, his observations were applicable, later, to the
division of opinion on European policy. He wrote in September 1961 of 'a rather interesting and quite deep divergence of view between Ministers, really corresponding to
whether they had old Whig, Liberal, laissez-faire traditions,
or Tory opinions, paternalistic and not afraid of a little
dirigisme'.[3]

It is within the context of such 'variables' that the capacity existed for individuals to 'make a difference' to the
outcome, the broad nature of which had been determined
by forces outside the direct control of the British government. Since the role of officials is to act as advisers and
facilitators for government policy, the preferences and perspectives of those senior civil servants also has a profound
impact upon the development of government policy. On the
European issue, it was the impact of particular civil service
personalities that directly affected the development of policy.

In this regard Brecher's study of the foreign policy system of Israel provides important insights. Brecher charac-
terizes the personality variables under the single heading of
the 'attitudinal prism' which, he suggests, has its roots in

the personality predispositions and life experiences of the politician or official concerned.[4] He shows that, while their attitudinal prism precludes, for some, serious consideration of a course of action, for others the same course of action would be viewed as a viable – and even welcome – opportunity. Another useful source for understanding how governments arrive at particular decisions is found in the work of I.L. Janis. Janis explores the impact upon decision-making groups of a syndrome that he calls 'groupthink'. The implications of this phenomenon for the development of British policy are explored in Chapter 5.

Because of all these factors, the development of a coherent and broadly acceptable policy was a long, slow process. As a consequence of this, recognition of the need for adjustments did not run concurrently with events. This flaw in the decision-making process, though, was (and is) by no means unique.[5]

As well as the particular configuration of attitudes and perspectives within government, outcomes are also dependent upon a number of other variables. These include the nature of the proposed policy itself; the timing of the introduction of the policy; the extent to which unity of purpose of government ministers and officials is achieved in advance of the promotion of the new policy; and the ability of the government (once such a solution has been agreed) to put it into effect. The latter depends not only upon the power derived by the government from the institutions of the political system but also upon the government's relative strength vis-à-vis opposition parties – and rebels in its own party ranks – at that particular time. A specific problem for Macmillan, just fifteen or so years after the Second World War, was to balance aspirations for Britain's greatness against the need for a once imperial power to find a new role in keeping with its reduced capabilities. In this respect, his cabinet opponents were well placed to undermine his own policy preferences through their capacity to 'subvert through neglectfulness'.

The essential element in the assessment of how one view or approach prevailed over another is the exploitation of power. The concept and definition of power has given rise to considerable debate among thinkers from many disciplines.

But for these purposes I rely upon the most fundamental definition of power – that is, the ability of A to make B behave in accordance with A's wishes.[6]

Within the operational structure of the British political system there exists two sources of power. The first, I shall call *formal* power and the second, *informal* power. Formal power consists in the clearly defined authority conferred by the political system itself. (The authority of the government to make decisions on behalf of the nation, subject to the constraint of parliament, falls into this category.) Informal power is less conspicuous and although it has its roots in the constitution, it is neither clearly defined nor readily identifiable. It consists in the means and devices available to government ministers and officials that arise *incidentally* out of the structure of the British political system. So, the first source or category of power is direct and formally recognized and the second is indirect and informally available.

The effective utilization of informal power depends upon the character and skill of the player. There are two broad types of 'devices' that are made available through the exploitation of informal power; they are *organizational* devices and *presentational* devices. These devices are available to a greater or lesser extent throughout the apparatus of government. Organizational devices include the selective exploitation of tradition and precedent, the imposition of a particular interpretation of division of responsibility, recourse to exclusion and secrecy, and the utilization of elite relationships. Presentational devices include the use of ambiguity, the effective direction of the political agenda and the skilful use of timing.

Since the effective exploitation of formal power depends to a considerable extent upon the effective utilization of the informal devices of power, it is the latter that is of greater interest. While remaining apart from the formal exposition of the British democratic process, these devices form the very stuff of day-to-day government and as such provide a vital ingredient in the explanation of how a particular decision was arrived at as well as how it was implemented. The variable ability of ministers and officials to exploit the informal devices of power had a profound effect upon the nature of the decisions made with regard to British European policy, especially in the months between April 1960 and April 1961.

It should be noted that while no particular value is attached to the ideas of officials and politicians, no value attaches either to the exploitation of informal power. The question is not whether it was right or wrong that officials and politicians should utilize these devices, but rather to ask to what effect they were utilized and what this tells us about the operation of democracy in Britain in the second half of the twentieth century. The informal devices of power are not illegitimate political tools, but neither are they fully legitimized. They exist in the grey area of the constitution and their accessibility depends to a large extent upon the nature and values of the government in office, the personality and skill of its leading members and the issues that arise for them to deal with. The evidence shows that informal power is an inevitable and necessary tool of the British version of democratic government.

To sum up then, this work is concerned with three particular aspects of the development of government policy toward the EEC in the late 1950s/early 1960s. At an empirical level the discussion centres upon how British policy with regard to the EEC evolved after the failure of the Free Trade Area (FTA) talks in November 1958. In this regard, insight will be offered with regard to the nature of the underlying cause for the change of approach that culminated in the statement made by the prime minister in the House of Commons on 31 July 1961. Secondly – also at an empirical level – the impact of the personalities and predispositions of the key players upon the development of government policy (which characterized policy-making mainly in the early part of the period under discussion) will be assessed. Thirdly, the question (which arose for the most part after April 1960) as to *how* the ideas and preferences of a particular group of politicians and officials gained ascendancy over those of the rest will be addressed. This aspect is of more theoretical value and will afford insight into *how* opposition to the policy, which was harboured by many key figures in government, was overcome.

This work serves to highlight, through the study of a particular case history, the *difference* that may be made, by the perspectives and personalities of a very few people, to the

nature and timing of response to a problem that arises – or
is determined by – the interaction of external and internal
forces. It also points up the serious ramifications of the
conflicting demands of ministers' cabinet and departmental responsibilities and draws attention to the eternal problem of contradiction between party loyalty and ineluctable
diversity of opinion within political parties, and between
cabinet unity and conscientious dissension. In this respect,
the application of Burkeian gradualism, which allowed ministers more freedom of manoeuvre than they would have
enjoyed under a more rigorously defined democratic system, appears (at least in the short term) to have served the
Conservative government well.

Since it is the aim of this study to examine and understand how the British government came to terms with a new
European outlook, it would be as well to set out what is
meant, for these purposes, by the term 'government'. For,
while there is general agreement that those who govern are
responsible for managing and directing the affairs of state
both internally and externally, the question of *who* is, or
should be, involved in this process remains substantially
unresolved.

The prime minister, although notionally first among equals,
traditionally enjoys the facility of gathering about him (or
her) like-minded ministers and advisers for the purpose first,
of developing a policy, and secondly, of deciding how best
to present that policy to the rest of the cabinet. Many of
the prime minister's closest advisers are senior civil servants
who have usually had many years' experience of government
and often know, better than their political masters, what is
and is not politically, socially and economically possible.
Serving at the heart of government, the work of senior officials in developing government policy, particularly in this
case, should not be underestimated.

All the members of the cabinet must also be considered a
part of government because the prime minister needs the
assured support of every cabinet member before he can
present his policy to parliament. His colleagues may disagree
with the prime minister, but as members of the cabinet they
are held to be as accountable for a government policy with
which they profoundly disagree as are its most enthusiastic

supporters. As well as acting as a constraint upon cabinet ministers, though, the imperative of cabinet unity may also, under certain circumstances, provide an opportunity for a confident cabinet minister to 'hijack' government policy.

As well as supporting the prime minister, cabinet ministers also have the responsibility of running their own departments and bringing before cabinet issues that need to be resolved and their suggestions for resolving them. When an issue such as British membership of the EEC arises, the reaction of ministers depends largely upon the likely ramifications of a decision for their particular departments. It was this aspect of cabinet government that was to tax the ingenuity of the prime minister in steering his colleagues towards, what had become by the spring of 1961, his personal goal.

Junior ministers hover on the edge of government, neither wholly in it nor wholly outside it. Their role depends largely upon the extent of the responsibilities that are delegated to them by their minister. Junior ministers often deputize for their minister in cabinet committees and by so doing have the power to affect the development of overall government policy.

Such is the diffuse nature of British governance that it is difficult to tell exactly where government ends. But it has certainly ended before it reaches the floor of the House of Commons. For, while parliament has many and substantial powers, it does not have the power to govern, i.e. the power to manage and direct the affairs of state. Its power resides in its responsibility for scrutinizing government policy and its ultimate capability of rejecting it.[7]

Finally, if the problems for historians arising out of the multifaceted nature of the EEC issue seem at times to be insurmountable, we would do well to spare a thought for those who were charged with dealing with the issue as the events unfolded. Within the Foreign Office (FO), for example, Britain's relationship with the EEC was dealt with in three separate departments: the Western Department, the Economic Department and the Mutual Aid Department. Not until 1960 was the European Economic Organization Department set up to deal with the issue, though even then, responsibility was to be shared with the new Western Organizations

Department.[8] Britain's relationship with the EEC was also an important and legitimate area of concern for the Treasury and the Board of Trade (BOT). It had severe ramifications too for the work of the Commonwealth Relations Office (CRO) and the Colonial Office (CO). Given this wide area of reference, it is only surprising that the question of whether or not Britain should apply to join the EEC, once raised, should have been so quickly settled.

1 No Easy Solution

The reasons why Britain did not seek to join the other six European states in their quest for formal unity – which began with the European Coal and Steel Community (1950), survived through the ill-fated European Defence Community negotiations from 1950 to 1954, and finally came to fruition with the signing of the Treaty of Rome in March 1957 – have been well detailed elsewhere. In short, the British attitude may be explained by the fact that, first, British political and strategic priorities were altogether and justifiably different from those of the European Six; secondly, British trade relied heavily upon Commonwealth connections; and thirdly, the federal ideal – which proved later to have been expounded with more enthusiasm than commitment – found no favour among the people of the United Kingdom. The British, clinging to the glories of war-time victory to blot out peace-time hardship, 'felt no need to exorcize history'[1] and, as Barzini points out, their leaders 'naturally found it unthinkable [for Britain] to join a condominium of defeated, weak, frightened, and impecunious second-rank nations'.[2]

This is not to say, though, that the British government turned its back on Europe completely after the Second World War. All three of Macmillan's post-war predecessors kept a close eye upon developments across the Channel, but only within the context of Britain's wider domestic and international interests, which were, in respect of day-to-day decision-making, altogether the more compelling. Issues such as the domestic economy, the role of sterling, decolonization, conflicts in the Middle East and the Far East, the development and containment of nuclear weapons and the ever-present danger of Cold War confrontation provided effective enough distractions for successive post-war governments from the apparently interminable machinations and grandiose ambitions of European idealists.

But soon after the Messina Conference of 1955, at which Britain was represented by a BOT observer, the first inkling of disquiet began to be felt. At a meeting of leading cabinet

11

ministers held in June 1956 to discuss trade talks with Australia, it became apparent that Britain would soon be facing a serious dilemma. Peter Thorneycroft, then president
of the Board of Trade, summarized the nub of the difficulty
that was to test the minds of politicians, publicists and later
even the British people themselves throughout the next
decade and beyond. He pointed out that, in the light of
the plans of the Messina powers, 'if we kept out of a European system we might have to face a discriminating bloc. If
we joined in one we ran the risk of disrupting the structure
of Imperial Preference.' He warned that, in any case, the
whole system of imperial preference was likely 'to erode'
and suggested that 'major decisions' would have to be taken
soon.[3] Harold Macmillan, then chancellor of the exchequer,
agreed that it would not be possible for Britain 'to enjoy
the best of both worlds indefinitely'. But, when faced with
the suggestion that it was time to consider the reorienta-
tion of British policy, Macmillan insisted that 'we were not
yet ready to make up our minds'.[4]

Perhaps because, as Churchill's minister of housing, he
pressed for more British involvement in Europe and, as prime
minister, he was responsible for Britain's first application to
join the EEC, Harold Macmillan has enjoyed a reputation
as a leading British Euro-enthusiast. Indeed, in the late 1940s,
when post-war idealism had yet to be tested in concrete
political and economic relationships, Macmillan, like
Churchill, displayed almost unfettered enthusiasm for the
'European idea'.[5] But after he was brought into Churchill's
cabinet in 1951, the higher demands of office meant that,
for Macmillan, the ideal of European integration, which had
once represented a Utopian vision, came at length to be
viewed as a real threat to British power and prosperity.

Sir Robert Rhodes James remembers Macmillan as 'an in-
comparable actor' and because of his romanticism 'the nearest
thing to Disraeli as we have seen in his time'.[6] But, battle-
hardened by his harrowing experiences in two world wars,
James recalls, the actor was also the real man – a showman,
an artist, yes, but also an adroit politician. His role in the
Suez crisis, described by Harold Wilson as 'first in and first
out', left Macmillan, in some people's eyes, with a reputation

for Machiavellian duplicity. As far as his political attachment was concerned, in common with his two predecessors, Macmillan had no great liking for the Conservative Party and the feeling, on the whole, was mutual. On the left of the party himself, it was not surprising that he should be disliked by the right, but he was also widely mistrusted by the left, who tended to regard him as 'slippery' and something of a cynic. For all this, or perhaps because of this, Macmillan remains a political enigma. James poses the question: 'did he actually believe in anything?' The evidence replies that he *did* believe in what he was doing – but, for Macmillan, there was no reason why the views that he held today should have anything to do with what he believed yesterday, nor indeed with the way he would act tomorrow.

His cabinet colleagues found in their prime minister an able politician, who, while clearly in charge, relied upon 'good lieutenants'.[7] In fact, Macmillan set great store by achieving a consensus with his ministers. He was particularly adept at appointing subordinates who were not only effective in their own right, but who provided for him a reliable shield from the worst political consequences of government policy. In cabinet, it was his practice, as it were, to lead from behind. In this, he was ably supported by his officials – notably Philip de Zulueta, plucked from a promising career in the Foreign Office in 1957, and Frederick Bishop, who served as Macmillan's principal private secretary before being appointed deputy secretary to the cabinet in 1960. These two men, along with Sir Frank Lee – moved from his post of permanent secretary to the Board of Trade to the equivalent post in the Ministry of Food in 1959, then to joint permanent secretary to the Treasury in 1961 – provided the PM with sound and well-researched advice on questions relating to European trade. Between them, they were able to weigh up the ramifications of government policy from an FO and BOT as well as from a Treasury perspective.

So how much was Macmillan a mould-breaking Europeanist and how much a steady and wary pragmatist? Certainly, on the European issue he was not what we would call today a conviction politician. In common with most of his colleagues he was perplexed rather than enthusiastic about developments across the Channel. According to Horne he had been inclined, while in Churchill's cabinet, to 'blow hot and cold over Europe'.[8] John Colville, Churchill's joint principal private secretary, recalls that in May 1952 Macmillan confided to him his belief that the 'development of the Empire into an economic unit as powerful as the USA and the USSR was the only possibility'.[9] David Carlton, a biographer of Anthony Eden, intimates that Macmillan was at best ambivalent about Europe.[10]

In assessing Macmillan's outlook with regard to Europe, care must be taken with the use of the epithet *Europeanist*. For to be a Europeanist in the late 1950s or early 1960s meant, at the very least, upholding a belief in the need, through membership of the EEC, for 'ever closer ties with Europe', ties which were clearly intended ultimately to result in federation. Macmillan, like his cabinet colleagues – with the possible exception, later, of Edward Heath – had no appetite for such an eventuality. Based on this criterion then, he could not be described as a Europeanist.

It is true that as minister of housing, Macmillan had argued for a more active British role in Europe. But for Macmillan this was desirable not for its own sake but rather as a check to the fervour of the federalists. He saw danger in the development of a federal Europe dominated by Germany, which would be tempted to side with the USSR. Macmillan, then, shared with Eden and Churchill a distaste for both the federal and the functional systems of European integration which were being sponsored by Jean Monnet and Paul Henri Spaak.[11] His vision, if he could be said to have had one, was that of a Europe of states held together by free trade, regular consultation and shared commitment to the Atlantic Alliance. His regret was not so much that Britain had missed the opportunity of being a founder member of the EEC but that the British government, through a lack of involvement, had missed the opportunity of 'redirecting' European aspirations to match British policy objectives.[12] In terms of defence, Macmillan was never convinced of the need for an overriding British military commitment to Europe.[13] He preferred to maintain a thin spread of British forces world-wide. But, while being prepared to discuss Britain's world role *capability*, he shied away from a discussion of Britain's world role itself. Setting great store by the possession of nuclear weapons and the effectiveness of nuclear deterrence, he saw the defence of Europe as a matter of power politics rather than simply a question of military power. It was through recourse to notions of power politics that he was eventually able to find a resolution to his European policy dilemma.

As prime minister, Macmillan favoured above all the establishment of a European free trade area which would incorporate the Rome Treaty states along with the other states of Western Europe. He was severely disappointed when it failed to materialize, and his disappointment turned to frustration as a tight-knit political and economic community steadily ground its way into existence before his helpless gaze.

Problems for Britain began to mount in 1956 as OEEC members – especially low-tariff countries such as those of Scandinavia and Benelux – pressed for a reduction of tariffs in intra-European trade. British ministers, with the Atlantic relationship and imperial preference in mind, preferred that any such arrangements should be made through the GATT. But for the short term, the secretary general of the OEEC (where Britain historically had enjoyed disproportionate influence, much to the irritation of the French) was encouraged to initiate a study of the whole question of trade between the Messina Six and other members of the OEEC. Thorneycroft and Macmillan were confident that the discussion could be kept going while, as Macmillan proposed, 'we have time to make up our minds'.[14]

Within three weeks Peter Thorneycroft and Macmillan had devised a plan that would safeguard Britain's world-wide trading interests while solving the problems occasioned by the plans of the Messina Six. The final draft of the cabinet memorandum is dated, perhaps appropriately, 27 July 1956, the day after President Nasser nationalized the Suez Canal Company, thereby striking a mortal blow to Britain's pretensions to world power status. Known as 'Plan G', the scheme would associate Britain, along with other OEEC countries, in a Free Trade Area (FTA) with the Six. The scheme would not extend to agriculture and would allow Britain to maintain its existing freedom of action with regard to imperial preference, since Britain would not adopt the common tariff of the Six against imports from other countries.[15]

Rising remarkably unscathed from the debris of the Suez débâcle as the new prime minister in January 1957, Macmillan was keen to advance his plans for an FTA. Even at this early stage, though, it was apparent that the French would be the hardest to please. It is illustrative, not only of Macmillan's lack of commitment to closer British ties with Europe but also of his interpretation of the problem as being one solely of trade – at least at this stage – that he suggested, if the French were not interested in forming an FTA, 'we might have to consider forming a Free Trade Area of our own'.[16] But the overall feeling was one of optimism. Still not totally cowed by the Suez experience, the belief that Britain had several options from which to choose precluded, for the time being, any anticipation of the difficulties to come.

By April, though, concern was beginning to grow – if only in the BOT. Officials there advised that 'if there was to be no Free Trade Area, the United Kingdom would have to consider trying to break the Common Market'.[17] In July, the PM wrote to Thorneycroft (then chancellor of the exchequer): 'we must take the lead, either in widening their project, or, if they will not co-operate with us, in opposing it.'[18] His own shrewd recommendation was that, in order to satisfy the eagerness of the Six for the establishment of European political institutions, the management of the proposed FTA should be left to a European managing board. 'This might well be called a supra-national institution', he admitted, 'but does it matter?' He suggested that 'we should not be unduly afraid of the risks to our own interests, since we could rely on support from a number of like-minded European countries.'[19] But he warned that any concessions likely to affect the Commonwealth must be agreed in advance with Commonwealth leaders.

In October 1957, David Eccles, the president of the Board of Trade met Jean Monnet. Eccles reported to Maudling Monnet's warning that nothing would be achieved in respect of an FTA until the European Commission was in place in January 1958. It was clear to Eccles that the French were not prepared to negotiate until they were able to make the Commission's view the French view.[20] But with negotiations in the OEEC underway under the chairmanship of Reginald Maudling, ministers remained hopeful if not, by now, wholly confident. Maudling spoke with uncharacteristic passion at the Council of Europe Assembly. He told his European audience that for Britain the Commonwealth was not only a matter of trade but 'a fundamental fact of British psychology' and 'a fundamental emotion which colours all our political life'.[21] But, perhaps in order not to appear too negative, he spoke of the possibility, in the proposed FTA, of agriculture being 'treated differently', instead of being excluded altogether.

The difficulties that Maudling encountered, arising out of his attempts to persuade the Six of British goodwill, point up the government's dilemma as it sought to strike an impossible balance between appearing to the Europeans to be ready to make at least some adjustments and indicating to the domestic constituency that no such adjustments were being contemplated. Maudling's allusion to a slight change in the government's position on agriculture was seized upon by the British press. At the press conference held after the meeting a challenge from a *News Chronicle* journalist elicited an assurance of 'a complete waiver' of tariff agreements by Britain for agricultural products. And in response to a searching question from a *Daily Telegraph* journalist about the role of the institutions that he might have in mind for administering the FTA, Maudling gave the further assurance that 'in our opinion, the supreme body must clearly be a Council of Ministers'.[22] So, not only were any gains that Maudling might have hoped to have made at the meeting effectively undone, but his subsequent assurance to journalists, by ruling out the possibility of British membership of a supranational body, signalled to the Six that Britain's commitment to Europe was strictly limited.

This relatively minor incident exemplifies the real dilemma for ministers of democratic government in weighing their perception of the national *will* against their perception of the national *good*. One of the weaknesses of the democratic system is that it makes it difficult for politicians to implement policies that may have long-term benefits but short-term costs. Schumpeter argues that 'voters ... prove themselves bad and indeed corrupt judges of ... [national economic] issues, and often they even prove themselves bad judges of their own long-run interests, for it is only the short-run promise that tells politically and only short-run rationality that asserts itself effectively.'[23]

But the problem for the government was not only one of

incompatibility between long- and short-run objectives, it was
also one of a lack of homogeneity of interest. The interests
of farming would not, for example, necessarily be advanced
by the same policy that would benefit industry. For government ministers in the late 1950s it was the interests of British industry that seemed to be under attack and it was the
interests of agriculture (among others) that were felt to inhibit
the government's ability to find an acceptable solution. But
this was not (yet) a matter of pressure-group politics, nor
of neo-corporatism, in its strictest sense, because Macmillan's
government was under no substantial pressure from interest groups, neither was it (yet) in regular or formal consultation with industrialists. On the European issue, Macmillan's
government was acting, for reasons of both electoral and
national exigency, on behalf of particular interests such as
agriculture and industry without incorporating these interests directly into the decision-making process.

By October 1957, it was clear that the three key areas of
concern for the government, in seeking a satisfactory trade
arrangement with the Six, were the Commonwealth relationship, British agriculture and British sovereignty. Even if
ministers had felt it appropriate to make concessions in these
areas – along the lines of Macmillan's European managing
board, for example – they would have been immediately
called to account by the British press, by the Opposition,
by leading members of their own party and – at the end of
the line – by the electorate. During these initial stages of
negotiation, it is likely that some important lessons were
learned by ministers with regard to the importance of choosing
words with care and the extent to which and the stage at
which ministers' intentions should be subjected to public,
parliamentary – or even to cabinet – scrutiny.

Notwithstanding the *potential* for dissent on the European
issue, the sentiments of the electorate (or public opinion)
and of their informer or reflector – the media – did not, at
this stage, provide the government with the sort of direct
and sustained challenge that was to be mounted during the
late 1960s and the 1970s. But there would soon be enough
interest, at least among the serious press and the political
elite, to prompt ministers to make use of political tools
such as secrecy, ambiguity and evasion whose justification

would be found in this inbuilt weakness of the democratic system.

Even taking account of the political weight of the farmers, the thorniest problem of all, in respect of Britain's trading relationship with Europe, was undoubtedly that of the Commonwealth relationship. This enduring affirmation of Britain's imperial past presented ministers with a peculiar challenge, as they found themselves constrained by the needs and preferences of peoples far outside their political constituency. While the Commonwealth relationship was significant for Britain as a source of preferential trade, strategic advantage and political prestige, it nevertheless carried the potential to encourage the government to act not always in the best interests of the British people. There is a fine point of judgement to be made here between how much the government's concern for the Commonwealth arose out of British interests and the preferences of the British electorate for maintaining strong links with Commonwealth countries, and how much ministers felt it incumbent upon them to act *on behalf of* peoples who were, in fact, separately represented by their own elected leaders.

Certainly, at regular meetings between both Commonwealth officials and ministers, British policy with regard to Europe was freely discussed. These meetings were conducted more along the lines of meetings between government departments than those between representatives of separate governments. This afforded officials and ministers from independent countries such as Australia, New Zealand and Canada an opportunity to influence British policy so that it would accord with their own country's interests. At a meeting held on 9 July 1957, for example, a New Zealand official was able to emphasize the need to exclude agriculture from the FTA because of the ramifications of its inclusion for New Zealand agriculture.[24]

This question of legitimate national interest versus old imperialist paternalism as the driving force behind the role of the Commonwealth relationship as it affected Britain's relations with Europe merits deeper study. For now, though, it is certainly worth bearing in mind the possibility that one of the key problems for Britain's relationship with the Six – throughout the period under discussion and beyond – was rooted, at least in some respects, in this anomalous political relationship.

By December 1957, eleven months before the negotiations were finally abandoned, it was becoming increasingly apparent that the French were not interested in reaching agreement on an FTA and the Germans, themselves unsure, were in no position to proceed without their prospective partners. The French feared that an FTA would deflect attention and commitment from the Common Market as well as proving economically disadvantageous. Maudling himself reported to the PM that the French were troubled too by public opinion, that they suggested treating the FTA as an experiment and that they felt it should not come into being, in any case, until 2–4 years after the Common Market was established. But, perhaps blinded by the lack of a viable alternative, Maudling clung to the hope that the French would accept an arrangement that would cater for their difficulties by making them a 'special case' in the FTA.[25] In January, Treasury officials were charged with the challenging task of constructing a formula that would be acceptable to the Six and that made no concessions on the exclusion of British agriculture or the retention of imperial preference.[26]

The reliance of ministers upon the eventual success of the FTA project is all the more surprising in the light of evidence to suggest that they had some access to French intentions through informal contacts in Paris. From these sources it was learned that the French, feeling that the proposed FTA would not be enough to safeguard their interests, planned to demand a treaty 'embodying a common policy and agreed objectives' as well as 'harmonization of social charges' and a 'common policy on agriculture'.[27] Whether or not the British official concerned was allowed sight of this French document for tactical purposes, it remains a clear indication of the lines along which French minds were working and should, perhaps, have commanded more careful attention.

But, in any case, for Macmillan, the need to secure consensus in his own government provided a steady distraction from giving serious consideration to the idea that the French would not be appeased. On 20 February 1958, his cabinet secretary, Sir Norman Brook, reminded the PM that, in view of growing unease, the cabinet should be consulted before any concessions were made.[28] Continuous consultation was still demanded too by Commonwealth ministers, particularly Robert Menzies of Australia. At the same time it was considered necessary to mollify interested journalists with promises that no concession was about to be made with regard to the three cherished political interests: the Commonwealth, British agriculture and British sovereignty. Indeed, when earlier the same month the paymaster general had put to the cabinet for the second time a request to be allowed to make some concessions on agriculture, he had again been turned down on the grounds that the issue was too sensitive both at home and in the Commonwealth.[29]

Now, even the PM gave voice to real fears about the prospects for a settlement. Macmillan summed up how he saw the situation in a memorandum to Maudling. He concluded that while Adenauer, the German chancellor, 'only thinks about the political issue', Hallstein, the German state secretary (later to become president of the European Commission), was actively antagonistic.[30] The protectionist French, he declared, were as 'jealous of Britain as the British people seem now to be of America'. The only hope, he suggested, lay in the French not wanting to be seen by Germany as 'guilty of destroying Europe'. This was a very slim hope indeed. It is not surprising that Maudling suggested to the cabinet ten days later that it might now be advisable to consider the policy to be adopted 'if it seemed likely that the Free Trade Area project would fail'.[31]

While the British government was feeling its way falteringly in Europe, British industry, in partnership with industrial organizations of countries on the periphery of the Messina Six, was taking positive action of its own. Anxious to keep up the pressure on their political representatives, the industrial federations and employers organizations of Austria, Denmark, Norway, Sweden, Switzerland and the UK issued a joint statement in April 1958 confirming that they had agreed between themselves 'on the principal features of a Free Trade Area'.[32]

The commitment of the FBI to finding a solution found resonance at the BOT. In May, David Eccles made an earnest plea to the PM to strive harder for agreement. Anticipating the tactics that Macmillan was to adopt in cabinet three years later (though with considerably less subtlety or success), Eccles painted for the PM an alarming picture of the consequences if the FTA should fail to materialize. He envisaged a neutral and united Europe, the withdrawal of America and the collapse of the Atlantic Alliance.[33] He suggested that the incoming president of France, General de Gaulle, would be likely to make an alliance with Russia – or even with Nasser. His grave warning to the PM was that 'either you lead or the bright day of Europe is done'. A report from Sir Gladwyn Jebb, Britain's ambassador in Paris, on his first meeting with the newly elected French president carried with it a similar air of bleak foreboding. He identified Europe as one of several areas where 'we are in for difficulties'.[34]

In the summer of 1958, though, Europe was by no means the only problem that weighed heavily on the minds of ministers and officials. At home there were industrial disputes, notably in transport and the docks. The economic situation was looking ever graver; British involvement in Cyprus, Lebanon, Egypt, Jordan and Iraq commanded a great deal of attention while in Africa, the first moves towards decolonization provided the government with a number of difficult judgements. There was no end in view of the Cold War and the vexed question of nuclear testing remained unresolved.

For Macmillan, faced with these many and various issues, Europe had become a worrying thorn in his side. A memorandum that he sent to the foreign secretary on 24 June betrays his frustration with the lack of progress with the FTA. Recommending that, if the Six did not cooperate, Britain should withdraw its troops from Europe and from NATO, he went on to proclaim that Britain should surround itself with rockets and 'say to the Germans, the French and all the rest of them: look after yourselves with your own forces. Look after yourselves when the Russians overrun your country.'[35] He suggested that Britain's position on this should be made 'quite clear' to de Gaulle and to Adenauer 'so they may be under no illusion'. Macmillan was probably aware from the outset that such an ultimatum was not politically or strategically possible. But his outrage is symptomatic of a psychological disposition, yet to be broken down, which precluded the possibility of Western European countries being able to evolve a joint policy without British involvement – or at least approval.

Meanwhile, Maudling, with as much commitment though considerably less passion than Eccles, struggled on in his attempts to find an acceptable formula. He put to the PM an FO suggestion that, as 'Assemblies are fashionable on the Continent', a Consultative Assembly for the FTA may be a good idea.[36] The PM concurred, though his meeting with de Gaulle on 29 June gave him little reason to believe that such cosmetic inducements would be rewarded. De Gaulle admitted to his erstwhile friend that the French economy 'was based on protectionism'.[37] Macmillan countered by pointing out that Britain was traditionally isolationist. He implied that a trade war resulting from failure to reach agreement would jeopardize Britain's commitment to maintain four divisions on the Continent. But in spite of Macmillan's best efforts – even attempting, at one stage, to turn to account de Gaulle's antipathy towards America – the General remained stubbornly non-committal.

By July 1958, no negotiations had taken place for five months and the president of the Board of Trade was setting about the bad business of seeking an alternative to the FTA. With regard to the prospect of joining with the Scandinavians in a UNISCAN agreement he commented: 'it would be a climb down – the engineer's daughter when the general-manager's had said no.'[38] Once the general-manager's daughter had been spoken for, however, the charms of the engineer's daughter were to prove a little more difficult to resist.

On 15 October, the foreign secretary met with M. Chauvel, the French ambassador. It was a strained encounter and little was achieved. M. Chauvel, while expressing sympathy for the British view, spoke of the 'compelling internal political reasons' for French prevarication.[39] The foreign secretary's allusion to new trade arrangements that Britain would be forced to make if the FTA failed to materialize, 'whose only beneficiaries would be the Russians', was met with the candid observation that 'the General himself knew nothing of economics and was not very interested in the subject'. But if economic matters were not at the front of the General's mind, they certainly exercised the minds of French industrialists. Alarming reports were now being received from the British delegation to the OEEC in Paris, outlining moves being made by French and German industrialists to enter into confabrication agreements. It was reported that talks were already underway between Citroën and Mercedes.[40] Here was material evidence of the threat posed by the Common Market for British industry.

Exasperation, now tinged with a touch of desperation, led Macmillan to revive his plan to challenge the French and Germans with the last weapon in his armoury, Britain's military withdrawal from continental Europe.[41] It may be noted at this stage that Macmillan's threat to denounce the WEU Treaty, in October 1958, sits uneasily with his later exhortations about the need to strengthen the unity – and hence the security – of Western Europe through British membership of the EEC.

Clearly, the PM's recommendation could no longer be ignored and accordingly officials from the Treasury and the FO met on 31 October to consider the options. It was quickly concluded that the withdrawal of British troops from Europe would mean the end of NATO and the tendency for Germany to seek accommodation with the USSR.[42] Since the establishment of the Common Market was to be carried out in accordance with the terms of the GATT there was no possibility, either, of mounting a challenge there. The recommendations that were put forward were, therefore, unsatisfactorily meagre. The first was that, if FTA talks should falter, which they now showed every sign of doing, the attention of the Six should be drawn to the effects of the political division of Europe that would be the inevitable result of the economic division. Secondly, it was proposed that while the establishment of an FTA with the Swiss and the Scandinavians would be both difficult to achieve and very much a second-best arrangement, it would be better than nothing.

On the day that Adenauer wrote to Macmillan to assure him that the negotiations were not in danger,[43] the PM set out his alternative plans in a cabinet paper. To the recommendations of the Treasury and the FO he added a proposal to approach the Americans with a request that, in the light of the 'strategic consequences' of this economic challenge to Britain, they would bring pressure to bear on the

French.[44] In spite of the findings of officials, the PM also wanted the cabinet to consider the feasibility of denouncing the WEU Treaty. The need for this may be averted, he suggested, by a meeting between himself, Adenauer and de Gaulle to thrash out a 'political' solution that would make considerable concessions to France. Fourthly, he wanted the cabinet to consider the arguments for and against taking discriminatory action against the Six and for and against the establishment of a second Common Market that would include Canada. Finally, the PM suggested that 'a realistic public relations case' should be worked out 'presenting this critical situation in such a way as to justify an eventual compromise'.

In the event, the Americans, with NATO, the WEU and now the EEC in place, had no interest in promoting an FTA that would discriminate against their own producers. It was considered too dangerous to denounce the WEU Treaty, de Gaulle was not interested in a compromise solution and the alternative Common Market was never likely to be a viable option. Ministers were left with the option of a second-best arrangement with the Scandinavians and the Swiss. It became evident that an attempt to alert the British public to the seriousness of the situation would not only highlight the government's own failure but, with not even a costly compromise in view, would serve no constructive purpose.

On 7 November, a meeting with Couve de Murville, French minister of foreign affairs, effectively confirmed Macmillan's worst fears. Not only did it now appear that the FTA was dead, but it was becoming apparent that it had never, in fact, been seen as a viable option by the French. The French economy, Couve de Murville explained, 'could not stand the competition of the Free Trade Area at the same time as that of the Common Market'.[45] Macmillan immediately wrote to de Gaulle urging him 'not to regard this as a technical issue' but to attend to it 'in its broadest political aspects'.[46] De Gaulle wrote back to say that the establishment of an FTA would be 'incompatible' with the French economy.[47]

Until November 1958, the Germans as well as the British had envisaged, in the FTA, an arrangement between the whole seventeen members of the OEEC that would be the same as that between the Six in respect of tariffs. Indeed, at the time of the ratification of the Treaty of Rome by the

Bundestag, Ludwig Erhard, Germany's deputy chancellor, had made it clear to the French that it was done so on the firm expectation that the FTA would follow.[48] Now, the French revealed that they had always believed that there was no possibility of extending the terms of the Six to the Seventeen. The notion that the Germans 'had sold out to the French on every count' pervaded deep into the British government.[49] But the plain fact that had to be faced was that the French were now in a position to veto any proposals that the other five might care to make and Britain was powerless to prevent it.

On 11 November, Maudling announced to the cabinet that it was now clear that the French would not accept the FTA.[50] As much to reassure himself as his colleagues he expressed the hope – which was never to rise to the status of an expectation – that some arrangement could be concluded with the other five, with special arrangements for France. On 28 November, Macmillan told George Humphrey, the US Secretary for the Treasury, that 'in Europe it looks as though we may be in for a trade-war'.[51] In case the nature of his concern should be misunderstood, he wrote to the foreign secretary on the same day: 'the British are being discriminated against with increasingly disastrous effects on their European trade.'[52]

Some important lessons were learned – and others were not – in this 'dry run' of negotiations with the Six. First, it became clear that ministers should, at all costs, avoid giving specific and unequivocal assurances at home and to Commonwealth ministers about what would *not* be conceded. While assurances were certainly necessary, they should be kept, it was found, as vague as possible, thereby allowing ministers room to manoeuvre in negotiations. This lesson was well learned. The seeds of doubt might also have been sown in Macmillan's mind about the wisdom of making a direct approach to the cabinet on this sensitive issue. He would have noted, for example, that Maudling's straightforward request for permission to make more concessions to the Six – in the interests of getting a much-needed agreement – failed to produce the required results.

Secondly, it had become all too apparent that, in dealing

with the European issue, no clear goal should be stated until the last possible moment. Pressure on those concerned with the negotiations would have been substantially eased had the desire for the establishment of an FTA not been so clearly stated. So confident had the government been at the outset of achieving a satisfactory solution that no thought had been given to the important and politically costly by-product of failure – that of losing face. On this point, it will be noted that even after the official negotiations for British membership of the EEC were underway, they were still (rather fallaciously) alluded to as talks to establish whether or not it would be feasible for Britain to join the EEC. One of the key lessons arising out of the FTA failure was that in dealing with the Six, secrecy, ambiguity and evasion would secure for ministers the best possible room for manoeuvre and ultimately the best possible chance of securing their goal.

The third lesson, though, was perhaps the hardest of all for ministers and officials to grasp. It was that the leading countries of Western Europe were capable of acting in concert without the need of a British conductor or the desire to play the British tune. And the reality that was the hardest to face was that any negotiations with the Six now depended ultimately upon the cooperation of the French. As the French motive for acceding to the Treaty of Rome was almost entirely political (economically, France was traditionally and avowedly protectionist), the French government was unlikely to cooperate, for some years to come, in any further moves that would subject French producers to more external competition. But, while ministers brought from the FTA defeat some valuable experience for dealing with the domestic constituency on this issue, the lesson that seems very clear in hindsight concerning the true position of France with regard to European trade appears, perhaps because it was so unpalatable, to have passed them by.

The contradictions faced by the British government at the end of 1958 were virtually insoluble. For commercial reasons it would have been beneficial for Britain if the Six had failed in their attempt to form a Common Market. For strategic reasons, though, the EEC had become, by now, an essential plank of Western security. A clear distinction should be made here, though, between the strategic value to 'the West' of the EEC, which is hard to challenge, and the strategic importance of achieving a trade agreement between the Six and Britain which was founded on much shakier premises. As for British 'commitment' to Europe, while it would have been commercially advantageous – certainly in the long run – to have sacrificed much in order to conclude a workable agreement with the Six, it was politically impossible at this time to do so. In the event, each of these contradictions proved to be more of a theoretical than a practical challenge, since the Treaty of Rome was always going to be signed and ratified with or without British approval and France, it seems, had never been prepared to enter into a free trade arrangement with Britain however much the British government would have been willing to compromise.

As for the prime minister, by November 1958, he had shown himself to be both intellectually ambivalent and characteristically pragmatic with regard to Britain's relationship with the Six. He was clearly shaken by his government's inability to secure a satisfactory solution to the problems arising out of the Treaty of Rome. The evidence shows, too, that it was the potential problems for British trade and industry that concerned him most – though there are the first indications that he had come to recognize political possibilities in the strategic argument.

In these early stages of the government's European difficulties, it was the paymaster general upon whom the PM relied for guidance. Already, though, the president of the Board of Trade was voicing his concern and the chancellor of the exchequer and foreign secretary were both being drawn into the deliberations. Because of the multifaceted nature of the issue, though, the PM himself was still taking the leading role. With Edward Heath serving as minister of labour, there were, as yet, no members of the cabinet capable of challenging the PM with regard to interest in or familiarity with the European issue.

As this complicated game begins to unravel, the areas of potential conflict within government have become clearer. The three-fold objection to anything more than the loosest of free trade arrangements, coupled with the apparently inextricable contradiction of Britain's international position and its politically anomalous relationship with the Commonwealth, provided some crusty grist for the government's mill. But the diversity of opinion, arising out of a variety of attitudes, perspectives and interests (including departmental interest), meant that the metaphorical mill was not a particularly well-coordinated machine. The grinding out of a consistent and credible approach to this issue was never, therefore, going to be a simple matter.

2 Finding a Way Forward

It will be helpful at this point to put into context the relationship between the different perceptions and responses of government ministers and officials to the European issue and the ramifications of this relationship for the development of policy. The substance and timing of a response to changed circumstances varies from individual to individual depending upon each person's particular *psychological environment*.[1] Whether and exactly when a particular response results in an adjustment of government policy depends upon the ability of those who favour that course of action to ensure that their view prevails. So the nature of the policy and the likelihood and timing of its enactment depends not only upon the facility of members of government to recognize and respond to changes in the external environment but also upon the distribution and the exploitation of power within government which determines which response, if any, is destined to become government policy.

On the issue of Britain's relationship with Europe, the problems were so many and so complex that the incidence of variability in respect of the timing and nature of responses by ministers and officials was very great indeed. It was in an attempt to align the ideas and preferences of individuals behind those of the prime minister and his immediate advisers that leading ministers and officials would eventually resort to the exploitation of informal power.

As yet (November 1958), though, there was little cause for dissent within government over the course of action that should be taken on the issue. The idea of applying for British membership of the EEC was still a long way from the prime minister's mind, let alone the cabinet agenda. Attention was directed instead towards agreeing a formula for a response to the failure of the FTA negotiations.

The ministerial Free Trade Area (FTA) committee set up in March 1957, with high hopes of securing a best-of-all-worlds agreement for Britain, now turned its attention to salvaging something in the way of a European commercial agreement.

The prime minister himself generally chaired the committee, whose membership included the president of the Board of Trade, the chancellor of the exchequer and the foreign secretary, as well as ministers from the CO, the CRO, and the MAG. Edward Heath, then parliamentary secretary to the Treasury, also attended, though not on a regular basis.

The committee met at the end of November to consider two separate reports.[2] The first was a set of proposals from the Treasury supported by Heathcoat Amory. The report concluded that a short-term *modus vivendi* should be sought – although it would be better, it was argued, to wait for an initiative for this from the Six. If a *modus vivendi* did not appear achievable, then the Treasury recommended commercial retaliation against France. But if a *modus vivendi* were to be achieved, the Treasury proposed that negotiations to establish an FTA should be resumed. The recommendation was that France should be offered 'a special position' in a wider permanent agreement embodying only temporary arrangements for the important question of 'origin', leaving 'other contentious issues' to be dealt with in three or four years' time. Treasury officials, like their political masters, found it hard to accept that the establishment of an FTA, on any terms, had effectively been ruled out by the French. They did, however, give fleeting recognition to the idea by concluding that if it did not prove possible to get an all-Europe FTA in the foreseeable future, then the same arrangement between the UK, Scandinavia and Switzerland 'would be well worth considering'. Treasury officials ruled out the denunciation of the WEU Treaty under any circumstances.

The other report was submitted by the paymaster general and reflects the extent to which a senior cabinet minister was susceptible to the almost wilful misinterpretation of the actions and intentions of his opposite numbers across the Channel. 'All the evidence accumulating, both in public statements and in private communications', Maudling's report declared, 'shows that the Six are now thoroughly alarmed at the situation and that they really intend to try and solve both the short-term and the long-term problem.'[3] Maudling might have been misled by a conversation with Professor Müller-Armack on 14 November, when the German secretary of state told him that he believed that the French had taken a 'new decision' that was not unrelated to their need for credits.[4] But subsequent reports from a French informant confirmed that the trend of French thinking was 'most unpromising' and that 'far from considering alternative ways of creating a free trade area, they were now not envisaging a convention of any kind'.[5] The only proposal that the French had in mind (leaked to British officials by the Dutch)[6] was for an insubstantial *modus vivendi*, which offered nothing more than some temporary adjustments of tariffs and quotas. The Dutch, themselves, were suspicious of the fact that no terminal date had been proposed for these interim arrangements.

On the basis of these reports the PM proposed that the two-fold objective must be a short-term *modus vivendi* and the long-term negotiation of an FTA.[7] He said that if a *modus vivendi* could not be negotiated, concerted 'defensive' (rather than retaliatory) action by the non-Six would offer a four-fold benefit. It would have 'a salutary effect on the Six', it would maintain solidarity among the non-Six, it would re-assure British industry and could well induce the US government to take some action. Not totally convinced by Maudling's optimistic assessment, he suggested that, with regard to the long term, 'urgent consideration should be given' to the proposals for establishing an FTA between the UK, Scandinavia 'and perhaps Switzerland'. He said that this would offer a means of promoting 'the type of ultimate association between the Six and the non-Six which we had always envisaged' as well as showing the Six that the UK was not prepared to accept 'a position of permanent inferiority in the markets of the Six'. The Swiss had already proposed a meeting of the 'outer' six[8] for 1 December, shortly after the FTA talks broke down. In the event, it was confirmed at this meeting that the non-Rome Treaty countries should, at the very least, concert their response to the action of EEC countries.[9]

Here, then, was the early rationale behind eventual British adherence to the Stockholm Convention. Though not quite constituting a 'knee-jerk' reaction, it is evident that the response owed more to understandable frustration and rumbling resentment than it did to reason. Given the attitude of the French, there was no logical reason to believe that membership of another trading bloc would improve the prospects of Britain coming to a satisfactory trading arrangement with the Six. On the contrary, as should perhaps have been anticipated, British membership of EFTA (known in its early stages of consideration as the 'UNISCAN agreement') was to pose an additional complication in Britain's troubled relationship with the EEC. But, in the light of what was seen as peremptory action by the French, the need to be taking *some* action evidently overrode the requirement for a proper assessment of the likely long-term ramifications of a restricted FTA. (After the EFTA negotiations were underway, the notion that the final convention would do nothing to advance the cause of a free trade arrangement with the Six would be so chilling as to be beyond contemplation.)

The second reason that the PM gave for looking into the possibility of an FTA with Scandinavia and Switzerland – that of 'showing the Six' that the British government was capable of acting independently of them – though a very human response, hardly amounted to a meticulously formulated strategy. Summing up, the PM added his personal view that negotiations were unlikely to succeed without the deployment of arguments 'of a political nature'.[10] To this end he suggested that it should be made clear to the Six that the British people 'would refuse to maintain indefinitely the existing political and military ties with Europe if no viable economic relationship could be established'. This argument, which Macmillan consistently put forward, was not that of a convinced 'Europeanist'. But it did represent the mark of an experienced and sophisticated statesman, who recognized better than many of his colleagues the essential link between commercial and political relationships.

The PM's assessment of the government's options was quickly shown to be more accurate than the paymaster general's. For, while Erhard (the German minister for economic affairs) expressed the personal hope that Maudling's OEEC committee was merely suspended, the French made it clear that they viewed the committee as dissolved and the matter to be in abeyance.[11]

A meeting between Macmillan and Erhard the following week was far from fruitful.[12] Erhard explained that, while the Six did not intend to negotiate, they planned to take action to minimize discrimination in Europe when the first

tariff reductions and quota enlargements came into effect
under the Treaty of Rome on 1 January 1959. He also proposed that the OEEC ministerial council should not convene
until January when it might do so in a calmer atmosphere.
Macmillan was made to realize here, perhaps for the first
time, the practical consequences of Britain's non-member-
ship of the EEC. Instead of being in the thick of negotiations, Britain was now accorded the status of a helpless
bystander – to be affected by but to have no control over
the joint decisions of the six EEC countries. It was not a
status that the PM regarded with any enthusiasm. It would
certainly have highlighted, in his mind, the unsatisfactory
nature of Britain's relationship with the Six.

At a further meeting of the FTA committee, the chancellor of the exchequer was charged with looking into the
possibilities for a UNISCAN agreement.[13] In the meantime
it was agreed that HMG would inform the US government
of 'its grave concern' about the possibility of Europe dividing into two economic blocs 'with all this might entail for
the future of European political and military co-operation'.
The UNISCAN proposals, then, almost by default, had become the main plank of the government's European commercial policy. The belief (or, more accurately, the hope)
persisted that the creation of a two trading-bloc Europe would
force the US and the European Six, both on their own account and as a result of the anticipated pressure from other
NATO and OEEC countries, to seek a solution that would
be satisfactory to the UK.

The chancellor convened an *ad hoc* ministerial committee
to assess the viability of Britain entering into a UNISCAN
agreement. The membership of this committee, which met
for the first time on 8 December, included the paymaster
general as well as representatives from the FO, the CRO
and the MAG. Sir Roger Makins attended from the Treasury
and Sir Frank Lee from the BOT. The consensus of the
meeting was that, while recognizing the danger of dividing
Europe into two blocs, it would be harmful to allow the
Common Market to develop unchallenged.[14] It was recognized that 'the prospect of such action [concluding a
UNISCAN agreement] leading to the building of a bridge
towards a full European free trade area was small'. It should

be noted that these were not the findings of a sub-committee of junior officials but of key ministers with the added weight of senior Treasury and BOT officials behind them. It is all the more surprising, therefore, that the notion of UNISCAN being utilized as a 'bridge' between the Six and the rest was to be cited regularly by senior ministers as the essential rationale for the UNISCAN policy.

The FTA committee considered the UNISCAN proposals again, in the light of the findings of the chancellor's *ad hoc* committee.[15] Agriculture (excluded, in the event, from the Stockholm Convention) was seen as the main sticking point. Summing up, though, the PM said that he was impressed 'by the mounting danger that the UK might find itself isolated in Europe'. The Scandinavians, he reminded the committee, 'had their own plans for a Nordic Customs Union'. 'If they established their Union and then decided to make their own terms with the Six', he warned, 'the whole development of this country's industrial trade with Europe would be imperilled.' This was probably the most cogent of all the arguments, but it was seldom reiterated – probably because of its negative overtones. The preferred version, put forward at the same meeting, was that UNISCAN was not to be regarded as a substitute for a European free trade area, 'but rather as the first step towards the achievement of a larger grouping'. Ministers were determined to put a positive slant on their proposals, both for their own peace of mind and for reasons of political expediency. In any event, the PM declared that potential problems over bacon and fish should not be allowed to damage 'the long term commercial interests of this country'.[16]

Macmillan's attitude at the FTA committee meeting represents a significant departure, indicating that the PM was, by now, prepared to view agricultural questions as negotiable. While the Stockholm Convention did not, in the event, require Britain to make agricultural 'sacrifices', such compromises – at least in the PM's mind – were plainly no longer out of the question. But, even while the ministerial committee was agonizing over Britain's trading predicament, not everyone was prepared merely to make the best of the unhappy situation. On 9 December, Sir Ashley Clarke, British ambassador to Italy, sent a cypher that caught the attention and

the imagination of the PM.[17] He wrote that it might be time
'to be guided a little by what we have been wrongly accused
of doing up till now' – i.e. turning economic questions into
political ones. He suggested that the British government
should link the EEC question 'with such matters as the Berlin
question' and even seek to break up the Common Market.
The British, he advised, should 'take a leaf out of the French
book and make it appear that we are ready and able to do
just that, allowing ourselves to be bought off at the last
moment with what will in fact be the terms on which for so
long we have been offering a free trade area'.

The prime minister wrote to his private secretary, Philip
de Zulueta: 'I hope the foreign secretary and others of my
colleagues now in Paris have read telegram 871 from Rome.
It is a pretty intelligent telegram.'[18] Macmillan, though, was
fully aware of the difficulties that such a course of action
would present not only in terms of Britain's relations with
the Six but also with regard to the views of some of his
colleagues and of his close civil service advisers. Even so,
the fact that Sir Ashley Clarke's cypher was so well received
by the PM – and supported by the president of the Board
of Trade – indicates that there still persisted among ministers something of the belief that, if it chose to, the British
government was still capable of getting its way in Europe.

A meeting in Paris of OEEC foreign ministers in the middle
of December was unproductive. Erhard's support for the
British *modus vivendi* proposal (for the removal of discrimination on important quota areas on a reciprocal basis) was
demolished by van Scherpenberg, his colleague in the German Foreign Ministry, even before the French themselves
were given the opportunity of rejecting it.[19] The meeting
has been described by Miriam Camps as 'the stormiest in
the history of the Organization'.[20] The intractable differences
between the British, who sought still to gain acceptance of
non-discrimination between all OEEC countries, and the
French, who were 'equally determined to preserve a clear
difference', were all too evident. The meeting was adjourned
until 15 January. In the meantime the French, in order to
prevent the charge of 'illegality' being made against them,
brought their liberalization undertaking to 90 per cent in
line with their OEEC obligation.

Shortly after the unhappy OEEC meeting, the question of sterling convertibility, which had remained an underlying source of suspicion among OEEC countries since the British undertook discussions with the Commonwealth and the Americans during the winter of 1952–3, was once again up for discussion.[21] But concerns among the Six that the British would use convertibility as a retaliatory measure – in so far as such a move would almost certainly spell the end of the European Payments Union (EPU) of whom the French were major debtors – were proved unjustified.

In the event, it was the devaluation of the French franc that set in train the convertibility of leading European currencies and the consequent replacement of the EPU by the European Monetary Agreement (EMA) – a modified payments system, the principles of which had been agreed in 1955. France was to be allowed to reschedule its debts to Britain and Germany. A tentative suggestion that the issue could be used as a 'negotiating card' to secure greater French cooperation with regard to the FTA was swiftly rejected as being counter-productive.[22] A currency row, which would have added to an already serious build-up of tension, was therefore successfully avoided.[23]

With the adoption of the EMA, the control of imports by quota among OEEC countries lost much of its rationale. Differences in the use of quotas between the Six and the other OEEC countries did little to improve relations over the following years, but with the movement towards convertibility, attention became more steadily directed towards the problem of tariffs.

By now, ministers and officials of all government departments were exercising their minds on the issue. One of the most far-seeing was the Earl of Perth, a minister of state at the Colonial Office. He had written to the PM at the end of November suggesting that Britain should apply for membership of the ECSC and Euratom and 'even now get somehow attached to the EEC Secretariat'.[24] 'Its importance grows daily', he argued, 'and of course in time creates a vested interest in its activity and success.' He advised the PM that the *Patronat* (a body of French employers) should be offered protection and markets in Britain. 'Once we are all in things can slowly be changed,' he explained. He also suggested that any contacts that the FBI might have with the *Patronat* should be exploited. While the PM was clearly impressed by Sir Ashley Clarke's earlier advice, there is little indication of how he viewed the opposing wisdom offered by the Earl of Perth. The fact that he agreed to have lunch with him might have been purely for reasons of friendship or courtesy.

At a meeting of the *ad hoc* committee, three days before Christmas, the postponement of the OEEC Council meeting set for 15 January was a source of considerable frustration.[25] This was to be the first in a long line of postponed meetings, missed deadlines and general prevarication – mostly, though not always, instigated by the French – which was to be a source of continuing vexation for British ministers and officials. Disturbing too were early indications that anticipated support from the US and Canada for Britain's position was not going to materialize. There was fear across the Atlantic that the successful negotiation of an arrangement between Britain and the Six would result in an intensification of dollar discrimination.[26]

As the year came to a close, recommendations on how to fill the policy vacuum were still arriving on the PM's desk from various quarters. De Zulueta advised the PM that there remained only two options.[27] The first was to break up the Common Market by threatening the Germans with a British withdrawal of NATO contributions. The second was 'to concentrate on watering it down and securing the best possible terms'. The PM, while showing no great enthusiasm for either course, indicated that he now favoured the latter. The president of the Board of Trade favoured a simple retaliatory approach, arguing that 'if we gave way our prestige would go down with a bang'.[28] In Whitehall too, fears were being expressed about whether or not 'we can afford another public rebuff'.[29] From Paris, though, Sir Gladwyn Jebb pressed for the abandonment of British insistence 'on the principle of complete non-discrimination' in the hope that the French would abandon their present 'take it or leave it position'.[30]

The *ad hoc* committee met for the last time on 20 January 1959. By now the extent of French non-cooperation even with regard to the establishment of a *modus vivendi* was becoming only too apparent. And it was noted that this failure to reach agreement was making UK industrialists 'increasingly restive'.[31] Reports from British delegates to the OEEC were beginning to indicate too the full ramifications for Britain of the Treaty of Rome. One of their number, Mr Warner, complained that 'it was all too frequent that our Ministers arrived in Paris to be faced by decisions of the six taken on the day before'.[32] It was under these strained circumstances that the UNISCAN proposals were identified as the best – and perhaps the only – available palliative for Britain's European difficulties.

It is evident from the way that ministers and officials communicated with each other during these difficult months that the 'bridge' idea was seized upon as affording genuine validation to a less than perfect scheme which seemed at the time to be the only one available. It is a clear example of how the development of policy can be affected as much by hopes and desires of ministers and officials as by the reality with which they were faced. They came to believe in it not because it was real but because they wanted it to be real. The fact that no attempt was made to examine the foundations of the so-called bridge – until it could no longer be avoided a year hence – indicates that, even in these exalted circles, hope could still triumph over expediency.

For senior ministers such as Sir David Eccles the hope persisted that the achievement of an FTA agreement with the Six was still a possibility – this, despite the fact that the French consistently indicated that, as far as they were concerned, the whole idea was dead and buried. The realization that the institution of the EEC and the declining role of the OEEC had brought about a marked diminution of British influence in Europe was dawning only gradually. Since it was still less than fifteen years since Britain had basked in battered glory as the sole victor of a devastated continent, it is not surprising that its leaders found the newly emerging order hard to comprehend.

By early 1959, it is evident that the question of Britain's relationship with the Six was still firmly based upon commercial considerations. In this regard the title, make-up and chairmanship of both ministerial committees is significant. They both had an obvious bias towards commercial rather than political or strategic considerations. This inclination was further underlined by the presence at committee meetings of two senior officials from the Treasury and the Board of Trade respectively. Where political or strategic policy was brought into the discussion, it was done so with a view to the possibility of it providing a *means* that might be used to secure what was emphatically still a commercial *end*.

3 EFTA: The Least Bad Option

Throughout the period under discussion, and particularly in these early stages of policy development, British public opinion with regard to Britain's trading relationship with Europe featured very rarely as a matter of ministerial concern – except, perhaps, for its proposed utilization as a threat with which to frighten the US and the Six. As far as particular interest groups were concerned, ministers were cognisant – especially as a general election loomed – of the concerns of farmers. They were also mindful of the interests of British industry, though this was more from the standpoint of Britain's overall economic well-being than for reasons of *direct* electoral appeal. The low-key treatment of the question by the serious press and its virtual neglect by popular newspapers owes much to the fact that it had not yet been *politicized* – that is to say that, as a predominantly commercial issue, it was of very little interest to the general public. Even if the government had sought to do so, it would have been hard-pressed to conjure up much public interest in Britain's quota and tariff arrangements with European countries.

Moreover, in the light of the failure of government policy with regard to securing an FTA and the paucity of ideas among ministers about how to proceed on the issue, there was little appetite among ministers for courting publicity. The government's account of the course of the FTA negotiations, published in the new year, was 'designed to demonstrate to world opinion the reasonable and constructive character of our policy'.[1] Evidently, it was *world* rather than *domestic* opinion that ministers hoped to inform. As Lieber points out, 'the general public paid little attention to Europe prior to July 1961' and, he adds, 'as far as the EEC was concerned, public opinion appears to have depended more on the Government than vica versa'.[2] There was undoubtedly an upsurge of interest and public debate following the July 1961 announcement. For the time being though, government ministers were content not to direct public attention towards Britain's troubled trading relations with Europe.

Throughout 1959, as ministers and officials examined and refined the UNISCAN proposals, it will be noted that such enthusiasm as had existed for tackling the underlying contradiction of Britain's relationship with the Six tapered off almost completely. Ministers and officials were able to assure themselves – and each other – that the question of Britain's trade with the Six was being dealt with when, in fact, no such dealing was being done. Confidence was placed, for the most part, in the likelihood, after the Stockholm Convention was signed, of securing a Six/Seven agreement. But, as will be shown, little serious thought was given in the meantime to what form this agreement would take. If it had been, it would soon have become apparent that the prospect for securing a tariff and quota agreement with the Six would be no brighter for Britain inside EFTA than it had been before that organization was instituted. In spite of the fact that it marked the establishment of EFTA, then, 1959 may rightly be regarded – in terms of Britain's trading relationship with EEC countries (which, even then, took two-thirds of Britain's European trade) – as a wasted year.

By the beginning of 1959, the machinery for examining the possibilities open to the government on the question of trade arrangements with Europe had been well developed. If the intermediate policy decisions were unimaginative, it was not for want of detailed appraisal of the problems involved. But the thinking of officials, like that of politicians, was channelled along a particular route which, hemmed in by tradition and loyalty – especially with regard to sovereignty, agriculture and the Commonwealth – precluded more than an occasional glance at broader horizons.

The *European Free Trade Area Steering Group*,[3] set up in October 1957 and chaired by R.W.B. Clarke (a third secretary to the Treasury), now submitted its findings, for the most part, through the new *European Economic Questions Official (EQ) Steering Group*, chaired in the first year by Sir Roger Makins, joint permanent secretary to the Treasury. Makins' steering group revised and enlarged upon the reports of the junior committee, before submitting them to ministers.

Makins' career had taken him, via the League of Nations and the UN, to America, where he had served as British ambassador from 1953 to 1956. An old friend of the prime minister,[4] he was an ardent Atlanticist and a powerful proponent of free trade. Makins' suspicion of the European 'idea' was not diminished by a vividly recalled encounter with Jean Monnet in London in 1950, when he was stung by the manner in which the proposals for the ECSC were presented to himself and Sir Edwin (now Lord) Plowden – as a 'take it or leave it' proposition.[5] The EQ steering group included among its membership Sir Frank Lee, permanent secretary to the Board of Trade, who was to take over from Makins both in the Treasury and as chairman of the steering group in January 1960.

On 22 January, Sir Roderick Barclay (from the FO) reported from Copenhagen on the activities of the industrial associations of Britain (the FBI) and the Scandinavian countries.[6] In their joint declaration they pointed to 'the parallelism between the [proposed] group and the E.E.C.', which should 'facilitate and encourage the fusion of the two'. Their statement gave added credibility to an ill-founded notion in which ministers were already about to invest too much confidence. But the proposals of the FBI together with the added assurances – with regard to the likely fusion of UNISCAN with the EEC and the probable exclusion of agriculture – were welcomed by ministers as fitting well with the direction of their own thinking.

The FBI's activities in late 1958/early 1959, though undeniably timely, should not be over-emphasized as a source of government policy. Since the advent of what has become known as *pressure* or *interest group politics* it has been all too easy to characterize the development of government policy in terms of government sensitivity to the demands and activities of such groups even though the demands of these groups have their roots as often as not in the changes that were already calling forth a response from government. In any case, as far as the FBI in the late 1950s was concerned, its consensus was a fragile one. Robert Lieber, who highlights the low-key contact that existed between industrialists and officials from the BOT and Treasury, admits that, at the UK Council of the European Movement held in February 1958, the delegations from both the FBI and the BEC (British Employers Confederation) were split over support for the FTA.[7]

Good news for British industry came in February, when the chancellor of the exchequer reported to the ministerial committee that a *modus vivendi* agreement on quotas had been reached with the French.[8] This objective having been achieved, discussion of Britain's short-term relationship with the EEC had arrived at something of a hiatus. Even now, though, ministers clung to the hope that, because of international developments (notably the Berlin Crisis) and the prospect of German economic hegemony, the French might yet accept an FTA.[9] At the same time, it was noted with some concern by the ministerial committee that the possibility of Britain joining the EEC was being energetically promulgated by a small though not insignificant minority of industrialists and radical political thinkers. In discussion, it was proposed that 'in view of current suggestions that our best course would be to join the E.E.C., it would be important to make known publicly and objectively the difficulties which such a course of action would entail'.[10] It was agreed that, among other difficulties, such a move would involve 'the abandonment of effective control over both domestic agricultural policy and external tariff policy, and would be irreconcilable with the Commonwealth preferential system'. The ministers present at this meeting, besides the PM, included Selwyn Lloyd, the Earl of Home, John Hare, Derick Heathcoat Amory, David Eccles, Reginald Maudling and the Earl of Perth. All, except Heathcoat Amory and the Earl of Perth were in the cabinet when Britain formally applied for membership of the EEC, two and a half years later.

The PM, in his summing up, called for work to be put in hand to find an appropriate formula should France be ready after all to accept an FTA. He also recommended that parliament should be solicited for its views on the whole question and 'in this connection', that 'an objective statement should be prepared [to which ministers may refer] setting out the difficulties which would be entailed if we were to join the E.E.C.'.[11]

In spite of the apparently negative attitude of the PM to

the prospect of Britain joining the EEC, there are grounds here for at least the suspicion that he was not so opposed to the idea as a first reading of this report indicates. For example, his proposal to initiate a debate in parliament seems to have been made in order to 'test the water' of opinion on the proposition. As has been indicated, it was clear by now that British membership of the EEC while not yet a significantly salient issue had at least been 'hatched' as an idea. He could well have been interested to see how much support there was in the House for such a move. The PM, after all, had no other reason to submit the government's current ideas on this question to parliamentary scrutiny. It would have been clear to him that the government would be unlikely to come out of such an encounter with a great deal of merit. In the event, as Camps points out, the debate gave an early indication that differences on the issue were greater within each of the main parties than between their leaders.[12] Another possible indication of the PM's attitude may be found in the wording of his closing recommenda-tion where he refers to the difficulties that would be en-tailed 'if we were to join the E.E.C.'. He might easily have pointed, instead, to the reasons why Britain *could not* join the EEC. By using this positive turn of phrase he indicated that he had at least recognized the possibility, however re-mote, of giving consideration to such a move.

If the PM himself was prepared to look at all possibilities, a report prepared in the Treasury and circulated to the cabinet by Heathcoat Amory indicated that the certainty of Britain's position with regard to membership of the EEC – at least from these quarters – was also showing early signs of erosion.[13] While ostensibly pointing up the reasons why such a move was not possible, the report gave some pre-viously unconsidered aspects of the question a guarded airing. For example, with regard to textiles, the report stated that 'Lancashire might approve, but our relations with India, Pakistan and Ceylon would be fundamentally changed'.[14] The use of the neutral term *changed*, where the more pejorative term *damaged* might have been expected, indicates a slight shift in emphasis. Even more telling was the assertion that 'the farmers might not object' to a common agricultural policy but that they and horticulturists would 'expect to get in such a system a satisfactory level of protection'. This was not so much an objection as the basis for a negotiating stance. In the same report the matter of a directly elected assembly – which was regarded by ministers as totally unacceptable – was played down, as it was pointed out that de Gaulle would ensure that it never came into being.

Finally, the report addressed the two points 'which were regarded as insuperable in 1955 but which might not be so today if all the Six were really anxious to include the United Kingdom and if on other grounds the United Kingdom wished to join'.[15] These were identified first, as the easing of the problem of Commonwealth free entry (under the terms of the Treaty of Rome, which already allowed for the free entry of East German goods into West Germany and products from the French African territories into France) and secondly, that although the existing arrangements of the EEC might not be to Britain's liking, they fell 'far short of being supra-national'. The shift of emphasis, though, should not be overstated. These were slight changes of nuance in a lengthy report whose substance provided a cogent case for Britain looking for a solution to its problems outside the EEC.

At a meeting held at the end of February, Clarke's committee ruled out both the threat of military withdrawal from Europe – on the grounds that it would increase the neutralist tendency in Germany – and the possibility of achieving worthwhile bilateral arrangements with the EEC within the terms of the GATT.[16] The committee identified a UNISCAN agreement as 'the only possibility'. And, in the face of all the contrary evidence previously cited, declared that 'such a grouping could subsequently negotiate with the Six' in the hope of 'eventually establishing something like free trade over the whole area'. The latter declaration owed more to the need to give weight to the committee's recommendation than it did to rational judgement.

Only the Treasury demurred from this line. A separate Treasury memorandum for the attention of the EQ steering group dated two days after Clarke's comprehensive report suggests that Treasury officials were not entirely convinced that UNISCAN would result in a better chance of negotiating agreement with the Six.[17] But the fact that Treasury officials felt that such an arrangement would 'have its own advantages' resulted in less attention being given to these doubts than might otherwise have been the case. It is likely that Treasury doubts never reached the ears of ministers because of the support of the EQ steering group – and notably its chairman – for the UNISCAN idea. On 3 March, Makins' committee concluded that 'we were left, by a process of elimination with a UNISCAN free trade area'.[18]

On 5 March, at a meeting of the ministerial FTA committee, the PM was forced to conclude, following a statement by the chancellor of the exchequer, that 'there was general agreement that the objections to our joining the European Economic Community were overriding'.[19] But, in the light of proposals favouring just such a course emanating both from the Continent and from 'influential public figures and journals' in Britain, the chancellor was charged with preparing material 'which might be drawn on as necessary' to give public expression to the government's conclusions.

Significantly, this report was to be far less 'liberal' in its approach to British membership of the EEC than the report that had been circulated to all cabinet members (though not discussed at a cabinet meeting) the previous month.[20] This is because the latest report was to provide an official rationale for the UK position. It was to be based on a statement made to the House of Commons by the paymaster general on 12 February 1959 and, as such, it was unequivocal in its rejection of the possibility of UK membership of the EEC. Maudling had put his indelible stamp on government policy. His peremptory statement illustrates clearly how the collective responsibility of the cabinet may be utilized by individual ministers (under certain circumstances) to keep government policy in line with their own preferences. Because, ostensibly, he was merely declaring publicly the government's view, Maudling could not be charged with abrogating his loyalty to cabinet colleagues. However, he was able, through making an emphatic statement in parliament, to ensure that – for the time being at least – there would be no softening of the government's position with regard to membership of the EEC as might have developed in the wake of the chancellor's earlier report.

It is important to note here though that while ministers were aware of the rising but (as yet) far from universal demand for serious consideration to be given to British membership of the EEC, they showed no sign of being influenced by it. Since, at this stage, ministers believed that the difficulties were 'overriding', their aim was to counter such demands with carefully formulated arguments rather than to explore the positive premises upon which those demands were based.

With the possibility of Britain joining the EEC effectively ruled out, ministers turned their attention, in March 1959, to the alternatives. They were either to do nothing or to work towards the conclusion of a UNISCAN agreement.[21] The chancellor stressed the need to do something on the grounds that to do nothing would not improve a disintegrating situation in which the UK was in danger of becoming progressively isolated. He argued that a UNISCAN agreement might provide a bridge between the Six and the rest (a proposition that had been specifically rejected by senior ministers and officials less than three months earlier); that it would give definite economic advantages and that it would reassure industrialists that the UK had a coherent trading relationship with Europe.

Now that the idea of UNISCAN becoming a 'bridge' to an agreement with the EEC was gaining currency with ministers, it could be utilized to offset the difficulties that were expected to be raised by British farmers and Commonwealth ministers. There was even a proposal that UNISCAN should be put forward as the first step of a plan not only to link the Six to the non-Six but also to link both with the US and the Commonwealth.[22] Although the idea was quickly dismissed as impracticable, now that the idea that UNISCAN would facilitate a Six/non-Six agreement had been developed and embellished in this way there was even less likelihood of its fragile foundation being re-examined. In any case, the PM concluded that UNISCAN appeared now to be the only possibility. However, the establishment of a Europe-wide FTA was to remain the government's 'ultimate objective'.[23]

On his return from a visit to the US in March, the PM was faced with mounting pressure to make a decision. He had received personal letters from Maudling and from Butler – the former arguing that if Britain failed to take up the

UNISCAN idea 'we should be left without a friend in Europe and we should thoroughly deserve such a fate' and the latter declaring that 'it is all very difficult but if we do nothing we are a sitting rabbit'.[24] Freddie Bishop, the PM's principal private secretary, urged the PM either to make a move on UNISCAN or to announce that Britain was not prepared to go ahead with the project. He expressed a concern that 'public opinion will increasingly solidify against the possibility of our forming a second economic grouping in Europe', adding that this would arise 'out of ignorance rather than malice'.[25]

On 3 April 1959, the ministerial committee finally came to the conclusion that 'the long-term interests of the country would best be served by an attempt to negotiate a European Trade Association'.[26] Macmillan recorded later that 'the Outer Seven was conceived of as a temporary measure pending the final unification of the economy of Europe'.[27] The decision, though, was not universally applauded. Peter Carey, a BOT official since 1953, who served as principal private secretary to successive presidents (1960–4), suggests that EFTA was viewed in the BOT as a *pis aller*. Many in the BOT, he recalls, wanted a customs union and 'quite a few' officials shared his own belief that Britain should have been in the EEC from the beginning.[28] Even Lord Sherfield (Sir Roger Makins) a leading proponent of the EFTA idea, says that he always regarded it as, essentially, a 'holding operation'.[29]

Sir Douglas Wass, the chancellor's private secretary (1959–61), describes EFTA as a 'half-way house' signifying an amalgam of FO Atlanticism and the commitment of the Treasury and the BOT to free trade. It also arose, he opines, because of the need 'to salvage something from the wreck'.[30] Sir Arnold France, who served on the EQ steering group and was chairman of the European Economic Questions (Official) committee, recalls that, after the FTA talks broke down, 'we got in rather a panic'. EFTA arose out of a deep-felt need to have *some* relationship with Europe, he explains.[31]

A month after the decisive ministerial committee meeting, the PM, as if to reassure himself and his colleagues that the decision they had reached was a sound one, itemized the three advantages of their action.[32] He confirmed that the proposed ETA (later to be retitled EFTA) provided not only the best route to an all-Europe FTA and a valuable trading arrangement in its own right, but also a safeguard against bilateral arrangements being entered into between the Six and the non-Six. The PM saw the first of these advantages, which had, by now, taken on an aura of certainty, as the most important. In discussion it was emphasized that the presentation of the new grouping as a rival bloc should be avoided. Instead, it should be presented abroad and to the British public as 'a bridge to an all-European solution'. This latter point was emphasized by the EQ steering group, whose report asserted that 'in public presentation, it will be of great importance to emphasize this and to stress particularly that the fundamental objective of the Government's seeking to establish an E.T.A. is to provide a new way to a successful European negotiation'.[33] In the Bank of England, where fears about the future role of the OEEC were giving rise to fears about the 'centre of gravity' shifting to the Six, the government's assurances were particularly welcome.[34]

While acknowledging the likelihood of opposition from various quarters – not least from the farming lobby – the PM said that the key objective was to safeguard British industry. It was upon industry, he argued, that farming and imports from the Commonwealth depended.[35] Agriculture and Commonwealth preference, despite their electoral significance, had become, for Macmillan, secondary considerations. Indeed, it was his recognition of the country's dependence above all upon its industrial strength that – when all efforts to achieve an acceptable trading relationship between Britain and the EEC had failed – would lead him to conclude that membership of the Community was the only sustainable option.

The proposals of the FTA committee were put to the full cabinet on 7 May.[36] The chancellor of the exchequer outlined the reasons for the proposals, emphasizing that 'the ministers directly concerned' believed that the ETA was 'the best means of eventually achieving an all-European Free Trade Area'. In dealing with the question of British membership of the EEC, the chancellor said that 'we could not ourselves join the Common Market on satisfactory terms'.

By now, at Maudling's insistence, the 'overriding objections' to British membership of the EEC had been officially re-established.[37] They were six-fold. The first was that it would result in the Six having to renegotiate and reratify the Treaty of Rome which had struck a 'very nice balance of obligations'. Secondly, majority voting on commercial relationships would not be appropriate for the UK whose trade was predominantly outside Europe. Thirdly, the common external tariff would mean the UK abrogating its obligations to Commonwealth countries. Fourthly, the proposed common policy on agriculture could not be reconciled to existing UK policy. The fifth objection was that the movement of workers and equal pay policies would cause problems for Britain; and the sixth, was that political integration, as envisaged by the Six, would find little support in the UK.

But, even at this juncture, six months after the FTA negotiations had broken down, there is evidence that senior diplomats still clung to the possibility of achieving an all-Europe FTA. Sir Ashley Clarke reported from Rome that the Italians were still aiming for an FTA. He suggested that, with the 'marked improvement in France's exchange position' the French may be less rigid in their opposition to the FTA.[38] But in London, the same men who had by now invested all their confidence in the negotiation of a free trade arrangement between the French-dominated EEC and the new grouping, would give little credence to the notion that France would be willing to change its existing position on tariffs and quotas. The contradiction of their position evidently eluded them.

The following months were taken up with negotiations leading to the institution of the European Free Trade Association. Fearful of the consequences of another rebuff, the British government arranged for Sweden to make the running.[39] Agriculture posed the biggest problem. In the event, it was excluded from the agreement altogether. The only other significant problem was the attitude of Commonwealth ministers, particularly from Australia and New Zealand who, according to officials on the Commonwealth Liaison sub-committee on European Trade Relations, 'still refused to recognize the realities of the situation and still appeared to regard the United Kingdom as blameworthy for developments in Europe over which we had no control'.[40] While safeguarding the Commonwealth relationship was to remain high on the government's list of priorities, there is a glimmer of recognition here that British interests and those of the rest of the Commonwealth might not, after all, remain for ever indivisible. The Stockholm Convention, setting up EFTA was signed on 20 November 1959 – a year after the all-Europe FTA talks had broken down.

The importance of the role of the FBI and the industrial organizations of the Scandinavian countries in bringing about EFTA is open to question. There is no doubt that their initiative was a useful one and there is no doubt either that their support for the policy provided added impetus to ministers. But the fact remains that the industrial arrangements upon which EFTA was based arose out of the ill-fated FTA negotiations over which, at the time, the FBI was split. If ministers had not been discouraged by the lukewarm reception of the FBI for their FTA proposals, there is no reason to suppose that they would have been unduly influenced either by the sudden flush of enthusiasm of the FBI for the UNISCAN idea. Furthermore, while some ministers and officials were giving way to early (and still barely iterated) doubts arising out of the unreasonable expectations of Commonwealth leaders, the FBI remained united and unequivocal in its attitude to the Commonwealth relationship. Pfaltzgraff points to an FBI statement published in *The Times* in June 1959 in which the FBI confirmed that 'we continue to regard the United Kingdom's links with the Commonwealth, and the system of mutual preferences and obligations among Commonwealth countries, as of vital and continuing importance to the United Kingdom. . . . We expect the Government's policy to be based on this fundamental premise.'[41]

While one of the key objections to British membership of the EEC was the problem it would pose for British agriculture, ministers and officials, believing that some sacrifices would be inevitable, had been prepared to make agricultural concessions in order to secure a UNISCAN agreement. They were also conscious that entering into such an agreement would be likely to cause friction with other members of the Commonwealth – another objection to British membership of the EEC. It seems, then, that the government was prepared to make (admittedly lesser) sacrifices in order to join a very much second-best organization. But the important point is that ministers *were* now prepared to make concessions both with regard to agriculture and the Commonwealth relationship. That they could not, at this stage, bring themselves to make a more far-reaching departure from previous policy owed much to the personality predispositions and psychological environments of the ministers and officials concerned. Sir Roger Makins was particularly influential in this regard. As a keen Atlanticist and free-marketeer, he chaired the most influential of the non-ministerial committees. It was largely upon the conclusions of his committee's reports that ministers based their judgement. Reginald Maudling's exploitation of informal power, drawn from formally sanctioned cabinet collectivity, was also significant, but more in terms of the government's longer-term attitude to the European issue than for its direct bearing upon the EFTA policy.

Government papers reveal, too, a tendency among both ministers and officials to invest all their hope and confidence in the prevailing government objective. Until November 1958 that objective had been to secure a Europe-wide FTA. Long after the French had made it clear that they would take no part in such an arrangement, it still figured largely in the plans and aspirations (particularly) of ministers. Only with difficulty did they adjust to a new agenda. When they did, they opted for the solution that resembled most closely the one that had eluded them. While a possibility existed to enter an (albeit very inferior) form of FTA, the less palatable alternative – membership of the EEC – could be resisted. The likelihood of being able to negotiate an EFTA/EEC agreement – upon which the whole *raison d'être* of EFTA came to be based – was seized upon, not because the arguments were convincing – ministers themselves had not been persuaded while other alternatives appeared to be available – but because the idea fitted well with ministers' preferred policy option.

But for all this, there was *some* indication of movement with regard to the question of British membership of the EEC. While the chancellor was not yet charged with looking into the pros and cons of such a move – he was, instead, merely to point out the difficulties involved – the fact that it was deemed necessary to compile such a report at all is worthy of note. For even a year earlier, it would have been considered unnecessary. Far from raising questions in ministers' minds, however, the upshot of the report was to confirm them still more solidly in their uncompromising position. Even so, the question of British membership of the EEC had at least been raised and, with the institution of EFTA, the attitude of British ministers with regard to the Commonwealth relationship and indeed to agriculture had undergone a barely perceptible but none the less material adjustment.

It was during the EFTA negotiations that the seeds were sown for the difficulties that were to come. First, little attention was paid to the sort of agreement that would be necessary to extend the tariff and quota arrangements of the Six to the Seven, without affecting the cohesion of the EEC. Secondly, far from showing that problems could be overcome, the Stockholm Convention by excluding agriculture illustrated all too clearly the magnitude of the difficulties posed by British agriculture and the Commonwealth for any future negotiations.

During this period too, the ramifications for Britain of its continued exclusion from the EEC, were beginning to make themselves felt. From the Commercial Relations department of the BOT, Miss Dennely, complained to her FO colleagues that 'the traditional U.K. suppliers of propellers to a French shipyard have said that licences have recently been refused for orders amounting to some 200,000 pounds on the ground that facilities were now available only for the import from Holland and Germany'.[42] This early indication of the potential disadvantage under which British manufacturers were now being placed was noted – and assimilated – by FO officials.

4 'What is it we want?'

Far from being a time of reconciliation with the Six, as ministers and officials had convinced themselves it would be, the next six months was to be a period of confusion and disappointment. The divisions among government ministers and officials were to become ever more evident as key players such as the paymaster general and the British ambassador in Paris attempted to mould government policy in accordance with their respective (and opposing) instincts and aspirations. Their efforts were facilitated by the very lack of a coherent or recognizable government policy on Europe. The PM's interest in the issue, which had become somewhat desultory since the EFTA decision had been reached, would be captured once again as the intractable nature of the difficulties still facing Britain became gradually more apparent. During this election period, though, one of the government's priorities would be to ensure that the issue did not damage the prospects of the Conservative Party. The best way to accomplish this, ministers judged, would be to keep the matter off the electoral agenda.[1]

While the problems arising out of Britain's trading relationship with Europe undoubtedly exercised the minds of certain ministers and officials a good deal during the late 1950s, as far as the cabinet as a whole was concerned, it was far from being at the top of the agenda. As an issue, it still had no fixed or permanent home in a particular government department. While it had obvious ramifications for the work of the Treasury, the BOT, the FO, the MAG and both the CRO and the CO, responsibility for finding a way of coming to terms with the developments across the Channel fell on no single ministry. As a result, the power of the PM was enhanced in that he had the option of including or excluding ministers in private discussions (where strategy would be formulated) according to the extent to which he trusted their views and judgement on this specific issue rather than, necessarily, in accordance with their particular ministerial responsibilities. This was to be a particularly useful source of informal power which the PM was able to exploit as his own views on the matter developed.

Conversely, it meant that the European question was, for many members of the cabinet, an unimportant side-show.[2] By the end of 1959 no minister – except perhaps the paymaster general, who had shown himself determined though unimaginative, and even a little naive, in his approach to the problem – had 'claimed' the European question for his own, nor had anyone addressed the long-term implications of the anachronistic assumption that Britain remained leader of a continent from which it was becoming ever more commercially and politically excluded. No one asked how a mutually agreeable arrangement with France would be negotiated once EFTA was established (when it had proved impossible to negotiate such an arrangement before) because no one had either the time or the inclination to immerse himself too deeply in an issue that clearly offered every opportunity for failure and very little opportunity for bringing off a political triumph.

Even for Macmillan himself, throughout the late 1950s and into 1960, the European question was not the most pressing of issues. It is evident that the questions that concerned Macmillan most related to contradictions and discord associated with other aspects of the changing world order. The vexed question of German reunification – and particularly the status of Berlin – together with Macmillan's own determination to retain Britain's position as a world power resulted in his preoccupation with the Atlantic relationship, with securing an 'independent' nuclear deterrent and with summitry. The challenge presented by decolonization especially, at this time, in east and central Africa – described by Macmillan as 'one of the most important jobs in our long history'[3] – also commanded much of the PM's attention, while at home, the demands of leading a far from united party to victory in the 1959 election and dealing with the threats to domestic economic equilibrium[4] provided him with further grave distractions from the challenging developments in Western Europe.

Maudling embarked upon the business of making a success of EFTA with enormous enthusiasm. He and the PM were conscientious in keeping the cabinet informed about the progress of negotiations in order to secure approval for any unpopular measures that might prove necessary. While the cabinet as a whole had hardly been involved at all in the development of the EFTA idea, the 'fine tuning' of the proposals was laid before them in great detail throughout the summer of 1959.

In July 1959, the British ambassador, Gladwyn Jebb – anxious as ever to bring the activities of the Six to ministers' attention – reported from Paris that M. Valéry Giscard d'Estaing (the French equivalent of the financial secretary to the Treasury) had warned him that pressure was building within the French government, if not from the president himself, for movement towards political unity between the Six. Jebb had told Giscard that the UK might well wish to be involved.[5] But, while the British ambassador's positive attitude might have eased the way in dealing with French ministers and officials, his tendency to see French responsiveness where none existed and his scepticism of Britain's position with regard to the EEC were liabilities that the government could ill-afford.

Lord Gladwyn says in his memoirs that, 'from the moment when I arrived in Paris . . . I began to press for some British political commitment to "Europe"'.[6] His motivation arose out of fear for the political consequences of British exclusion from European political institutions which would, he believed, expose continental Europe to 'the inexorable pull of the Kremlin'.[7] In the light of this, he claimed that it was necessary to 'partially sink our identity in Europe'. This was needed too, he suggested, from the purely British point of view as he warned of the development of a 'Third Force' from which Britain would be excluded.

Well liked and respected in French political circles, Jebb also enjoyed what he described as a 'personal friendship' with de Gaulle. He further admitted to having been influenced by M. Wormser[8] (who had responsibility for France's trade relations). But this 'closeness' with the French establishment, while proving invaluable in affording him easy access right to the top of the French government, also left him little room to stand back and calculate objectively the true intentions behind French declarations. By his own admission, he 'got it wrong' several times when dealing with de Gaulle.[9] Added to this, his acknowledged misgivings with regard to HMG's policy resulted in a tendency for him to put his own interpretation on his government's priorities. It was quite clear, for example, that the British government had no wish to be involved in a movement towards political unity among the Six in July 1959, as Giscard d'Estaing would have been well aware. By claiming otherwise, Jebb would have been in danger of undermining his own and his government's credibility.

But, if Britain's ambassador in Paris was open to the charge of immoderate Europeanism, the same could not be said of the paymaster general. Maudling placed far greater emphasis on Britain's world role and Atlantic relationship. Even so, on 28 July, he wrote to the PM proposing that the Free Trade Area office should be wound up and its duties handed over to the FO.[10] Since, in 1959, the FO still shared (for the most part) his own priorities, the paymaster general felt confident that Britain's conservative policy with regard to the EEC would be safe in the FO's hands.[11] This was a confidence that he would later come to realize had been severely misplaced. For the time being, though, Maudling remained optimistic that a solution that would fulfil all Britain's requirements could yet be found. His optimism was not wholly without foundation. For example, in August, John Profumo, minister of state in the FO, had reported that various indications, including statements made by Giscard d'Estaing and M. Joxe, suggested that the French were anxious to get an agreement between the Six and the Seven.[12]

M. Wormser, though – as British officials had learned to their cost during the FTA talks (and would do again) – was an astute and even an artful negotiator. He might well have put out deliberately contradictory signals in order to exploit the resulting weakening of resolve in London. His frequent changes of mind and mood throughout the series of talks with Sir Roderick Barclay in the winter of 1960/1 bear out this interpretation of his intentions. British officials and ministers, who had been inculcated, mostly from their public school days, with a reverence for consistency and fair play, were thrown into some disarray by the (apparently) constantly changing outlook in Paris, much though not all of which appears to have been orchestrated by M. Wormser. The upshot was that, when British ministers or officials met

with their French counterparts, they did so with little knowledge of what line the French would be taking.

It should be said, however, that by no means all the confusion about French motives arose out of the tendency of
M. Wormser and his colleagues for inconsistency. Confusion often arose too out of differences between the Quay
d'Orsay and the president and between them both and the
European Commission. The fault in London – and perhaps
even more in the British embassy in Paris – lay in a failure
to recognize, even after the FTA experience, that French
views, as expressed by senior ministers and officials, might
bear no relation, in the event, to the enactment of policy
by the French government. Had ministers and officials been
able to shrug off their own hopes and aspirations through
which they interpreted French declarations, they would have
been better able to reflect upon recent experiences, from
which they might have drawn very different conclusions about
French intentions. A more realistic outlook might have been
encouraged too, if more note had been taken of the steady
stream of information arriving in the FO from Kenneth
Christofas, head of the UK Delegation to the European
Commission in Brussels, who had close contacts with both
Professor Hallstein (president of the Commission) and
M. Marjolin of the French delegation.[13]

Ironically, though, the first real blow to British hopes of
securing an agreement between EFTA and the EEC came
not from Paris but from Washington. Early reports of American objections to any such agreement were now being borne
out. It had become clear to Sir Harold Caccia, British ambassador to the US, that the Americans had a very negative
attitude indeed towards EFTA.[14] The reasons for this were
three-fold. First, it represented another source of discrimination against America with the potential to worsen what
was already a worrying balance of payments deficit; secondly,
as a 'rival' for the EEC, it was viewed as hardening the rift
in Europe; and thirdly, unlike the EEC, it had no political
attractions for America to offset its commercial disadvantages.[15] Even so, Caccia was not altogether disheartened. He
was confident that, once EFTA was established, the Americans would bring influence to bear in order to secure an
agreement. This belief could have been based on nothing

more than his faith in American goodwill towards Britain arising out of the so-called special relationship.

Douglas Wass, in the chancellor's office, was one of a handful of officials who had a clear understanding of the difficulties ahead. In an update for the PM on progress in the EFTA negotiations, he took the opportunity to warn Macmillan that 'at present there is no sign of French willingness to make an agreement. Nor can we see how, even in more favourable political circumstances, we could expect to get an agreement within our previous conditions [i.e. with regard to agriculture and the Commonwealth]'.[16] Towards the end of November, de Zulueta drew the PM's attention to another missive from Wass – this time about the ongoing discussions of the Six. Wass had concluded that, even though the Six had not adopted the views shared by the Commission and the French that a Six/Seven agreement was 'disadvantageous in principle', there was 'no basis whatever among the Six for discussions for an agreement between the Seven and the Six'.[17] Sir Douglas has since suggested that the difficulty for ministers and officials in coming to terms with the true situation lay first, in their misunderstanding of the motivation behind the Common Market which militated against 'dilution' by EFTA and secondly, in the 'traditional weakness of British policy-makers of believing their own hype'.[18] Dissenting voices, he claims, tended not to be heard.

Notwithstanding the considerable doubts that were now being raised in the Treasury about the achievement of any sort of working trade arrangement with the Six, the EQ steering group examined three possible courses of action arising out of a report prepared by Clarke's EFTA steering group.[19] The first was to seek an immediate agreement with the Six. The problems here were obvious; first, it was conceded that the French were unlikely to be amenable to such an idea and even if they were, such an agreement would require substantial British concessions with regard to agriculture and the Commonwealth. The second suggestion was that the UK should seek world-wide tariff reductions to make for a better climate for Six/Seven negotiations later. But here again they believed that, although this course might well attract the approval of the US and Commonwealth countries, the plan would probably be blocked by the French.

It would also mean that the UK would have to make tariff reductions which would pose difficulties of their own. Moreover, it was felt that it might be difficult to hold the Seven together in the course of lengthy multilateral negotiations. The third option that presented itself was for an interim arrangement whereby countries of the Six and the Seven would agree to the tariff reductions that they planned for 1 July 1960 being applied to all OEEC members. But this plan would not be acceptable to the US nor to the Commonwealth since it would increase discrimination against them. Furthermore, officials feared that, if adopted, it could well result in powerful pressure on the UK to enter into a form of closer association with the EEC 'with all that meant for the Commonwealth'.

The conclusions of the steering group were that an interim agreement would not be in Britain's interests at this stage, though consideration would have to be given to any approach made by the Six. Before proposing world-wide tariff reductions, careful consideration would have to be given to Britain's own situation in this regard. It was recommended that the chancellor should discuss these problems with his colleagues. In effect, the steering group had no constructive policy to recommend. So, even before the Stockholm Convention was signed, officials had come to realize that EFTA held no answers to Britain's dilemma.

The ministerial FTA committee did not meet again after July 1959. But, at the end of October, the PM convened the *European Economic Association committee* comprised, like its forerunner, of senior ministers from key government departments. Freddie Bishop was appointed to the secretariat of the committee. The terms of reference of the committee were 'to consider all questions relating to the establishment of closer economic association between the United Kingdom and other European countries'.[20] Inevitably, though, the early meetings of the committee concentrated upon short-term questions arising out of the proposed Stockholm Convention. Instead of taking a broad view of Britain's economic relationship with the rest of Europe, ministers found themselves embroiled in matters such as how to come to terms with their EFTA counterparts over tomato purée.

In November, Makins' steering group met again, turning

their attention to 'next steps after Stockholm'.[21] By now the pressure to try out 'the bridge' was growing. This emanated not only from the Swiss, the Danes and the Austrians but also from British industry. Voices were even being raised on the subject in parliament. But now that 'the bridge' was theoretically in place, there was no great desire on the part of officials to test it. All the difficulties and contradictions that had been so conscientiously overlooked while EFTA was being presented as the key to trade harmony in Europe were now making themselves felt. Clarke's committee had prepared a paper setting out preferred options which required both a change of heart by the French and 'tangible progress' towards the freeing up of world trade – neither of which seemed likely.[22] Only two practical options were identified. The first was to encourage EFTA countries to delay moves towards closer association with the Six, by pointing out that a speedy attempt at negotiations might threaten the cohesion of the Seven, and the second was to make proposals that the French would be sure to reject.

In truth, Makins' committee had belatedly concluded that the peculiar combination of Britain's agricultural arrangements, Commonwealth relationship, existing tariff system and (now) membership of EFTA did not lend itself any more easily to the achievement of an acceptable trading arrangement with the EEC than had existed a year earlier. Officials had come to realize that agriculture, left out of both the failed FTA proposals and, in the event, the Stockholm Convention, could not be excluded from a Six/Seven negotiation. Neither British farmers nor Commonwealth producers, though, had been primed for this eventuality. The so-called 'bridge', then, was reminiscent of the king's new clothes: totally lacking in substance, though widely applauded and constantly alluded to by everyone on the assumption that everyone else was familiar with its intricate details. That 'the bridge' was a fabrication of desire rather than reality began to be appreciated as soon as its theoretical construction was complete. Faced, not for the first time, with the intractable contradiction of Britain's trading interests, all the steering group had to offer was to propose 'playing for time', hoping Micawber-like that something would turn up.

In the light of the conflicting reports emanating from

various government offices and departments and the lack
of positive suggestions from the EQ steering group, Freddie
Bishop (now serving as deputy secretary to the cabinet)[23]
advised the PM that the matter should not be raised in cabinet. The PM was to meet a few ministers and officials at
Chequers – to which, Bishop suggested, 'I presume you will
not refer at the Cabinet.' After the Chequers meeting, the
ministerial committee on European Economic Association
would meet to consider the findings of officials.[24] Bishop
recommended that, as far as the cabinet was concerned, 'it
would do no harm to lay down the provisional rule that we
should concentrate on consolidating our position, and avoid
any premature move towards "bridge-making" at least until
the Convention is ratified.'[25]

The meeting at Chequers was restricted to the PM, the
foreign secretary, the chancellor of the exchequer and their
officials. Maudling (serving, since the election, as president
of the Board of Trade) was not included, nor was there any
other representation from the BOT.[26] At this informal meeting, the insubstantiality of the EFTA agreement in terms of
its main purpose – a Six/Seven agreement – was quickly
acknowledged. Ministers agreed that 'the Seven had come
into existence ostensibly as a bridge with the Six'. But the
next logical step, the beginning of negotiations between the
Seven and the Six, did not now seem likely. It was 'United
States opposition to any European trade arrangement' rather
than French objections, or indeed British difficulties, that
was seen as the main obstacle. It was noted that, if there
seemed no likelihood of achieving a Six/Seven agreement,
there was a danger of 'defections' from the Seven, so it was
important to keep the 'momentum of negotiation' going. It
was now openly acknowledged that 'there was little reason
on present evidence to suppose that negotiations between
the Six and the Seven would be any more successful than
had the original negotiations about a free trade area'. The
three ministers concluded that an assessment was necessary
'to decide how far the United Kingdom could live with the
Common Market, and how best to mitigate its effects'.

Having been only too ready to believe that the institution
of EFTA would bring rich rewards in respect of Britain's
European trading difficulties, the PM now found himself once

again cut adrift from any firm line of policy. His early instinct was to abandon the uneven struggle and look for ways in which Britain could live with the effects of EEC tariff barriers. But after ruminating overnight on the various ramifications of the latest findings, he concluded that there must still be something that could be done. Unclear, though, as to what the next step should be, he handed the problem over to Heathcoat Amory in the hope that the chancellor would be able to offer some insight that he himself had missed.[27]

The following week the PM met the foreign secretary in his room.[28] Selwyn Lloyd expressed his concern that Britain should still be seeking a solution through an all-Europe FTA. He was convinced that such a solution was not available, though he realized that Britain's EFTA partners would continue to press for it. He feared that, in the light of this, Britain might be pushed into a position 'which would be inconsistent with our domestic, Commonwealth and international obligations'. Lloyd favoured a more low-key approach which would leave discussions to the *Commission de Contact*.[29] It was agreed that Douglas Dillon (US under-secretary of state) should be told that Britain had always envisaged EFTA as a unifying force in Europe. He was also to be warned that it would be dangerous 'to base United States' policies on the assumption that this temporary situation [the success of the EEC] would continue'.

That ministers were not successful in their attempts to convince Dillon was made very clear by reports in the British press. On 10 December, *The Times* reported that the Americans 'were evidently reluctant to encourage the Six to negotiate with the Seven as a group'.[30] Furthermore, it asserted that if the US were forced to choose, it would stand by the Six rather than the Seven. Macmillan's characteristic response was to argue that the need for a *political* solution should be emphasized.[31] It should be argued, he said, that the Seven was a valuable political asset in preventing the disintegration of Europe. Obviously rattled, he wrote to the chancellor: 'unless some way can be found of avoiding the economic damage which we should otherwise suffer from the Six, the whole of our political relationship in Europe will have to be revised.'[32] This is a clear indication that it was Britain's *economic interests* rather than *political* considerations that were at the forefront of the PM's mind.

The political usefulness of EFTA in 'preventing the disintegration of Europe' – an unconvincing proposition since the Stockholm Convention was a purely commercial agreement with no political content – was to be emphasized to Dillon in the interests of securing a *political* response from the US which would bring about a solution to Britain's *economic* difficulties. As the months – and years – went by, the political emphasis would broaden and deepen until the economic foundation of the policy was almost obscured under a welter of political and strategic arguments and exhortations. Inevitably, as those arguments were practised and refined, they took on a certain credibility of their own. Even so, in his handling of European policy, there is no question that the PM was motivated over the coming months and years not by political and strategic concerns but by the overriding fear that Britain was in danger of sustaining irreparable 'economic damage'.

Under the burden of this fear, while fully exploiting the opportunity, as occasion demanded, of consulting with only a few close colleagues – opportunities of which he was to avail himself regularly as a new and controversial initiative presented itself as the only solution to Britain's difficulties – the PM did not demur from plundering the cabinet as a whole for ideas. This he did in December 1959. However, as leader of a political party which demanded strength and authority from its incumbent prime minister, he was careful to avoid any suggestion of doubt or failure with regard to the Stockholm Convention. In this respect the limit of the PM's formal power militated against the possibility of full cabinet involvement in his underlying dilemma.

The style and content of the chancellor's presentation of the Stockholm Convention to the cabinet, prior to its ratification, was illustrative of the necessity to ensure that cabinet morale was maintained, not only for the good of the government and the Conservative Party but also for the political security of the PM himself. As previously noted, the cabinet as a whole had not been involved in the development of government policy on this issue. But cabinet approval was required for the policy to be enacted. As a

result, the tone of the chancellor's report was more reminiscent of a presentation to a potentially hostile constituency than to colleagues.[33] The advantages of the policy –
such as the proportionately higher incomes and foreign trade
of EFTA partners compared with EEC countries – were played
up while the potential difficulties – arising out of the cold
response to the scheme from Washington – were played down.

The written report circulated earlier to the cabinet by the
chancellor had contained a rather more realistic appraisal
of the situation by acknowledging, for example, that the
possibility of 'a bridge' now 'looks like a dead end'.[34] Even
so, in his written report, the chancellor claimed to have
been encouraged by Dillon's attitude which, he said, indicated that the US was keen to work more closely with Europeans on trade problems. His recommendation was that 'we
should be unwise to make any drastic reassessment of policy
at this time'. An FTA agreement should remain Britain's
objective, he asserted, while recognition should be given to
the fact that 'it may be unrealisable or at best that we shall
make very slow progress towards it'.

Summing up the cabinet discussion, the PM argued that
the economic problem which faced Britain with regard to
the EEC would not be solved 'until we had reached a political understanding with the French Government'.[35] He emphasized the validity of French aspirations for representing
the 'natural leadership of Europe' and of Britain's important relations with the Commonwealth and the US. This
somewhat surprising declaration, recognizing French hegemony in Europe, compared with Britain's broader relationships and world-wide commitments, serves to illustrate the
confusion in his own mind arising out of the contradiction
of Britain's position. The response of his cabinet colleagues
offered the PM nothing new in the way of a possible solution; if anything it merely emphasized the importance that
the cabinet still attached to a free trade solution in the context
of the Commonwealth and the Atlantic relationships. But
the lack of a constructive and realistic approach by cabinet
members was due not only to a lack of imagination, but
also to a failure on the part of the ministers most involved
to take the cabinet into their confidence from the outset;
to signal the gravity of the situation and to expound the

need, as the PM declared in private, for a complete revision of Britain's political relationship with Europe in order to solve its commercial difficulties.

A meeting between de Gaulle, Macmillan and Eisenhower at Rambouillet later that month produced nothing to encourage a more optimistic outlook.[36] Macmillan took the opportunity to declare that it would be impossible 'to keep troops and aircraft in Germany at a cost of 60 million pounds a year if France and Germany were waging economic war against the UK'. De Gaulle simply denied that any intention of such an economic war existed. The attitude of the US administration in the months following indicated that Eisenhower, too, was unmoved by the British prime minister's threat. The only positive outcome of the meeting, as far as Macmillan was concerned, was an agreement to set up a New Economic Committee of OEEC members, the US and Canada where difficulties arising out of trade relationships could be discussed along with other issues of concern to industrialized countries, such as Third World development.

It was during the Christmas period that the barrenness of Britain's European policy struck deeply into the PM's psyche. He called again on Heathcoat Amory, with whom, unlike the chancellor's predecessor, he felt a strong rapport.[37] He asked him directly: given that an FTA was not possible, 'what it is we want?'[38] The chancellor's response is not recorded but it is unlikely that he had a ready answer. There was no enlightenment for the PM either in the paper produced for him by the EQ steering group. He commented to Freddie Bishop, 'it is a very good paper but I still do not know what to do. The paper is rather like the Delphic Oracle.'[39] Freddie Bishop was as discouraged as the PM himself at the steering group's unsatisfactory recommendations: 'Can we rely only on tariff bargaining in the G.A.T.T. to reduce the commercial advantages of the Six?' he enquired rhetorically.

Similar doubts were expressed by the foreign secretary, who wrote to the PM a few days later, 'my own difficulty is to be certain that I know what we are trying to get and how we want to try to get it'.[40] His only suggestion was that the UK should 'take on the Six'. 'We have 80 to 90 millions of people in the Seven with high standards of living,' he argued, 'there are 160 million in the Six, but they include the Italians and perhaps the Six will have the Greeks and Turks round their necks.' It is unlikely that he was much convinced himself by this argument; the fact that he put it forward at all reveals his own recognition of the shortage of viable options.

The only glimmer of hope, as 1959 came to a close, rested in the New Economic Committee, which at least provided a forum where disagreement over trade arrangements could be tackled.[41] This development, though, would pose problems of its own in so far as the British government was not yet clear about what it wanted to achieve. Once again, in the absence of a coherent strategy or even a clearly defined aim, hope was invested in finding a solution through dialogue with political allies who, to the growing discomfiture of British ministers and officials, openly expressed their satisfaction with the existing arrangements. Far from improving the chances for finding a solution, British membership of EFTA was now adding to the government's difficulties. For, besides being committed to safeguarding the interests of British colonies and the Commonwealth, there was now an extra obligation on Macmillan's government: to take into account the interests of Britain's EFTA partners in any further discussions with the Six.

The PM, constrained by the need to preserve both cabinet unity and the strength of his own position, felt unable to share his difficulties with the cabinet. Freddie Bishop's assumption that the cabinet would not need to be fully apprised of the gravity of the situation, nor of the PM's meeting at Chequers, reveals that this was not a particularly unusual practice. It also serves to illustrate where the loyalties of the deputy secretary to the cabinet lay. But the exclusion of the cabinet from involvement in the *essence* of the problem was to lead, in the end, to its own difficulties. For, while a few interested and involved ministers would, through their immersion in the substance of the issue over many months and years, come gradually to appreciate the need for a radical solution, their colleagues, who had been largely shielded from the reality of Britain's circumstances, would find it hard to make any such psychological adjustment.

For now, though, the question of British membership of

the EEC, having been raised and determinedly resisted, had been effectively excised from the agenda. There was to be more tortured negotiation, bewilderment, disappointment and even desperation before the question was to be asked again – this time with a measure of tentativeness and finesse which, in the light of other developments, would make it considerably harder to dismiss.

While, at the end of 1959, the tendency persisted among some ministers and officials to allow their own aspirations to colour their perspective – to hear what they wanted to hear and to ignore the rest – it is evident that a number of senior ministers, including the PM himself, had, after the short respite of confidence in the 'bridge' nostrum, been assailed by new and even more deep-seated doubts about how to proceed.

British confusion had not arisen out of a lack of information – lines of communication with Paris, for example, were extremely good – but rather out of the need for a more careful interpretation of that information and of the will to act constructively upon it. At the same time, government policy was constrained by its commitment to the Commonwealth relationship, British farming interests and the vexed question of sovereignty which, hinging as it did upon the legitimacy of British aspirations for world status and an Atlantic outlook, amounted to more than fears about purely domestic autonomy.

Already the PM was beginning, more or less consciously, to gather around him ministers and officials whose minds were not closed to the possibility of a radical departure from existing policy. Reginald Maudling was not one of them. Though his new position as president of the Board of Trade, together with his previous assignment as chief British negotiator for the FTA, would indicate his close involvement in the development of European trade policy, he was conspicuously absent from the meeting at Chequers. Significantly, Sir Frank Lee appeared to command the PM's confidence. Indeed, he was moved to the Treasury in January 1960 to replace the 'free trade Atlanticist' Sir Roger Makins, whom Macmillan had invited to chair the Atomic Energy Authority.

But, if answers were still elusive, the questions, at least, were becoming clearer. They related, coincidentally, to the three 'circles' of British influence expounded by Winston Churchill. The Atlantic relationship, so painstakingly repaired by Macmillan after Suez, was once again giving rise to uncertainty. It was plain that the US administration was not willing to accord the British government the support it required; indeed, reports indicated a fundamental antipathy from the US towards the British-dominated EFTA. As far as the Commonwealth was concerned, although it was still almost universally acknowledged as a source of wealth and influence, it was now clear that the Commonwealth relationship was contributing to Britain's problems. Closer to home, in the European 'circle', the old assumption that Britain's *economic* hegemony in Western Europe was assured by its *political* and *strategic* contribution was shown now to be unfounded.

5 Dissonance and Drift

In making an assessment of how the British government arrived at the situation in which it found itself in 1960, it is worth at least alluding to the condition that I.L. Janis has described as *groupthink*. Many decision-making bodies are susceptible to this syndrome which impairs the ability of decision-makers to arrive, through a process of rational debate, at the optimum solution; instead, the group tends to light on a particular idea or suggestion and to *build into it* the reasons why it should be adopted.

Peculiarly susceptible to groupthink, Janis suggests are, first, those decision-making bodies made up of people with particular personality predispositions (such as those marked by a fear of disapproval or rejection); secondly, those groups where there exists a marked degree of amiability and *esprit de corps;* and thirdly, those where 'members are undergoing high stress from external threats of losses to be expected from whatever alternative is chosen'.[1] 'Whenever a policy-making group displays most of the symptoms of groupthink', Janis claims, 'we can expect to find that the group also displays symptoms of defective decision-making.'[2] Although he relies heavily, for his examples, upon what he describes as American foreign policy 'fiascos' such as the Bay of Pigs invasion of Cuba and the escalation of the Vietnam War, he also intimates that the groupthink syndrome may occur in less momentous action taken, for example, by boards of directors or governors of large organizations.

The seven symptoms of groupthink are listed as follows: 'an incomplete survey of alternatives; an incomplete survey of objectives; failure to examine risks of preferred choice; failure to reappraise initially rejected alternatives; poor information search; selective bias in processing information at hand and a failure to work out contingency plans'.[3] Apart from the fact that officials could not be accused of carrying out an inadequate 'information search', most of the other symptoms were displayed to a greater or lesser extent during the period in which the government struggled to come to terms with the developments in Europe.

Groupthink symptoms were most apparent in the way that ministers and officials arrived at the decision to negotiate the EFTA agreement, on the premise that it would afford greater opportunity for arriving at an agreement with the Six. The survey of alternatives was hampered by an emotional attachment to the Commonwealth and by a traditional British antipathy towards 'grand designs' such as the EEC. No clear objective of what the Stockholm Convention should achieve was set out, save a vague and ill-thought out suggestion that EFTA would lead to a bridge between the Seven and the EEC. The risks of such a course of action, such as the possibility of Britain finding itself in an even more intractable situation *vis-à-vis* the Six were not even considered. There was no reappraisal either of the initially rejected alternative – that of seeking British membership of the EEC. As the idea of EFTA gained support, the information both given and sought was coloured by a substantial bias in favour of the plan. Finally, the failure of ministers and officials to work out contingency plans reflected all too clearly their lack of a specified objective or a workable agenda.

By the beginning of 1960, the confusion in the minds of senior ministers as to what it was that Britain wanted, and how the government should set about getting it, resulted in a period of drift. The EFTA policy had provided no answer to Britain's difficulties, yet no new plan had been put forward either by officials or by ministers themselves.

The new year opened with approval being recommended by the EQ steering group for an American proposal that the OEEC should be reconstituted with American and Canadian involvement.[4] The American plan, signalling an end to notions of European dependence on the US in favour of a more responsible and (it was hoped) responsive partnership, was to result in the institution of the Organization for Economic Co-operation and Development (OECD) in December 1961. The FO was charged with the responsibility of looking after British interests in the matter. Suffice to note here that the proposed adjustment represented another warning to the British government that the pattern of economic relationships in the western world was in the process of being remoulded. The post-war arrangement upon which Britain had relied for its political and economic hegemony in Europe was coming to an end. But, as the economic climate in Europe was becoming more demanding, so Britain's capability to ameliorate its worst effects was diminishing.

At the first cabinet meeting of the new year, the chancellor of the exchequer told the cabinet about the New Economic Committee where, he hoped, some progress would be made.[5] Summing up the short discussion on the issue the PM stressed the need for strengthening the internal institutions of EFTA, in the hope of convincing the US of its worth. When it came to recommending further action, though, he was at something of a loss. His only suggestion was that the UK should seek to establish 'some procedural machinery for considering future developments', though in the light of the uncertainty among his officials, he added that 'there might be advantage in securing that this did not work too fast'. Macmillan left for his 'winds of change' tour of Africa the following day and did not return to London until 15 February.[6]

At the meeting of the New Economic Committee held in Paris on 12 and 13 January, Dillon made a broadly neutral speech with regard to EFTA and the EEC calling only for a solution to the dangerous friction caused by the divisions in Western Europe.[7] Afterwards, the chancellor expressed his disappointment to the cabinet that the inter-governmental committee had concentrated almost entirely upon procedural issues.[8] The Six/Seven problem had not been discussed at all. Nevertheless, he was pleased to report that it had been agreed to set up a working party to look into the Six/Seven problem. While allowing his disappointment to be recorded, this key minister was still at pains to avoid transmitting to the cabinet as a whole any sense of urgency or gravity with regard to the European issue. Indeed in a memorandum circulated later to the cabinet, the chancellor remarked that he and the president of the Board of Trade had been involved in 'four days of exhausting but (in the end) not unsatisfactory discussion'.[9] But Sir Paul Gore-Booth in the FO did not share the chancellor's satisfaction. His reservations arose out of the comments of France's chief negotiator M. Wormser, who asked him after the meeting: 'What is this Trade Committee going to talk about anyway?'[10]

The optimism of Hugh Ellis-Rees, reporting from the UK

delegation to the OEEC in Paris, was plainly unfounded. He claimed that Dillon was now convinced of the need to find a Six/Seven agreement and that the French were now ready to renew discussions.[11] A more accurate account of the attitude of the Americans, though, was given by Mr Greenwald of the US Embassy in a meeting with J.A. Robinson of the Foreign Office. Greenwald said that, in spite of Dillon's speeches, he did not contemplate the Trade Committee being anything more than a 'talking shop'.[12] By now it was known in London that Dillon was sceptical, not only about the government's claim that a Europe-wide FTA was essential to prevent political division in Europe but also about the feasibility of securing such a grouping.[13] On his return to the US, Dillon spoke openly of the committee as a 'purely consultative' body. In the light of this Greenwald said that he found British optimism 'difficult to understand'. He told Robinson that he hoped he would be given some warning 'when you propose to stop smiling'.

Maudling's was evidently one smile that Greenwald had in mind. The president of the Board of Trade commented to the US under-secretary of state, Mr Livingstone Merchant, on the surprisingly successful outcome of the Paris meeting. It was important to have established, he enthused, 'that the problem of the Six and the Seven was one that must be dealt with'.[14] The chancellor, too, despite the mounting evidence against such a possibility, remained convinced that the government would yet achieve the setting up of some form of FTA. On this point he wrote to the PM to warn him against getting concessions from de Gaulle which the French president would then see as a settlement. Such an eventuality, he said, 'would weaken our ultimate ease for getting a proper free trade agreement between the Six and the Seven'.[15]

Sir Frank Lee (now chairman of the EQ steering group) expressed a more realistic disappointment with the outcome of the New Economic Committee meeting. Uninhibited by the political considerations that moderated the statement of the chancellor, he said bluntly that the meeting had shown that the division between EFTA and the EEC 'had never been more apparent'.[16] Nevertheless, he pointed out that EFTA was still united and the OEEC had been retained for the time being as 'an important symbol of European unity'. Furthermore, the UK had avoided the danger of a committee of the thirteen countries becoming established, 'which would have caused embarrassment all round'. For want of an alternative, the hope of the EQ steering group rested in the proposed working party and in the newly-established Twenty Government Trade Committee which would consider (it was believed) the whole question of European trade.

But, with no firm proposals to advance, and indeed, with no clear and comprehensive objective at which to aim, ministers and officials watched helplessly as the question of European trade slipped further down the international agenda. Britain was alone among the foremost countries of Europe and their Atlantic allies in being dissatisfied with the existing arrangements. This situation was made worse by the lack of a consistent and viable policy objective. Ministers and officials found themselves calling for discussions without any idea of what they wanted to get out of them. They were clear only about what they did *not* want: the establishment of an Atlantic trading community, British involvement in a customs union, the loosening of EFTA ties and any development that would embarrass Britain with regard to the Commonwealth or the GATT. They spoke of an *association* between EFTA and the EEC without any clear idea of the form such an association would take.[17] Talk of 'a bridge' between EFTA and the EEC had all but evaporated; the matter was now referred to, instead, as the *Six/Seven problem*.

During the lull in international activity between the meeting of the New Economic Committee and the meeting of the 'Twenty Governments', the EQ steering group considered the Dutch proposals, which had been put forward at a meeting of the EEC Council of Ministers three months earlier. The Dutch had suggested that, on 1 July 1960 (when EEC countries were due to lower their tariffs with respect to each other), EFTA and EEC countries should make reciprocal tariff reductions on an mfn (most favoured nation) basis. Third countries would be asked to make compensatory concessions within the framework of the GATT. The proposal had already received some support from the Germans and

Belgians, though it had been opposed, as might have been expected, by the French. The Overseas Office of the Bank of England urged support for the Dutch approach,[18] and for their part, the BOT had concluded that 'for the moment we can think of no better idea for loosening the deadlock between the Six and Seven'.[19] On these grounds it was noted in the FO that 'we should provide artificial respiration if it [the Dutch proposal] shows signs of flagging' to allow time for progress to be made towards a wider European settlement.[20]

Lee agreed that, despite French opposition, the proposal should be given serious consideration. More vigorous and less patient than his predecessor, he expressed the view that 'we could not let the present situation go on indefinitely'.[21] There followed a discussion by the steering group on the best way to handle possible Commonwealth reactions. To save embarrassment, it was agreed that it should be suggested to Commonwealth ministers that the other six EFTA countries wanted Britain to consider the plan. They would then be told that it would be discussed without commitment, and that the Commonwealth would be informed of the outcome.

Although, in the event, the Dutch proposals came to nothing, the way in which Lee and his colleagues proposed to 'handle' the Commonwealth marked a significant departure from previous government practice, which had habitually entailed close Commonwealth involvement. Britain's membership of EFTA no doubt contributed a certain amount to a slight but perceptible weakening of the Commonwealth relationship. Sir Douglas Wass suggests that by the beginning of the following year, the PM was 'moving away from the Commonwealth as a power base and as a major political concern'.[22] It is noteworthy, though, that it was a steering group under Sir Frank Lee's leadership that first signalled this departure. Long after the Dutch proposals had been shelved, the method suggested for handling the Commonwealth would be employed for a far more far-reaching purpose.

The significance for the government's European policy of the appointment of Sir Frank Lee as permanent secretary to the Treasury and as chairman of the EQ steering group cannot be overstated. Sir Roderick Barclay, deputy under-secretary of state at the FO who conducted lengthy discussions with representatives of the three key members of the Six during the winter of 1960/1, recalls that Lee was highly regarded by everyone. With a strong and likeable personality, he says, Lee had a considerable influence on the PM. With regard to Britain's application to join the EEC, Sir Roderick maintains that 'Lee had a big hand in the decision to apply to join – there is no doubt about that'.[23] Sir Arnold France was a member of Lee's committee and chairman of its associated sub-committee. He describes Lee as 'a very forceful and powerful character',[24] while Sir Peter Carey, who worked alongside Lee at the BOT, remembers him as a man of vision who took a very broad view of things.[25] Sir Douglas Wass, too, remembers Lee as a strong and powerful personality, a 'very dynamic, highly opinionated man . . . who would work for seventeen hours a day'.[26] According to Sir Douglas, Lee was very gregarious and, as a consequence, had many contacts, particularly with industrialists. 'If he was converted to something', Sir Douglas recalls, 'he would embrace it with all the passion of the convert.' Referring to Britain's application to join the EEC, Sir Douglas says: 'I think he wanted this and the way he played his hand was softly softly . . .'

As yet (February 1960) though, Sir Frank Lee, contrary to Camps' assertion,[27] was not (quite) yet converted to the idea of British membership of the EEC. Even so, through his own reckoning, the options were running out. With regard to a proposal for a treaty of association between the EEC and EFTA, he concluded that the idea 'was full of dangers for the United Kingdom'.[28] His unequivocal dismissal of the only potentially constructive British proposal as 'a barren institutional association' underlines his incipient impatience with a situation where policy options, within the constraints of the existing political premises, were becoming markedly rarer.

The ministerial committee considered the Dutch proposals at a meeting on 9 February.[29] Ministers noted that BOT officials had 'not yet formed a final view'. They also took note of the advice of the steering group that only after approval for the plan had been indicated by the US and

EFTA should the Commonwealth and colonies be brought 'into the picture'. The sterility of British policy was indicated clearly by the ministerial committee's conclusion that it would be tactically advantageous for the UK to show a willingness to consider the Dutch plan for the very reason that EEC countries would be likely to reject it.[30]

A subsequent meeting between British officials (one of whom was Sir Frank Lee) and two senior US officials, Mr Leddy and Mr Corse, confirmed that the Dutch proposal was 'totally unacceptable to the Six'.[31] In case any misunderstanding of the US position should remain, Leddy pointed out that 'the US had come forward with the idea of a Trade Committee in the previous discussions because there was evidence that the United Kingdom wished to cope with practical short-term arrangements'. 'The U.S. would be concerned', he said, 'if the meetings developed into discussions of a free trade area.'[32]

The steering group, meanwhile, persevered in their attempt to negotiate in advance the difficulties that would almost certainly arise out of the Twenty Government Trade Committee set for 15 and 16 March. A note from the MAG intimated that as far as that department was concerned, 'the main objectives of the establishment of a special agricultural working group in the Trade Committee would be to prevent any discussion of agricultural concessions as part of a general industrial agreement'. This was necessary, it was asserted, 'both to protect UK farmers *and to ensure that Commonwealth agricultural interests in the UK market were not impaired'.*[33] While the attitude of some ministers and officials towards the Commonwealth was no longer one of totally unfettered enthusiasm, it is apparent that the belief still prevailed that the interests and preferences of Commonwealth countries (whose people enjoyed autonomous democratic representation) had a legitimate role to play in the development of Britain's European policy. It is particularly telling that the steering group was urged to bear Commonwealth interests in mind, not by CRO officials but by officials from the MAG, whose only brief for safeguarding Commonwealth interests was an emotional one.

The question of how to make a positive approach to the Trade Committee remained unresolved and was, indeed, further complicated by US insistence that the idea of an FTA should not be reactivated.[34] The fear was expressed that the US delegation might walk out of the meeting if the matter was raised – taking others with them. Sir Harold Caccia in Washington proposed that in order to 'make life easier for the U.S.', the UK should water down its objective from 'the creation of a single European market' to ensuring 'that nothing should be done which would put barriers up in Europe'. But his suggestion was poorly received in London.[35] Sir Christopher Steel's assertion that despite the fact that the Germans were 'growing into the Common Market',[36] there was still a possibility of achieving an FTA, was greeted with much more enthusiasm.

If the PM had hoped that some progress would have been made – or even some agreement secured – on the European question while he was in Africa, he was to be disappointed on his return to realize that little had changed. His failure to provide his colleagues with instructions on even a broad approach to be pursued during his absence is characteristic of his uneven and sporadic interest in the European issue. This attitude arose in no small way out of the lack of consensus on the issue in his party – and even in his cabinet.[37]

In fact, as the deadline of 1 July drew nearer, a siege mentality was developing in Whitehall with respect to the European issue. The PM was accosted immediately on his return by a testy memorandum from Philip de Zulueta, who declared that 'the Americans have been ganging up with the French' to put back the date of the Trade Committee meeting.[38] The truth was that the issue was of little consequence to the US or to the French, whose shared interest was only that the integrity of the EEC should not be threatened. The postponement of the meeting for two weeks was of significance only to members of EFTA.

While officials contested with their American counterparts the formulation of an agenda for the forthcoming meeting, the Treasury concluded its own report with the unhelpful comment that 'we cannot therefore yet say what solution for the July 1st problem will be practicable'.[39] The PM's immediate reaction was to ask for the preparation of a 'cabinet statement'. 'We are drifting,' he declared. Fresh from his successful and widely acclaimed trip to Africa,[40] Macmillan was in no mood for failure. Having been out of touch with the European problem for several weeks, he had yet to be habituated again into the vacillation and uncertainty that characterized Britain's trade relations with Europe. To add to his discomfiture, the idea of 'acceleration' of the Treaty of Rome was now under active consideration by the Six.[41] This would mean that trade discrimination against the UK would be greater and come sooner than had hitherto been contemplated.

The PM himself chaired the next ministerial meeting. He emphasized the seriousness of the situation and spoke grimly of the 'political consequences of a permanent economic division of Europe'.[42] He was well aware that it was on this premise that he would be most likely to achieve consensus. While attempts to address the economic arguments would undoubtedly give rise to predictable responses from ministers owing loyalty to their own departments, the *political* ramifications of the issue fell outside the remit of any particular minister (except that of the foreign secretary who enjoyed the PM's confidence in this matter) and could be considered as being of general interest to all. Even so, once discussion was underway, attention inevitably came to focus upon the economic aspects of the problem. If Britain made no move, the PM argued, acceleration of the Treaty of Rome would be more likely, resulting in still more discrimination.

Significantly, ministers agreed that the main problem with the Dutch proposals was not the objections of the Commonwealth and British farmers but the opposition of the US, France and the European Commission.[43] Taking account of the report of the steering group, ministers concluded that the best course of action under the circumstances was for Britain to show support for the Dutch proposals (but only to Britain's EFTA partners) and use new Swedish proposals (for reducing though not eliminating discrimination) as a 'fall-back' position. The latter, they believed, would probably be acceptable to Commonwealth countries 'if carefully presented to them'. Britain's position though was to be camouflaged inside the recommendations of the EFTA countries. No direct reference was to be made to British preferences. Instead, it would be stated that 'a completely non-discriminatory solution had been advocated by some (the less that such a proposal could be attributed to the United Kingdom, the less alarm this would cause to the Commonwealth) and that they themselves would prefer a solution of that kind'.[44]

The day before the EFTA meeting, where it was planned to put together an approach to the problem behind which all the partners could unite, reports were received suggesting that the European Commission's idea of 'acceleration' appeared – much to the relief of officials – to be meeting with a mixed reaction in Paris and somewhat firmer opposition in Bonn.[45] But this welcome news was soon overshadowed by the difficulties of finding agreement between the EFTA partners. Britain's partners pressed for a solution that would eliminate discrimination altogether between the EEC and EFTA. The British delegation, though, opposed this suggestion on the grounds that it would be seen by the Six as 'provocative' and would therefore weaken EFTA's position in the Trade Committee. The communiqué that was issued after the meeting reflected in its blandness the lack of agreement among the Seven. It intimated only that the EFTA countries were ready, in accordance with GATT principles, to extend to the Six, on a reciprocal basis, the tariff reductions that they were due to make between themselves on 1 July.

By this time two questions, at least, had been resolved. The first was that the Dutch solution was patently not acceptable to the US or to the French. The second was that the Americans, having previously stood somewhat 'aloof' from European trade problems, had now 'thrown their weight heavily on the side of the EEC' and against an exclusive trade agreement between the Six and the Seven.[46] This last development, which had been anticipated for some time, now had to be faced. Under Lee's guiding hand the steering group at last concluded that Britain could no longer work (either covertly or openly) towards the creation of a full European FTA.[47]

But, having decided that a policy based upon securing an FTA was untenable, officials were faced with the fact that Britain's EFTA partners, as well as Germany and the Benelux countries, appeared to favour just such a solution. As well as this, it would be seen as an admission of defeat for

Britain if it was shown that HMG had no proposal for reducing the division in Europe. The steering group concluded that the most likely outcome would be first, that the UK would have to live with tariff discrimination from 1 July, and secondly, that the UK would have to live with the situation for the next 18 months while hoping to secure a good result from the GATT negotiations in January and making the best of EFTA.[48]

On the whole, the ministerial committee concurred with the steering group's latest conclusions.[49] They also came at last to acknowledge a truth that had long been avoided: that for the Six, discrimination was a necessary component of the EEC in that it emphasized the political unity upon which the whole concept was founded. 'It was therefore most unlikely', it was conceded, 'that they would accept any proposal for the complete removal of barriers between them and E.F.T.A. countries.'

But for the PM, the passive acceptance of discrimination against British industry – for whatever reason – was unthinkable. He insisted that some form of association with the EEC should be sought even if it proved to be 'contrary to the G.A.T.T.'.[50] Such was the PM's frustration that besides finding himself proposing that Britain should undermine the GATT, he was also thrown back upon the old and fruitless reasoning that associated Britain's strategic role with its trading relationships. He proposed that ministers and officials should look into the possibility of action 'not limited to the commercial field' which might be taken 'if the EEC insisted on implementing fully the Treaty of Rome with no relaxation in our favour'. But as bluster gave way once more to disenchantment and frustration, the PM again handed over the problem to his ministers and officials with the exhortation to look afresh at ways through which a tolerable compromise might be achieved.

The options available for Britain now looked as meagre as they had ever done. As the PM saw it, the alternatives were: to look again at a plan that the French had already rejected; to cobble together a compromise that would break the rules of the GATT; or to threaten Britain's NATO allies with political or strategic non-cooperation. Because of various considerations – from the attitude of the US and the

French to the interests of the Commonwealth and British farmers and a lack of consensus on the matter at both official and ministerial level – the UK had no ideas of substance to put forward. As for Macmillan, his tendency to vacillate between a determination to make Britain's strategic role count and handing the issue over to colleagues and officials, is symptomatic of his frustration. Europe, after all, was only one issue on his agenda. His readiness – once the going got tough – to light upon other policy areas (such as decolonization), where he could at least hope for some progress, was, if not helpful, at least understandable.

As if to mark this unhappy period of frustrated ambition, Frank Figgures, under-secretary at the Treasury (who later became EFTA secretary general), submitted a paper to the FO which amounted to a post-mortem on Britain's conduct of the FTA negotiations. It represented an indictment of British attitudes and presentation.[52] Figgures proposed that his observations should be taken into account when the UK embarked upon any further negotiations. His criticisms were many. The first was that the UK mistakenly felt it was 'wanted' in Europe. Secondly, he pointed out that not enough attention had been paid to the attitude of the French. Thirdly, he argued that the negotiations were hampered by 'the continued repetition of the pledges both to the farmers and to the Commonwealth' giving the French an opportunity to complain 'while they thought up a host of other objections'. Fourthly, he said, the UK had failed to appreciate that the EEC was essentially a protectionist grouping which would not fit into an FTA. Finally, he declared that the British attitude was inflexible and British propaganda was poor compared with the French. R.W.B. Clarke added that, in the light of the absence of involvement of the cabinet and parliament, the UK also suffered from a lack of 'political weight'. But, despite Clarke's subsequent suggestion that the government had learned from its mistakes, there were very few points on Figgures' list that had not been, or were not even now being repeated.

Even so, alongside the frustration, the confusion and the vulnerability to groupthink, a new attitude was being moulded out of the multifaceted nature of the problem. For example, in a curious way, the fact that the US and the French objected so vehemently to the Dutch proposal resulted in a new perspective being adopted towards the difficulties arising out of any such settlement with respect to the Commonwealth and British farmers. Had there been no external objection to the proposals, it is likely that more would have been made of Britain's difficulties in this respect. As it was, the problems associated with Commonwealth preference and the British system of agricultural support were eclipsed by broader international objections. In the minds of some senior ministers and officials, the *status* of Commonwealth and agricultural objections in the development of Britain's European policy would never fully recover from having been relegated to a secondary consideration.

6 A Momentous Plan

As the government's predicament worsened, the language used to express its aims is especially worthy of note. The particular idiom used to describe Britain's relationship with the EEC – or British objectives with regard to that institution – was, for the most part, indicative of the attitude and objective of the speaker or writer concerned. It will be noted though that, as the perspective and attitude of the PM and his closest advisers altered through 1960, their language was carefully chosen so as not to cause alarm or controversy among their colleagues. It is helpful to draw attention at this stage to the particular language used by officials and politicians to express their fears and aspirations, since it was in the spring of 1960 that the fundamental stipulations of Britain's European policy were at last to be challenged.

Up to the end of 1959 the government's objective with regard to relations with the EEC was almost invariably described as *agreement* or *solution*. But the winding up of the ministerial *Free Trade Area* Committee towards the end of 1959, and its replacement with the *Economic Association* Committee (with virtually the same membership) hints at the dawning of a new realism.[1] Ministers were now charged by the PM with finding ways – not necessarily through the establishment of an FTA – of bringing about British economic association with Europe. As time went by, however, the term *association* gave way to terms such as *settlement* and *arrangement,* which implied the necessity for Britain to make some concessions. Later still, the term *accommodation* was coined to suggest the need for even greater concessions and adjustment but still indicating that the government was not fully committed to a new European orientation. Finally, ministers spoke of *consolidation* and *membership,* but this was not until after government policy was fully and publicly directed toward the goal of British membership of the EEC.

As suggested above, while some choices of terminology were 'involuntary', that is to say, they accurately represented the perspective of the ministers and officials concerned, policy-makers were also able, through a deliberate and calculated choice of terminology, sometimes to promote and sometimes to obscure their particular policy objectives, as the need arose. For example, Sir Frank Lee moved forward during April 1960 from seeking a *solution* to promoting a closer *association*. By the end of the year he was recommending the need for a *settlement*.[2] For his part, it will be seen that Edward Heath began with recommending closer *involvement* and moved on to the advisability of seeking an *accommodation* in the space of one meeting.[3]

The result of this exploitation of the richness of the English language was that potential opposition, within government as well as from outside, was often left with no sure target at which to aim and no clearly defined objective to challenge. In terms of the language used to describe it, government policy developed through slightly shifting nuances and vaguely worded statements of intention rather than through carefully detailed descriptions.[4] One of the reasons for the virtual absence of opposition to Macmillan's EEC initiative was that potential opposers were faced with the fact of a changed policy without ever having observed the stages through which it had come to pass. This is evidenced by the fact that the Anti-Common Market League did not come into existence until August 1961.[5]

In the middle of March 1960, the PM was revitalized in his quest for a solution after a short visit to France. Horne suggests that the PM believed that he had convinced the French president of 'Britain's desire to play her full part in Europe', although he did warn that it remained to be seen how far de Gaulle was prepared to go to prevent a permanent economic division in Europe.[6] In any case, as something of a francophile himself,[7] the PM made great play of the fact that he had succeeded in 'revitalising an old friendship' with the General. This warmth of feeling, though, might have made him less heedful of de Gaulle's attitude with regard to Anglo-French relations. After all, de Gaulle stated quite plainly that 'France can and must lead Europe' and that, as far as he was concerned the 'Anglo-Saxons' were 'not sufficiently sympathetic to French ambitions or to the traditions of Europe'.[8] The optimistic conclusions drawn by the PM from this meeting represent an early indication of his capacity to draw out of de Gaulle what he wanted to hear from him and to gloss over the General's more trenchant observations. This tendency was to be exhibited to even more telling effect during his meeting with de Gaulle at Rambouillet in January 1961.

On another plane, the doubts that already existed in the PM's mind about the value of the Commonwealth in respect of Britain's future trading relationships were unwittingly strengthened by the action of one of the champions of the Commonwealth relationship, Reginald Maudling. The president of the Board of Trade had written a long paper to promote his suggestion that Britain should strive, in the long term, for a single European market formed by a treaty between EFTA and the EEC, each of which would retain its own identity.

In summarizing the paper for the benefit of the PM, though, Frank Glaves-Smith, from the Cabinet Office, warned that the 'Commonwealth link . . . is inevitably becoming looser as time goes on'. 'As we lose power in relation to the new economic rival in Europe', he added, 'our influence may become less and some of the remaining Commonwealth links disappear.'[9] His argument – which was to be taken up by the PM and other ministers later on – was that the Commonwealth link could only be sustained through sacrificing, to some extent, the favourable terms of trade, currently shared by Britain and other Commonwealth countries, in order to secure a profitable trading agreement between Britain and the EEC countries.

But while the relative value to Britain of Commonwealth preference (set against an agreement with the EEC) was now being questioned in some quarters, in other areas of government the arrangement was still viewed as non-negotiable – and not always for fear of an unfavourable public reaction.[10] In the development of policy it is noticeable that it was the officials and ministers charged with finding a solution to Britain's trading difficulties who would be most inclined to take a more flexible view with regard to the interests of the Commonwealth. Those who had no direct responsibility for finding a solution tended, not surprisingly, to be more uncompromising on the matter of Commonwealth preference.

The extent to which the protection of Commonwealth interests was still seen as a legitimate activity for British government departments is indicated by a report from the BOT to A.W. France's EQ committee on the effects of the EEC's special ('List G') tariff arrangements.[11] Of the fifteen paragraphs detailing potential damage, nine concentrated on the likely effect of these measures on Commonwealth producers and only six on the effects that the action would have on British producers. While the conclusion of the BOT was that no 'large' damage would be sustained in either case, the fact that the BOT concerned itself so thoroughly with the potential problems of Commonwealth (not colonial) producers illustrates a peculiar psychological attachment that can probably be best accounted for by residual feelings of imperialistic paternalism. Since Britain could not have been held responsible for EEC action, the BOT's concern would not have arisen out of fear of a bad public reaction. This deeply ingrained feeling of responsibility towards Commonwealth producers was an ongoing source of controversy up to July 1961 and beyond.

But, in the spring of 1960, the internal pressure for the government to 'hold the line' was matched by external pressure that demanded some sort of positive response to ongoing developments. Sir Harold Caccia reported his concern about the lack of publicity that EFTA was attracting in Washington compared with that of the EEC. For example, he pointed out that, notwithstanding reports received in London a fortnight earlier, President Eisenhower and Chancellor Adenauer had just concluded a meeting by issuing a joint communiqué approving a plan to accelerate the operation of the Treaty of Rome. Maudling, in particular, was most disconcerted at this news.[12] Dillon's reaction to British indignation was one of surprise. He said that the US had always supported the EEC and did not understand the strength of the British reaction.[13] Freddie Bishop advised the PM to take a firmer line with the Americans, arguing that 'we have been too gentle with people like Mr. Dillon'.[14] British smiles, it seems, were at last beginning to fade.

In the event, though, the PM's visit to Washington at the end of March to negotiate the Skybolt deal did little to enhance Anglo-American understanding over Europe. It was with some alarm that the FO received published reports that the PM had threatened to cut its contribution to the support of troops in Europe unless a satisfactory solution was found to the Six/Seven problem. Reuter quoted 'American sources';[15] Caccia claimed that the report was based on 'an unauthorised and inaccurate leak'. Nevertheless, the news agency was able to quote Macmillan as saying that the EEC would cost the UK between 100 and 200 million pounds in foreign exchange. The particularity of the figures, and the fact that the PM had been proposing that he should make just such a threat for some time, point to the accuracy of the report.

The repercussions in Europe were considerable. Sir Christopher Steel was incensed by reports in the German press – and with good cause. One of the more inflammatory accounts referred to 'Britain's historical role to prevent Napoleon's planned economic integration of Europe'.[16] Another claimed that 'Britain's real motives towards Europe – hostility to European integration – are now unmasked.' Steel complained, 'we now appear as separated even from the Americans in just that isolation where Hallstein and Company would like to see us.' Reaction in other EEC capitals, though, was less resounding. Sir George Labouchere in Brussels even ventured that it would do no harm for the Belgians to appreciate how strongly the UK felt about the issue.[17] From The Hague, Sir Paul Mason reported that many Dutch editors took the view that the report was in fact 'a leak engineered by Washington', while others were politely critical of the PM's alleged comments. One Liberal journal even proposed that the leak was contrived by the Americans who feared Macmillan's ideas about rapprochement with the USSR.[18]

While the political wrangling, innuendo and counter-innuendo continued, the senior advisory group, reconstituted as the Economic Steering (Europe) *Committee*, but still under Lee's chairmanship (and with much the same representation as before) met at the end of March to consider the developments – such as they were – and to arrive at a viable recommendation to present to the ministerial committee.[19] It was at this apparently routine meeting that questions arising out of particular policy positions, previously regarded as non-negotiable, were at last raised.

After dealing briskly with recent developments, Lee called on his colleagues to reconsider many of the assumptions upon which a framework for finding a solution to Britain's difficulties had come to be based. Not yet having arrived at any firm conclusions of his own, but spurred on to greater efforts by the confidence placed in him by the PM, Lee was evidently keen to encourage a different way of thinking that might result in a new approach to the problem.

He restated the fundamental difficulty. This was that Britain needed to minimize the effects of discrimination but 'could not agree to the political links which were inherent in the Common Market'.[20] Since neither the US nor France favoured the establishment of a wider FTA in Europe, it might be wise, he concluded, 'to suspend discussions for two or three years after which time some looser association with a more established EEC would be possible'. Evidently not totally convinced by his own suggestion, though, he added that 'ministers should be warned that, given our G.A.T.T. obligations, our policy of free entry for the Commonwealth, and agricultural protection in this country, the chances of any such association were extremely slender.'

But this sudden recourse to unfamiliar realism did not end there. 'It was equally unlikely in the foreseeable future', he went on, 'that the United Kingdom would be able to join the Common Market.'[21] The UK would not be admitted, he asserted, 'unless we were prepared to accept the common tariff against the rest of the world including the Commonwealth, and this was something which ministers would not contemplate'. This last sentiment is particularly striking. Because the ideas and aspirations of ministers with regard to the European question were well known – and for the most part shared by officials – it was usual for officials to refer to the party or parties who determined policy on behalf of the nation as 'we' or 'the UK' or 'Britain'. Lee might have been expected to say, for example, that 'this was something which the UK would not contemplate'. But, by singling out 'ministers' in this instance, Lee detached himself somewhat from the firm line hitherto adopted by his political masters. Besides drawing attention to his own newly-formed doubts, Lee evidently hoped to encourage ministers to reconsider *their* position on the question. This subtle device, while undoubtedly having the desired effect on his fellow committee members, was, nevertheless, either missed or ignored for the most part by the ministers concerned. Even so, in finally facing up to the unpalatable facts of the UK's trading position, Lee had opened for himself and his committee new avenues to explore.

He concluded his explication by casting doubt upon what was to become the government's key (though essentially baseless) rationale for their action the following year. 'The time was approaching', he suggested, 'when we would have to decide whether we should continue to argue that economic division in Europe would lead to political division.' The implication here is that this argument could be abandoned if it was seen to complicate matters for Britain. As Lee regarded the political argument as 'optional', it was evidently – at least as far as he was concerned – lacking in legitimacy.

The second meeting of Lee's new steering committee was held less than a week after the first.[22] The attention of officials was directed to a report from Arnold France's EQ committee, which was devastating in its conclusions: 'The proposal for a treaty of association between the European Economic Community (E.E.C.) and the European Free Trade Area (E.F.T.A.)', it said, 'would be against our wider trading interests.' The reasons given were three-fold: first, such an arrangement could well encourage the development of other preferential areas; secondly, preferences all too often led to bilateralism in trade, which would tend to lower the volume of trade world-wide; and thirdly, Commonwealth countries – notably Australia – would be likely to seek, to Britain's disadvantage, a 'revalorization' of their preferences in the UK market. Lee's committee concluded that the best hope now lay 'in making the most of the forthcoming GATT negotiations'.

On 8 April the ministerial committee met, with the PM in the chair, to consider the findings of Lee's steering committee.[23] Macmillan was furnished with the advice of Freddie Bishop – delivered only that morning – that 'this situation demands a fundamental rethinking of our attitude towards Europe during which the courses which are already being examined, and perhaps others, will have to be considered'.[24] The PM quickly discovered, though, that his colleagues were unready to countenance any shift in the government's position.

But if ministers were stuck in the rut of past illusions and failures, Sir Frank Lee at least – galvanized by the instruction handed down by the PM at the previous ministerial committee meeting – was moving forward with his ideas. It was at the third steering committee meeting of the year, held only a week after the second (an indication, in itself, of his growing preoccupation with the European question) that Lee first imparted to colleagues the results of his private deliberations.[25] The subject to be discussed was entitled: 'The European Trade Problem: Longer Term Aspects'. Leading the committee in defining 'the basic objectives of United Kingdom policy towards Europe', Lee presided over a discernible shift of emphasis – a move away from seeking an EFTA/EEC solution toward examining the prospects of a UK/EEC 'association'. Having identified, and systematically disposed of, non-viable alternatives, Lee set about replacing them with a series of radical though delicately constructed propositions. His carefully chosen language was such as to render almost incontrovertible his findings and the conclusions drawn from them. Indeed, so light was his touch that the change of approach that he invoked could, initially, barely be discerned. Only after his early surmises had been accepted did the far-reaching consequences of his line of argument become apparent.

Lee spoke to his colleagues of the need 'to reach some form of closer association with Europe' in which, he believed, 'it might well be possible to maintain also some of our economic links with the Commonwealth such as the free entry of Commonwealth products'. There are two points of interest here. The first is Lee's reference to *closer association* with Europe rather than closer *economic* association: he was evidently not discounting an arrangement that had some political content. The second is in his assertion that it *might* be possible to maintain *some* economic links with the Commonwealth *such as* (but, by implication, not necessarily) Commonwealth free entry. This two-fold uncertainty, to which Lee gave subtle expression, amounted to a considerable departure from the rigorously adhered to line with which ministers and officials were equally familiar.

Then, effectively marginalizing all the well-rehearsed objections to British membership of the EEC, Lee observed that Britain would be unable to join the EEC because such an action would upset the balance of the Treaty of Rome. The matter for deliberation now was not why Britain could not join the EEC but why it would be difficult for the Six to accommodate Britain. The implication was clearly that the main stumbling-block consisted in the technicalities involved rather than in British objections to the idea. Furthermore, in the suggestion that 'it might . . . be impracticable to reach satisfactory arrangements' for the colonies and the Commonwealth, the likelihood of being able to do so was manifestly implied. And, with the stress firmly placed on the question of the *possibility* rather than the *desirability* of such a move, fundamental objections were skilfully set aside.

From this point the committee concluded that the proposal to ministers should be that the UK should aim for 'as close a form of association as possible with the EEC'. In a further bold departure from existing policy it was suggested that this should include '*provisions for the harmonization of external tariffs* and possibly for *the acceptance of some of the social and other commitments of the Treaty of Rome*'. In this, officials agreed, 'we should need to carry with us *as many as possible of the E.F.T.A. countries* and to devise some other form of association for those of them which were not prepared to be so closely linked with the E.E.C.'. It was recognized that *some concessions on agriculture and horticulture* would have to be made and that 'a close association with the E.E.C. *could not be combined with the maintenance of the present Commonwealth preferences*'.[26] The question of the threat posed to British sovereignty by these proposals was neatly dealt with. By pointing out that a different form of association could be worked out for the 'neutral' members of EFTA who 'would be unwilling to accept the provisions which involved concessions on national sovereignty', British acceptance of some such concessions was cleverly insinuated.

A measure of the impact that such conclusions would be likely to have on ministers is indicated by Lee's announcement at the end of the meeting. He told his colleagues: 'although some time must elapse before a paper on these lines would be ready for submission to ministers, there was no immediate

urgency.' In the meantime, he said that he would personally report to ministers on the progress being made by the
committee.[27]

These were important developments which marked the
leading edge of a turning point in the British perspective.
Under Lee's guiding hand the whole question of Britain's
relationship with the EEC had been reassessed. Imperatives
such as working in concert with Britain's EFTA partners;
giving priority to Commonwealth preference; safeguarding
the interests of British farmers and horticulturists; and, perhaps most startling of all, preserving every aspect of national
sovereignty, had been called into question in pursuance of
a larger objective. It is important to note, though, that there
was no suggestion here that Britain should apply to *join* the
EEC; only that there should be as close an association between the EEC and the UK as it was possible to achieve. It
is entirely possible, though, that this as yet unwritten report
represented for Lee the first step towards the goal of full
British membership of the EEC.

By taking responsibility for communicating with ministers,
Lee had won for himself a free hand in addressing those
ministers who would be most receptive to the committee's
findings. Lee was mindful of the fact that the ministerial
committee, representative as it was of a variety of departmental responsibilities and loyalties, would be likely to reject his committee's recommendations and, knowing that
such a rejection would spell the end, for some time, of his
own aspirations for Britain's future, he set about the task of
winning over his political masters via a different route.

It is evident from the coincidence and content of their
memoranda (addressed, respectively, to the PM and to the
chancellor of the exchequer) that, sometime during April
1960, Freddie Bishop and Sir Frank Lee had come to a
consensus with regard to the European issue. The fact that
the deputy secretary to the cabinet and the joint permanent secretary to the Treasury were 'old friends'[28] lends
credence to the assertion that the timing and content of
their respective missives was carefully coordinated.

The first of the two memoranda to arrive on the PM's
desk was from Freddie Bishop.[29] It began by outlining
for the PM the main objections to what Bishop called the

'minimum discrimination arrangement' between EFTA and
EEC countries that had been considered and rejected by
Lee's committee. This is a disappointing finding', he admitted, 'but it is not easy to challenge it.' By way of preparing
the ground for Lee's substantial and detailed report, Bishop
then observed that 'the experts are increasingly coming round
to the view that in the end we shall have to come to terms
with the Six, in some form of association which would be
very close to accepting full membership of a common market.'

Sir Frank Lee's memorandum, dated the same day, was
addressed in the first instance to the chancellor of the exchequer. The PM – not surprisingly, since he had asked
Lee to look into the European question – expressed a wish
to read it.

Lee's memorandum to the chancellor of the exchequer
of 22 April 1960 stands out as the definitive document that
was to set Britain on a new course, not only in terms of
trade but also in terms of Britain's political role and outlook. But, although it set in motion the process towards full
British membership of the EEC, the memorandum did not
directly propose such an action. There was to be much more
in the way of debate, prevarication, persuasion and counter-
persuasion, manoeuvre and counter-manoeuvre before the
proposal that Britain should apply to join the EEC – as a
means of finding out whether or not satisfactory arrangements could be worked out – was finally put to the House
of Commons in July 1961. Nevertheless, despite doubts and
setbacks – the PM himself would not yet be wholly convinced
of the feasibility of Lee's proposals – the substance of the
memorandum formed the basis of an argument which ministers would eventually (and unevenly) come to recognize
as irrefutable.

The memorandum ran to ten pages and, as a hitherto
untapped source, is worthy of careful scrutiny. Entitled *The
Six and the Seven,* the document is divided into six sections
beginning with *The Immediate Outlook* where Lee expressed
the hope that, in the face of discrimination and division,
'countries will be concerned to avoid recrimination and
reproach', showing themselves instead 'prepared to seize any
future opportunity of an accommodation should one present
itself'.[30] Already, then, he had established the necessity of a

constructive approach and hinted at the possibility that Britain would be able to find some sort of 'accommodation' with the Six.

Section two dealt with the *Implications for the United Kingdom* of the division of Europe. Here, Lee seized upon the argument made, fortuitously, by the PM himself, to warn that 'economic divisions may weaken the political cohesion of the West'. Although Lee had already expressed severe doubts about this proposition, he was certainly not disposed to leave untapped such a weighty political adjunct to his own essentially economy-driven reasoning. In this section, too, he warned that although not too much damage would be done to the British economy in the short term, longer-term prospects were less favourable. He pointed out that British exclusion from the markets of the Six, where the high rate of economic growth was likely to continue, would be 'a serious matter' for the British balance of payments. In the longer term, Lee added, because of the strength derived from 'their large internal market', the Six might also constitute a severe challenge to Britain's share of 'third' markets.[31]

While first conceding that the Seven was not 'a despicable grouping in economic terms', Lee went on to describe it as one brought together by 'ties of common funk', which was unlikely to develop 'real cohesion or even continuity'. Then, in a passage that betokened his close informal contacts with industrialists, he asserted that 'there is great uneasiness, amounting almost to dismay among leading industrialists at the prospect of our finding ourselves yoked indefinitely with the Seven and "cut off" by a tariff barrier from the markets of the Six.' Stressing the fact that Britain's trading position *vis-à-vis* the Commonwealth was 'likely to weaken rather than grow stronger', he referred to the prospect of 'three powerful economic groupings – the U.S.A., the U.S.S.R., the Six – able to develop internal markets of scale and therefore strong and competitive industries based on such markets'. He concluded his review of the economic implications by upholding the view that 'the Six are going to come out on top in Europe' – an eventuality that would 'almost certainly lead to a diversion of U.S. investment – which otherwise might have come to this country – to the Six'. This could well be matched, Lee warned, by UK industrialists themselves diverting their own investment to the Six. 'The conclusion', Lee claimed, 'was inescapable.' Even if the political factors were discounted, he said, 'from an economic standpoint we *must* maintain our broad objective of having the U.K. form part of a single European market'.[32]

In section three of his memorandum, Lee considered *Some Critical Factors*. Of these, timing was considered particularly significant. Since no immediate solution was possible, Lee concluded that the government should, in the meantime, direct its attention to (a) defining the broad objective; (b) deciding how it would best be achieved; (c) settling on the right tactics; and (d) setting an agenda for the short term. In this, he emphasized the need 'to carry the Seven with us', although he conceded that EFTA's neutral members 'may limit our freedom of manoeuvre in certain important respects'.[33] As far as the Commonwealth was concerned, Lee recommended that ministers should argue that 'the Commonwealth is not likely to flourish under the leadership of a United Kingdom shut out of growing European markets by tariff barriers and diminishing economic strength'. He added that there was already 'a quiet realisation' in Commonwealth countries of this fact.

On the domestic scene, Lee envisaged some difficulty in securing acceptance of the necessity (as he now saw it) for more than an economic commitment to Europe. Hitherto, Lee pointed out, the UK had paid only 'a purely "industrial" subscription', but, he argued, 'we shall have to face the ineluctable fact that a higher price will have to be paid.'[34] The 'higher price' that he envisaged had three elements. The first was the requirement to enter into an agreement for the harmonizing of social policies (which would be unpopular with many sections of UK industry); the second was the need to make concessions on agriculture (which would not necessarily be damaging in the long term but would be 'difficult to explain politically'); and the third element, he suggested, was 'some surrender of sovereignty'.

Lee had been careful, especially at the beginning of his memorandum to draw attention to the best possible outcome under existing circumstances and to stress the advantages afforded by membership of EFTA and the Commonwealth. The power of Lee's argument, then, lay in his conclusion that a change of direction was necessary – even after having included in his assessment all the advantages of the status quo and all the difficulties that a change of policy would occasion.

Section four of the memorandum – the most detailed and expansive part of the document – was entitled *The U.K. Objective.*[35] Lee prefaced this section by stating that what followed represented a purely personal view and should not be taken as the 'collective judgement of Whitehall'. He was anxious neither to pre-empt the report from his committee nor, in view of considerable confusion on the issue among ministers as well as Whitehall officials, to make himself vulnerable to charges of imperiousness.

He began by pointing out bluntly that 'we are not desperately needed in Europe' and that 'we shall have to be prepared to pay for the sort of settlement we want'. The costs, according to Lee, included inconveniencing or even damaging 'our cherished interests'. He numbered among these: the Commonwealth, domestic agriculture, UK policy on tariffs and 'perhaps indeed our political pride and sense of self-reliance'.

The proposition that the UK should join the Common Market, Lee pointed out, was now supported by notable converts such as Lord Plowden and Lord Robbins.[36] But, even though it constituted, in Lee's view, the most advantageous solution for the UK (if an Atlantic arrangement was discounted), such an option was fraught with political difficulties – not only from Britain's point of view but also from the point of view of the difficulties it would raise for the Six, for the Commonwealth and for the cohesion of EFTA. It is likely, though, that Lee's underlying sympathy and long-term aspirations were, by now, rooted in just such a proposition. It was necessary for him to clarify and even to emphasize the difficulties in order to afford credibility to his reasoning. Although he seems to have been convinced that such a course of action would not be possible for some time, he was already preparing the ground through pointing out that 'the pressures on us to adopt this clear-cut solution, notwithstanding the difficulties, are likely to grow in strength and insistence'.[37] He expressed the hope that 'if the time came when the Government felt that this was the course which the U.K. must follow . . . the country as a whole (and perhaps indeed informed opinion in the Commonwealth), would be ready to respond to a deliberate act of statesmanship.' Statesmanship, as Lee well knew, was a term that had considerable allure for political leaders.

The final alternative that Lee brought to the chancellor's attention – and the one which, he claimed, would be the most advantageous for the UK – was one of his own construction. Entitled *Near-identification with the Common Market*, the proposal was that the Seven would go as far as possible towards accepting 'the essential features of the Common Market' without actually becoming formally absorbed into it.[38] The arrangement would involve acceptance of a harmonized external tariff (referred to by Lee as 'an inevitable condition'); 'agreed arrangements for agriculture and horticulture' (probably consisting of 'European-wide managed markets'); 'acceptance of harmonization of social changes' (upon which the French would almost certainly insist); and compensation taxes (in lieu of Commonwealth free entry). Lee acknowledged that even such an imperfect solution would raise considerable difficulties. In fact, he described here much the same difficulties as he had suggested would be raised by full British membership of the Common Market. His deduction was that if the UK could not join the Common Market, this was the objective 'which seemed at once the most practicable, the least harmful to our basic political interests, and that most likely to secure for the U.K. the great economic benefits of a single European market'.[39]

In section five, Lee dealt with short-term tactics. He proposed that the government should strive to 'keep the temperature down' by eschewing recrimination or retaliation even if the Six agreed on acceleration of the Treaty of Rome. Secondly, he counselled that the government and British industry should do all it could to 'build up the Seven' even though this would mean 'going against the grain' in many cases. The 'ultimate objective' of the government, he advised, should be made 'known and accepted'. He proposed that Britain's EFTA partners, the Commonwealth, the US and the Six should all be apprised of Britain's ultimate objective 'and the sincerity with which we are ready to seek it'. 'Above all', he added, 'we shall have to convince the U.K.

people of the necessity of our being ready to pay a real price (not possible to quantify or specify in advance) in order to secure our objective.' He did not underestimate the magnitude of this task since, he said, 'there is still an assumption that we can get the full benefits of a European club on the basis of a cheap subscription'.[40] Finally, he advised that the UK should play a major part in the GATT negotiations – not least in order to make 'a resolute effort' to get British tariffs down, which, he argued, were 'unconscionably high by almost any standards'.[41] Lower tariffs, he suggested, would 'facilitate any later negotiations for a European settlement'.

Section six of the document ran to one sentence. 'Let us hope', Lee reflected, 'that Pitt will still have the last word: "We will save England by our exertions and Europe by our example".'[42]

Despite his protestations to the contrary, there is every indication in Lee's memorandum of an underlying belief that the UK should begin immediately to work towards full membership of the EEC. His memorandum constituted both a rationale and a programme for just such a move. But by indicating that full membership of the EEC was not yet possible, Lee was able to draw the sting out of a good deal of potential opposition. It left him still on the side of those who could not yet contemplate such a radical step. At the same time, though, by proposing 'near-identification with the EEC' – an objective that he might well have known was unachievable – he was able to offer ministers the opportunity of raising questions about previously non-negotiable components of policy such as Commonwealth free entry, agricultural support and British sovereignty. Once such topics were opened up for debate in the context of *not* joining the Common Market, it would soon be apparent that it was a nonsense not to discuss them with a more positive eventuality in view.

As well as signalling the beginning of a long process that would lead, albeit unsteadily, to Britain's first application to join the EEC, Lee's memorandum also marks a watershed, in analytical terms, in respect of the internal determinants of policy formulation. For, as the once unthinkable began to be thought about – and talked about – and positions were taken up and their rationalizations formulated, the nature and direction of policy development would come to owe less to cognitive dissonance on the part of ministers and officials and more to their capability for the exploitation of both formal and informal power within the machinery of government.

7 Pressure, Politics and Persuasion

The account given so far tends to support the proposition that ministers and officials were able to develop European policy for the most part independently of the people, of parliament – and even of the cabinet. In so far as this was true, it was due primarily to the low salience attached to the issue by the public and parliament alike. While the government might have found difficulty in discouraging interest in an issue that was seen by the people to affect their everyday lives, the same could not be said of a question that held very little broad appeal. Here, ministers were able, through their own low-key approach to the matter, to effect policy with the minimum of interference either from the public or from its representatives in parliament.

Hitherto ministers had been disinclined to draw attention to their European policy because of its deficiencies in both definition and achievement. From the spring of 1960, though, ministers would strive to keep the matter off the public – as well as the parliamentary and even the cabinet – agenda, not because of governmental *inadequacy* but because of the potential for *controversy* arising out of the new ideas that were beginning to gain the attention and the interest of certain ministers.

It is true that a policy could not be presented to parliament without cabinet approval, nor could it come into effect without the approval of parliament.[1] But before each of these stages was reached there was a good deal of scope for ministers and officials to see to it that, by the time formal approval was sought, the main objections would have been largely 'neutralized' by ensuring the apparent lack of an alternative course.[2]

But, in the British democracy – as in many others by the second half of the twentieth century – the potential for influencing government policy was not confined to parliament and the electorate. The various sources of pressure being

102

exerted upon government from the domestic constituency, during the period under discussion, have been well documented – notably by Robert Lieber and R.L. Pfaltzgraff. Both writers describe a 'second wave' of influence exerted on government by pressure or interest groups, which were, themselves, responding to the primary effect of the developments in Europe. Through focusing carefully on government documentation, though, it is possible to contrast, accurately, the extent to which Macmillan's government was affected by 'second wave' domestic demands, with the extent to which ministers were influenced in their decision-making *directly* by primary external forces.

Sir Frank Lee's memorandum evinced his close personal contacts with particular British industrialists. To this extent, then, some influence from domestic interests was brought to bear on the government decision-making progress. Beyond this, though, two important factors should be noted. First, it was, and had been for some time, the PM's concern to safeguard the interests of British industry that coloured his whole attitude to the European question. It is likely, therefore, that the concerns of Lee's contacts were already largely the PM's own. Secondly, while the directors of larger British firms saw advantages early on in British membership of the EEC, their views were not shared on the whole by the myriad of medium-sized and small companies that still made up a large proportion of British industrial activity. Lieber finds that between 1959 and 1961, 'the 200 largest firms tended to become increasingly outspoken advocates of accession to the EEC, while the small firms and trade associations took a more hesitant view'.[3]

A result of this hesitancy was some ambivalence on the part of the FBI, and other trade organizations, throughout 1960 and even up to July 1961 with regard to the issue of British membership of the EEC. For example, a statement made in Berlin by Sir William McFadzean (former president of the FBI) in May 1961 – that business leaders in the UK were 'very much in favour of the United Kingdom joining the EEC'[4] – was sharply at odds with the statement issued by the FBI Grand Council two months later, which was described in *The Times* as 'too negative'.[5] Indeed, the Federation expressed deep misgivings about a solution that meant that 'the Commonwealth was to pay a substantial part of the price for British association with the Common Market' or which reneged on Britain's moral commitments to EFTA.[6] In effect, with regard to British membership of the EEC, the FBI was arguing – even by the summer of 1961 – on a 'no unless' as much as on a 'yes if' basis. The role of industry's influence as an interest *group*, in the development of Britain's European policy, then, was far from decisive. This is true, despite the exhortations of particular industrialists and the mediation of first, the Palmer Working Party (where FBI leaders met with officials from the BOT and the Treasury),[7] then the Consultative Committee for Industry (where officials from the BOT met with representatives of the FBI, the TUC and the NFU)[8] and, eventually, the Export Council for Europe (established by the president of the Board of Trade in November 1960).[9]

Lieber also finds that the large banks did not 'visibly play a strongly pro-European role'. In fact, he points out that 'not until the year-end statements for 1961' did any of the banks advocate 'outright Common Market entry'.[10] This is borne out by the recollections of Sir Eric Faulkner, who, as managing director of Glyn Mills Bank and a director of the Royal Bank of Scotland (as well as serving on the Finance Committee of Vickers and, later, as president of the British Bankers Association), says that the EEC issue was a favourite lunch-time – rather than boardroom – topic, over which views were fairly evenly split.[11] The greatest concern for bankers, Sir Eric recalled, was the prospect of European-style regulation being brought into the British banking system which had operated hitherto quite satisfactorily on a self-regulatory basis.

In the City, the issue was widely regarded as the business of politicians although Sir Eric ventured that the view of insurance companies might well have been coloured by their interest in the lucrative US market which was subject to less stiff competition than that of Europe.[12] In other financial institutions, however, many looked upon closer relations with Europe – which was seen to be outstripping the Commonwealth with regard to exports – with undisguised favour. There was certainly no firm line of opposition in the City to the government making overtures to Europe.[13] Indeed, Lord Perth (a City figure close to Edward Heath) suggests that it was because of his weight in the City that he was brought into the government[14] – though this serves as much to indicate ministers' attempts to influence the economic and financial sectors as it does the reverse.

As for the broader public, Lieber points out that 'only after Macmillan's July 1961 announcement did the panoply of public opinion channels come into noticeable operation'.[15] Pfaltzgraff asserts, conversely, that the press was noticeably 'in advance' of the government on the issue, though his own suggestion that there was a continuous exchange of ideas between the editorial writers and their contacts in the civil service,[16] hints at significant 'official' input into press opinion. It will be seen as no coincidence, in the light of the date of Lee's memorandum, to note that *The Observer*, the first convert to the idea of full British membership of the EEC, became so in April 1960, followed by *The Guardian* in May and *The Economist* in June 1960.[17] *The Financial Times* followed suit in the latter part of 1960 (having already disclosed to government officials in June that it was about to move gradually in that direction),[18] and the mainstream Tory press (*The Sunday Times*, the *Daily Mail*, the *Daily Telegraph* and *The Times*) 'during the first half of 1961'.[19] The Beaverbrook press remained implacably opposed throughout. So, while a large sector of the press might have appeared, at the time, to be well in advance of government thinking, it was, in fact, only in advance of government thinking *as it was disclosed at the time*, which is a very different matter.

Public opinion polls taken at the time indicate little more than a widespread indifference to the issue. Opinion varied according to the way the question was framed. For example, in March 1959, 54 per cent favoured Britain joining the Six countries of Europe 'for the purpose of trade', whereas in May 1961 only 8 per cent thought that Britain should 'leave the Outer Seven and apply for membership of the European Common Market'.[20] Mostly, though, the polls show that the people were happy, by and large, to trust the government to do the right thing. For example, roughly half of those questioned in January/February 1963 expressed their support for the government if it felt that Britain's interests would best be served by joining the Common Market. Almost the same percentage, though, indicated that they would also give their approval to stay out if the government could not get the terms it wanted.[21]

There is little here to suggest that the government was unduly influenced by domestic public or press speculation and exhortation. As Lieber says: 'Macmillan's decision is sufficiently explainable by political and economic factors . . . so that there is no reason to believe the arguments presented by the press acted to sway him directly'.[22] In fact, a combination of circumstantial and documentary evidence[23] suggests that Lieber was correct in assuming that 'insofar as the European decision was concerned, he [Macmillan or, perhaps more accurately, his officials] influenced the press more than they did him'.[24]

As for other interest or 'pressure' groups, such as the NFU and the TUC, the question was rather one of the government helping them to come to terms with changing policy than of those groups being able to bring influence to bear on that policy. And, as previously noted, the role of genuine one-issue pressure groups for and against a British application for membership of the EEC – such as the Anti-Common Market League (against) and the Common Market Campaign (in favour) – did not even begin until after the decision to open negotiations had effectively been made.

In the years to come, public and interest group opinion, juxtaposed in the mass media with the various orthodoxies of the competing political parties (or sections of parties), would become a significant source of government policy on the European issue. During the period under consideration, though, government policy continued to develop largely as a response to the 'primary wave' of external events. Domestic pressure, where it did exist, was piecemeal, low-key and often divergent.

Lee's April memorandum quickly set up a new tension in the decision-making process resulting in a divergence of view that flowed swiftly through Whitehall and was soon lapping at the doors of the cabinet room. Among the leading players on the 'Europeanist' side of this division were Sir Frank Lee, Freddie Bishop, Sir Richard Powell (BOT) and Sir Paul Gore-Booth (FO).[25] Among those who took the traditional view were Reggie Maudling, Cyril Sanders (BOT), a number of CRO, CO and MAG officials, Rab Butler and Viscount Hailsham. The contest was now on to win the hearts and minds of uncommitted Whitehall officials and – even more importantly – for winning round the majority of cabinet ministers who, while still largely inclined towards Maudling's perspective, were becoming, in the light of the government's failure to find an alternative solution, potentially open to persuasion along the lines that Lee set out.

Although the traditionalists enjoyed the advantage of at least three senior cabinet ministers on their side, the Europeanists, for their part, had recourse to informal power arising out of their particular roles in government. While as yet they had no champion in the cabinet, they did have a direct line to the PM (through Freddie Bishop), and (through the steering committee) direct access to and considerable control over the very latest information. In this respect, they were not short of tactical advantages.

Early in May, export figures produced by the Treasury added impetus to Lee's initiative. They showed an increase in UK exports to EEC countries of 10.2 per cent in 1959 over the previous year. Apart from an increase in exports to Canada (that was roughly comparable), for the rest of the sterling area the figures showed a reduction of exports by 6.2. per cent.[26] It was also evident that the pattern of British exports was changing. The percentage of exports from areas of production where Britain had traditionally excelled (especially within the sterling area), such as shipbuilding and the manufacture of aircraft and railway vehicles, was down by about a quarter between 1958 and 1959.[27] Over the same period 'five groups of products – non-electrical machinery, road vehicles, steel, chemicals, and electrical machinery' accounted for a very large part of the rise in British exports.

At the same time, the bi-monthly trade statistics published in the National Institute Economic Review illustrated the extent to which the UK was losing out to its economic rivals in Europe. Statistics concerned with the exports of manufactures by industrial countries, published in March 1960,[28] showed that the volume of manufactures exported by the UK had risen by less than a quarter since 1953 while German exports of manufactures had risen by over 60 per cent and

French by nearly a half. Over the same period Britain's *share* of the world export market for manufactures had fallen by 4.6 per cent, while Germany's share rose by 6.5 per cent and France's share by 0.8 per cent. Figures produced by the Treasury two months later confirmed the trend.[29]

No opportunity, it seemed, was now to be missed to proselytize on the basis of the new wisdom. In advance of the next cabinet meeting, Freddie Bishop submitted a memorandum to the PM outlining his ideas for the position to be adopted by the UK at the Trade Committee meeting, set now for 8 June.[30] Having established that a settlement on the basis of either a world free trade system, or an Atlantic FTA, or an accommodation between the Six and Seven were each either unattainable or undesirable, Bishop concluded that 'other than outright joining the Common Market, the only other alternative is "near-identification" with it'.

But the PM came to the cabinet meeting with a different approach in mind. Only recently emerged from a torrid meeting with Commonwealth prime ministers[31] and just three days after the failure of the summit which he was later to refer to as 'the most tragic moment of my life',[32] the PM was inclined, more than ever, to put the issue into a global context. Still not fully convinced, despite the best efforts of his officials, that he could not achieve a satisfactory solution through a process of 'strategic bargaining' with Britain's allies, he suggested that 'the present circumstances . . . might make it possible to consider solutions which would not otherwise have been acceptable to the United States'.[33] He had in mind the old ill-defined notion of 'an economic accommodation' between the Six and the Seven. Proposing to exploit, for Britain's gain, the unhappy international situation, he said that 'the need to consolidate the Western Alliance might provide a better opportunity for a satisfactory settlement of the problem of our economic relations with Europe'. Macmillan told his colleagues that arrangements would be made for consultations between the UK, France and the US, which, he intimated, 'might lead the French government to be more favourable towards an accommodation'.

At the risk of repetition, it is worth noting that the PM referred to the problem as one of 'our *economic* relations with Europe', even while he saw the opportunity for a *solution* to that problem through exploiting Britain's position at the heart of the *strategic/political* alliance. Moreover, it is evident from the record of the PM's observations, at this meeting, that his conversion to the idea of British membership of the EEC certainly did not arise spontaneously out of the failure of the May summit.

But, whatever type of 'accommodation' the PM had in mind, unless it reflected the UK's commitment to EFTA, it would not find favour with the president of the Board of Trade. Sir Arnold France recalls that, as the British minister most involved in the establishment of EFTA, Maudling set great store by British membership of it.[34] Sir Roderick Barclay too believes that Maudling was anxious to preserve EFTA because of his commitment to it, which was an inevitable consequence of his involvement in its inception.[35] Sir Douglas Wass suggests that, coming from an economic background based on Anglo-American Keynesianism, Maudling was sceptical of the EEC, which he saw as formal, bureaucratic and governed by classical economics.[36] Maudling was an Atlanticist who had no affinity with Europe, Sir Douglas recalls. In common with his one-time colleagues, he believes that Maudling's investment of political capital in EFTA 'meant that he was unwilling to retreat'.

Because of his involvement with EFTA, his economic perspective and his political orientation, then, Maudling would be the hardest of the key government ministers to convince that a radical change of direction was necessary. This is true despite the fact that his attitude was by no means shared with all the officials in his own department.[37]

No doubt aware of an undercurrent of change, the president of the Board of Trade now set out his own counterarguments for circulation to members of the ministerial European Economic Association committee.[38] Outlining his proposals for the conduct of future policy he asserted that the Six should be pressed to take a position in the context of seeking long-term negotiations. Any solution, though, he warned, should not threaten the political cohesion of the Six nor the political independence of the Seven. The strength of his argument against Britain applying individually for EEC membership was contained in his refusal even to entertain the possibility. 'Our starting point', he insisted, 'is clearly something like the free trade area which we still believe to be the ideal solution.'

By now, though, the steering committee had developed a line of reasoning which, they hoped, would convince members of the ministerial committee of the need to adjust their perspective. Their report, dated the day after Maudling's, contained very different sentiments and came to very different conclusions.

In content, it differed little from Lee's original memorandum to the chancellor of the exchequer. As well as stating plainly the likely consequences of doing nothing, it set out in stark terms – with considerably more detail than that contained in Lee's original memorandum – the difficulties arising out of the pursuance of a 'near-identification' policy, which was, nevertheless, the policy recommended for adoption.[39] In a further clarification of Lee's original document, the committee concluded that Britain would be unable to negotiate on behalf of the Commonwealth and that, as a consequence, Commonwealth countries would press to participate in any negotiations. While no opinion was ventured on the desirability or feasibility of this possibility, here at last was recognition of the fact of Commonwealth autonomy in matters of international trade.

The tone and content of the steering committee's report reflected the need of officials to set out in detail the difficulties likely to arise out of their recommended course of action. Had they failed to point out all the potential difficulties, or objections, their case would doubtless have been weakened by the later 'discovery' of these same objections by particular ministers, who would then have used them to counter the steering committee's proposals.

In the FO, R.W. Jackling briefed the foreign secretary for the forthcoming meeting of ministers. He suggested that Sir Frank Lee's proposals would have 'a good chance of success' if they were given 'political content'.[40] He expressed doubts, though, as to whether anything short of an offer to join the Common Market would succeed. Although the necessity for converting other ministers to Lee's perspective was not specifically referred to, just such a requirement was implicit in Jackling's comments. As if to emphasize the severity of this task, the following day Maudling reported from his meeting with the Seven in Lisbon that 'joining the Six is clearly ruled out'.[41]

The day before the ministerial committee was due to meet to consider these findings, Freddie Bishop addressed a seven-page memorandum to the PM suggesting ways in which the PM might approach the matter with his colleagues.[42] Bishop set out to anticipate the questions that ministers would be likely to raise and to brief the PM on how to deal with them. He advised the PM that 'it might be best simply to express some general doubts, and then to examine the proposal for near-identification'. He proposed that the PM should present the matter as a choice as to whether the UK should go into Europe 'whole-heartedly, with the object of controlling it politically' as well as aligning Britain economically with the Six or whether Britain should maintain its traditional policy of 'remaining aloof from Europe politically' while attempting to mitigate the economic dangers. Bishop warned the PM that ministers would be unlikely to be attracted sufficiently to the idea of 'near-identification' to propose pursuing it straight away. 'Nevertheless', he said, 'whatever doubts there may be about the validity of near-identification, it would be right to ask officials to continue with the detailed study of this solution which they are making.' 'The right course at the moment', Bishop counselled, 'is perhaps to avoid making a final choice.'

Bishop's recommendations were aimed at ensuring that the PM would not allow Lee's plan to be dismissed 'out of hand' by the ministerial committee. He would also have been aware that the prolongation of discussion, in any case, had its own rewards. For, as had been seen with the EFTA policy, concentration even on the shortcomings of a particular policy tended to lodge that policy in the minds and on the agenda of ministers, who would then seek to find solutions to the problems it raised instead of looking for alternatives.

It is evident that, although Bishop's official role was now that of deputy secretary to the cabinet, there existed an understanding between himself and the PM whereby he acted, in certain respects, in his previously held role as the PM's principal private secretary. In spite of his own change of designation, the appointment of Tim Bligh and the special responsibility allotted to Philip de Zulueta for overseas affairs, Bishop continued as before to advise the PM on European matters. This was a situation that admirably suited Sir Frank Lee, who was assured of having his way to the PM well prepared by his friend and colleague.

The agenda for the ministerial committee meeting was deceptively short. The first item to be discussed was *The Six and the Seven: Long Term Objective* and the second was *The Six and the Seven: Short Term Tactics.*[43] The PM was in the chair and, unusually, Rab Butler attended from the Home Office. As home secretary, Butler was by no means an obvious candidate for the European Economic Association committee. His attendance at this important meeting indicates an awareness on the part of the PM (or his advisers) of the dangers of excluding from the discussion a potentially vociferous opponent of any radical change of policy. Butler's presence would also afford the PM the opportunity to gauge the strength of support among his colleagues for Butler's conservative approach to the European issue. The president of the Board of Trade did not attend the meeting. It is likely that he had already left for a trip to Canada.

The committee had before them both the memorandum from the steering committee and Maudling's report on the first meeting of the EFTA Council of Ministers together with a summary of his views on the Six/Seven question. Taken at face value, the PM's opening comments indicated that, despite Lee's powerfully worded recommendations, he remained far from convinced of the necessity for making any radical adjustment to existing policy. He asked his colleagues to consider whether or not 'near-identification' was really the only viable long-term objective for Britain. He questioned the belief that all hope was now lost for the achievement of an industrial free trade area 'once the Six had fully consolidated their economic and political union'. He also proposed that the possibility might still exist for the establishment of a single European market with a preferential position for the Six. This might still be attained, he ventured, through eliciting American support to secure 'at least the acquiescence, if not the approval' of other signatories of the GATT.[44]

Turning next to consider what he called the 'formidable' objections to "near-identification"', the PM went through a litany of the potential disasters that the enactment of Lee's proposal might bring down on the government and on Britain. But he did not, as his colleagues must surely by then have been expecting, propose the straightforward rejection of Lee's plan. Instead, in an act of elegant political stealth, he harnessed the power of the objections to the proposal to underpin an even more audacious proposition. 'It was for consideration', he said, 'whether, if we were prepared to contemplate "near-identification" with all its difficulties and dangers, we should not do better to go the whole way and secure the full advantages of membership of the Common Market.'[45] To 'go into Europe fully', he observed, 'would at least be a positive and an imaginative approach which might assist the Government to overcome the manifest political and domestic difficulties.' 'Near-identification', the PM argued, held most of the dangers of full membership of the Common Market and few of its advantages.

In the course of his statement then, the PM had outlined all the possibilities (which might or might not still have existed) and highlighted all the difficulties arising out of Lee's plan. At the same time, though, he contrived to conclude his statement with the offer of a choice – not between 'near-identification' and some less radical course but between 'near-identification' and full membership of the EEC. After a lengthy debate which brought to the fore once again the disadvantages – and some of the advantages – that a decision in favour of a British application to join the EEC would incur, the committee concluded that the matter should be looked into by officials and the arguments on both sides set out.

Summing up, the PM again expressed the view that if ministers were contemplating 'near-identification', they would do well to consider full membership instead.[46] Then, borrowing unreservedly from Freddie Bishop's briefing, he said that the important decision was between 'initiating a dramatic change in direction in our domestic, commercial and international policies, and maintaining our traditional policy of remaining aloof from Europe politically while doing all we could to mitigate the economic dangers of a divided Europe'. The PM was anxious to impress upon ministers the gravity with which he viewed this issue. 'This would be another of the historic moments of decision', he said, 'and would need much careful thought.' He told the committee that, in consultation with the chancellor of the exchequer and the foreign secretary, he would circulate a list of questions for ministers and their officials to consider. He took the opportunity, though, to warn his colleagues that 'these were primarily matters of judgement which could not be answered definitively'.

The committee agreed that further consideration would be given to the matter after officials had reported back on the questions raised.[47] In fact, there was no further meeting of the ministerial committee until 30 August, a lapse of some three months, during which time the PM made important changes in his cabinet and turned for advice to the particular group of officials and ministers whose views he was coming gradually to share. Meanwhile Maudling's concern, expressed to his permanent secretary over the telephone from Canada, that a decision should not be reached with regard to the UK and the Six while he was away, received a double-edged reassurance from Sir Richard Powell. The president of the Board of Trade was reminded that, following a meeting in Switzerland, which Maudling himself had attended, it was clear that nothing short of full British membership of the EEC on the same terms as the rest would satisfy the French.[48]

There are several important indicators here for the interpretation of the later management of policy development. The first is that, throughout their discussions, ministers referred to the organization of the European Six as the *Common Market*. The choice of terminology (which was not particular to this committee) is illustrative of the preoccupation on all sides with the trade problem as opposed to the political ramifications of Britain's exclusion from the Community. Indeed, where political difficulties were discussed, they generally centred upon those that would be raised by economic problems in the domestic constituency. And, when the question of Britain's international political position *was* referred to, there was a measure of consensus in the committee that the UK might even do better, politically, from outside the Community than from within it.

Secondly, it is noticeable that even in the privacy of 10 Downing St, ministers could not bring themselves to refer, more than was strictly necessary, to the possibility of British

membership of the Common Market. After the initial out-
line of officials' proposals had been put by the PM, the terms
'near-identification' and 'membership' were avoided by ministers in favour of the euphemistic term 'association', which
betrayed less in the way of commitment to a particular course
from which ministers might later wish to retreat.

Thirdly, while the PM was not yet totally converted to the
idea of British membership of the EEC, he apparently saw
enough in it not to rule out the possibility. (The allusion,
in his summary, to the 'historic moments of decision' probably owed something to Lee's reference to 'statesmanship'.)
Nevertheless, Macmillan's assessment, both of the alternatives to Lee's recommendations and of the difficulties attached to this radical course of action, was by no means
cursory. He was evidently prepared to approach the Rubicon
but would have been grateful if colleagues had abrogated
the necessity for him to begin the crossing by picking up
and developing with enthusiasm one of the alternatives he
had offered. They did not – and this is a matter of the greatest
significance. For in the discussion that followed, Lee's proposals (or their enhanced version) were not set against alternative proposals but against their own intrinsic difficulties.
The question had unexpectedly catalysed into whether the
UK should seek 'near-identification' with (or membership
of) the Common Market or . . . not.

8 The Cabinet Says 'No'

This chapter explores the relative effectiveness of the formal and informal power of civil service officials set, in this instance, against the formal power of their political masters. The events described serve to highlight both the opportunities and the limitations of the power of civil servants in directing the development of government policy. The same events show how the operation of cabinet government constrained the prime minister to consider short-term political costs before (his interpretation of) the long-term national interest.

Despite the positive reaction of the PM and certain of his colleagues to Lee's proposals, the new thinking was to encounter some difficult obstacles in the coming months, even in the minds of those who now found themselves no longer wedded to traditional policy. And the result of the ongoing tendency for equivocation was that the government as a whole was in danger of developing a split personality over the European issue. The two separate identities manifested themselves not only through the diverse opinions and stances of particular ministers (many of whom, outside the ministerial committee, were as yet unapprised of the seriousness with which a momentous change of direction was being contemplated), but also through pronouncements made by the same ministers dealing respectively with short-term and long-term government objectives.

When addressing long-term objectives ministers in committee were prepared to consider the radical solution, but when attention focused once again on short-term considerations they displayed a tendency to fall back upon their old assumptions about Britain's requirements – holding out the prospect, still, of the eventual achievement of a Six/Seven agreement or even a Europe-wide FTA. It was almost as if their mental excursion into the uncharted territory of European economic integration had been an aberration – a flight of fancy embarked upon by different people in a different age.

The same ministers, though, were soon to be presented with a report from the steering committee which would

demand some decisive action. This would come to be seen
as all the more necessary in the light of the growing rift
between Britain and the US over the Six/Seven issue. In
this regard, the president of the Board of Trade did little
to advance the British cause by consistently promoting abroad
a policy that was, at the very least, now under review. When
the matter did finally come before the cabinet, in July 1960,
it would be Maudling's view that would prevail. It will be
seen, though, that this was due less to constructive opposition to Lee's plan than to a lapse into uncharacteristic naiveté
on the part of the PM which was to set back the development of a realistic policy for another year.

At the end of June, Freddie Bishop was still anxious to
avoid a full cabinet debate on the issue calculating (rightly)
that the cabinet would be unlikely to come out in favour of
Sir Frank Lee's proposals. In recommending that ministers
should nevertheless be consulted about the findings of officials, he advised the PM that 'there would be much advantage in making it an *ad hoc* meeting of ministers rather than
the whole cabinet'.[1] He evidently believed that, in this way,
a careful balance could be struck which would frustrate
potential opposition before the matter was brought before
the full cabinet.

Acting on Bishop's advice, the PM attempted to convene
just such a meeting at Chequers for either the next or the
following weekend. But after several efforts to arrange and
rearrange the date of the meeting to allow for the various
commitments of the ministers involved, the PM – fatefully,
as it transpired – abandoned the attempt.[2] Now his patience
was exhausted. 'It must be the whole Cabinet', he wrote,
'that is the point of the exercise now.'[3] Freddie Bishop saw,
immediately, the folly of the decision. He wrote to Edward
Tomkins at the FO: 'There is still some idea that the Cabinet as a whole will discuss this enormous subject at a meeting in the following week, but I have serious doubts as to
whether a discussion in those circumstances and in that forum
will produce any useful result at all.'[4] He pointed up the
need for an authoritative government statement, adding: 'it
is hard to see how we can get any steadying statement of
this sort unless ministers are prepared to have something
like the Chequers weekend.'

The nature of these exchanges and their outcome points up the difference in priorities between the government secretariat and its political masters. Freddie Bishop's priority was to hold the cabinet together while gaining acceptance for Lee's proposals, which were tacitly supported by the PM. The PM, though, identified in this process the potential for political disaster. Where he calculated the risk to be between the successful implementation of the new policy and his own standing as prime minister, he was prepared to jeopardize the former in favour of the latter. It might not have been apparent to his officials that he was not yet committed enough to the new thinking to allow for the possibility of disaffected colleagues instigating a cabinet revolt. For the time being, at least, Macmillan believed that the safest policy was to consult his colleagues and do what he could with the outcome. There was always the possibility, after all, that, having been presented with the arguments, the cabinet would look favourably upon a radical solution – a possibility that would have had great appeal for the PM.

The answers to the PM's questions (circulated to the departments after the ministerial meeting) were issued by Lee's steering committee at the end of June. In a covering note it was conceded that, with regard to Britain's relationship with the EEC, the choice between 'joining' and 'near-identification' amounted to a 'substantial difference in public presentation but probably little in substance'.[5] Having captured the interest of the PM and his closest advisers, the steering committee under Lee's guidance now pointed out that the 'near-identification' policy had little to commend it when set against an application for full membership of the EEC. Lee's committee asserted that the former would take longer and incur higher costs with fewer benefits. Moreover, officials suggested, France would be less able to object to a straightforward application to join the EEC than it would to a half-way approach.

It was at this stage that the presentational conversion of the issue from an economic to a political imperative received a further boost. Lee proposed that the foreign policy reasons for joining the EEC were even more powerful than the economic.[6] The potential loss of influence if Britain was left outside was cited, as was Britain's apparently unique ability to prevent the EEC from disintegrating. The fact that neither of these points had been given serious consideration until *after* the economic imperative had been established suggests that, as happened with the EFTA proposal, once the proposition had found favour it became imbued with a rich variety of previously unsuspected advantages.

The main problems were then outlined and ministers were warned to be prepared for the possibility that 'the whole of the preferential arrangements [with the Commonwealth] would begin to crumble'.[7] Lee had concluded only the previous day that it would not be 'practical politics' given Britain's wider objectives, to press for the maintenance of free entry for Commonwealth manufactured goods.[8] Public opinion though, his officials noted, would present a considerable problem. They pointed out that 'we should have to contend with the ordinary Englishman's almost innate dislike and suspicion of "Europeans"'. Opposition, they advised, 'would require careful handling' involving 'intensive re-education'. The public must be made to realize, it was stressed, that 'in the modern world even the United Kingdom cannot stand alone, and that if we are excluded from the powerful European Community our influence and standing in the world at large – including the Commonwealth and the uncommitted countries – would be bound to diminish.'[9] It is likely that this assertion was made as much to convince the PM and his colleagues of the need for a change of policy as it was to provide them with the necessary information with which to handle such a change.

The main part of the document, which consisted of answers to the PM's questions, was prepared in the particular government department to which each question was most closely related. The whole document was put together by Lee's committee and ran to some 50 pages.[10] Even then the answers were given in shortened form. The steering committee pointed out that the editing had 'not been agreed inter-departmentally' but was based on longer papers which were discussed by a group of officials 'under Treasury chairmanship'. The longer papers were circulated as addenda to the main paper.

The first few questions reflect the PM's preoccupation with seeking a political rationale for British membership of the EEC. For a number of reasons, not least for the necessity of securing cabinet approval, the existence of sound political reasons for such an important decision was essential. Macmillan was well aware that the British would be more easily moved to accept change in the interests of preserving British power, prestige and security than for reasons related to the complicated and obscure niceties of European trading relationships. The complex economic arguments would have to be buttressed by a measure of political rhetoric that would be more readily assimilated.

On the whole, the FO responded to the questions in a positive vein.[11] They pointed out that British influence would grow – especially if Britain were to become a *full* member of the EEC.[12] Officials were not averse to playing the political card where it had the potential for enhancing the likelihood of ministerial acceptance of their primarily economic objective. For their part, Treasury officials, while keen to emphasize the advantages to be gained from British membership of the EEC, were at pains, as before, not to conceal the potential difficulties.[13] The contribution from the MAG was uncompromising, pointing out the potential losses, particularly for horticulturists.[14] The CRO was even more pessimistic, stating unequivocally that free entry would have to end and that Britain would stand to lose preferential treatment on 20 per cent of its exports.[15] A 'vast amount of paper' on the issue was produced by the BOT. It was Herbert Andrew, contributing for the BOT, who spelled out that 'we face a choice between the Commonwealth and Europe'.[16] The BOT's view (perhaps not entirely accidentally, given the differences of opinion within the department) was obscured by the very volume of its explication.

Although Lee's committee had attempted, both in the covering note and in its own contribution to the main text, to offset some of the points made by the MAG and the CRO, the resulting document by no means amounted to a definitive rationale for embarking upon an historic change of direction. While there was much here for the PM to use in promoting an application to join the EEC, there was also much that might be utilized for the opposite purpose. For all this, though, the document was *not* 'neutral'. It reflected the views of the officials who compiled it – setting an agenda rather than providing raw information.

If the PM was, by now, convinced that membership of the EEC was the best answer to Britain's problems, he would also have been aware that it was not yet time to publicize this conviction. There was a good deal of work yet to be done both in securing the support of his colleagues and in seeking a way round the dilemma posed by the Commonwealth relationship. It was this problem that remained the most intractable. The answers to his questions indicated to Macmillan that the possibility existed for dealing with all the other troublesome considerations. Even the problems associated with British agriculture and British sovereignty appeared to be soluble given time, careful planning and skilful presentation. But the problem of reconciling British membership of the EEC with the Commonwealth relationship – underpinned as it was with ties of history and emotion and by the long-standing free entry arrangement – was of an altogether different order. In a subsequent clarification from the steering committee, the PM was forced to recognize the fact that it was not going to be a matter of how much free entry would have to be conceded but rather of how much could be retained[17] – an apparently subtle difference of emphasis, but one which implied a huge shift of economic and political orientation for the UK.

If the Commonwealth relationship was at the heart of the PM's dilemma, the attitude of the president of the Board of Trade was not going to make the task of finding a solution any easier. Already, on a visit to Ottawa, he had warned the Canadians that if they did not adopt a helpful attitude towards the British objective of securing an FTA, the UK 'might be forced into a settlement and something close to joining the E.E.C. which', he said, 'would not only be unpalatable to us but might also have unsatisfactory consequences for Commonwealth countries'.[18] Now, in early July, the record of a conversation between Maudling and Dillon showed the extent of his alienation from the 'new wisdom'. Maudling said to the US under-secretary of state that British membership of the EEC 'did not make sense for a variety of reasons'.[19] Subsequent ill-timed warnings, by Maudling, against 'economic threats from the European Common Market' raised embarrassing questions for the PM to deal with in the House of Commons.[20]

Despite the well-known resistance to change of several members of his cabinet and contrary to the advice of its deputy secretary, the PM brought the European issue before the cabinet on 13 July. The agenda was summed up in one word: 'Europe'.[21] Ministers had received copies of Lee's report summarizing the answers to the PM's questions.[22] The debate was opened by the chancellor of the exchequer, who quickly set about the business of making the required presentational adjustment, which the PM had calculated was likely to inspire his colleagues with a little more temerity. 'A decision to join the Community', the chancellor said, 'would be essentially a political act with economic consequences, rather than an economic act with political consequences.'[23] (It is of interest to note that, following the lead given by Sir Frank Lee, the term *Community* was now adopted in place of the more usual *Common Market*, a term which not only implied economic rather than political emphasis, but which also had disagreeable associations for ministers.)

In setting out the arguments for and against British membership of the EEC, though, the chancellor's personal misgivings held sway. He spoke of the *surrender* of British control over its commercial policy, a requirement to *abandon* the special relationship with the Commonwealth, and the *sacrifice* of Britain's loyalties and obligations to its EFTA partners.[24] Summing up, he expressed the view that 'we should be ready to join the Community if we could do so without substantially impairing our relations with the Commonwealth'.[25] He argued forcefully that the point should not be pressed to the extent that it would endanger the Commonwealth relationship.[26] As a great Commonwealth enthusiast who did not have much to do with 'continentals', Heathcoat Amory was far from convinced that membership of the EEC would be right for Britain. At the same time, though, he was a man of great loyalty and discretion.[27] It was the fact that the PM had not yet come out in favour of British membership of the EEC that allowed him to give such forceful expression to his own objections. Had the PM persevered in his attempt to convene a Chequers meeting, the chancellor might well have been persuaded to take, at the very least, a more ambivalent line.

The president of the Board of Trade then gave voice to

his own grave doubts, after which he proposed that the government should issue a statement to the effect that 'this was not a suitable moment for negotiations with the Community'. Further discussion led to cabinet agreement that the UK 'could not accept membership of the Community on the terms of the Treaty of Rome'.[28] Any looser form of association was also ruled out since it was seen to entail few of the advantages and most of the disadvantages of full membership. Agreement was finally procured for encouraging a greater awareness of the problem and of the choice which would eventually have to be made, 'by consultation with the Commonwealth, by discussions with the agricultural and horticultural industries and by informing public opinion generally'.[29] It was this proposal, from which it was hard for any minister to demur, that left the door open for the prime minister and his closest advisers to set about their task of bringing Britain, a year later, to the brink of EEC membership.

The PM, perhaps betraying thoughts that were travelling in the opposite direction, said that it was important, in any event, that the cabinet should be kept 'closely in touch' with policy developments.[30] He agreed that the statement to be given to the House of Commons on 25 July would explain that 'there were insuperable difficulties in the way of our accepting membership of the Community under the existing provisions of the Treaty of Rome', but that Britain would 'continue to seek for a mutually satisfactory arrangement between the E.E.C. and E.F.T.A.'. It was a measure of Macmillan's disillusion with the whole business that he charged the president of the Board of Trade, in consultation with other ministers, with preparing a statement to this effect.

Maudling lost no time in preparing a speech for delivery at the forthcoming parliamentary debate and FO officials lost no time, either, in proposing its revision. Paul Gore-Booth complained that Maudling's draft 'slammed the door finally' on any possibility of the UK joining the EEC.[31] The speech was redrafted in the Treasury and was approved by the chancellor of the exchequer but still FO officials were not happy, arguing that it emphasized British attachment to EFTA as an alternative to the EEC rather than as a means of coming closer to it. Suggestions for the speech were received also

from John Profumo and Iain Macleod but it was Maudling,
Lloyd and Heathcoat Amory who finally came together to
hammer out a text.[32] Inevitably, though, it took Lee to propose an acceptable compromise.[33] Freddie Bishop summed
up the difficulty. The intention, he said, was to avoid saying
explicitly that the UK would consider joining the EEC if
the terms were right, but at the same time implying that
this was so.[34] Somewhere among the deliberations it was
agreed that the foreign secretary rather than the president
of the Board of Trade would open the debate in the House
of Commons.

In the foreign secretary's statement to parliament on the
25 July, it was made clear that the government did not believe that the time was ripe for negotiations with the Six.[35]
What exactly the negotiations might have been about, had
the time been ripe to open them, and when they would
now be likely to take place, remained unspecified. But while,
in the ensuing debate, Lloyd's calculated ambiguity leant
towards the possibility of eventual British participation in
the EEC, Reginald Maudling – despite the best efforts of
FO officials – spoke more emphatically about the advantages
for Britain accorded by its membership of EFTA and of the
desirability of seeking an association with the Six in the
context of a Six/Seven agreement. Not surprisingly, given
the deliberate obfuscation, the reception for the foreign
secretary's speech both at home and abroad was muted.[36]
Hallstein typified European impatience with the British attitude. He made the point to Paul Gore-Booth, over dinner,
that every time the Six had an initiative for tighter coordi-
nation, the UK had responded by attempting to dilute it to
'something wider and weaker'.[37]

If the PM had hoped for some new enlightenment or input
of ideas from his cabinet colleagues, he would have been
sorely disappointed. Ministers generally displayed a marked
lack of enthusiasm for addressing the intricacies of the issue in a constructive manner. In the end, though, it was
the PM's own inconsistency that gave rise to his greatest
problem in dealing with his cabinet. First, the attempt by
the PM to present the issue as political rather than economic – thereby freeing ministers from their departmental
obligations – turned out to be counter-productive since it

gave the impression that the economic factors were less important and *ipso facto* that, in the absence of a specific political exigency, no drastic departure from existing policy was really necessary.

Secondly, having first heeded the advice of his officials to rule out any in-depth discussion of the European issue in cabinet, he then gave way to an impulse, not only to bring the matter before the full cabinet but there to seek a decision on the specific matter of whether or not Britain should apply for membership of the EEC. Having only a limited acquaintance with the carefully accumulated findings and the sound reasoning of Sir Frank Lee – and with all that had gone before – it was only to be expected that Macmillan's cabinet colleagues would be less than vigorous in their support for what many of them would have viewed as an uncalled for leap in the dark.

Ironically, it had been one of the PM's most loyal colleagues, the chancellor of the exchequer, who opened the way for other ministers to give powerful expression to their objections. Had the PM taken the cabinet into his confidence at the outset and faced his colleagues early on with the serious nature of the economic difficulties that now confronted Britain, it is possible that – at this later stage – they would have seen the matter in a different light. Alternatively, had the PM heeded the advice of Freddie Bishop and cultivated an inner circle of support (including that, particularly, of the chancellor of the exchequer) before taking the matter before the full cabinet, the outcome might again have been different. Discouraged and dispirited, Macmillan wrote to his friend, Lady Waverley, 'this week has been a very difficult one'.[38]

The consequences of the tactics (or the lack of them) adopted by the PM at this pivotal stage in the development of British policy amount of to more than an historical nicety. For, had the cabinet approved the proposal, in July 1960, that Britain should apply for membership of the EEC, the timing, nature and outcome of Britain's negotiations with the Six might well have taken a different course. Among many other considerations, the claim that de Gaulle was able to make (by virtue of his newly acquired political security) in January 1963 – that Britain was unfit for membership of

the EEC because of the Nassau Agreement – would not have
been possible a matter of months before. Macmillan himself told his biographer that although after the Rambouillet
meeting of December 1962 he believed that de Gaulle 'didn't
want us in', he also felt (before Nassau) that 'we would leave
him no excuse to exclude us'.[39]

The cabinet reshuffle came little more than two weeks
later, though its timing in respect of the European issue
was as much propitious as it was deliberate. Its necessity
was signalled in the PM's mind by the obvious discomfiture
of the chancellor of the exchequer, who was, in Macmillan's
opinion, 'tired and overdone'.[40] Indeed, Heathcoat Amory
had himself expressed the wish to step down after the election the previous October but had been persuaded by
Macmillan to stay on.[41] As always, the departure of a single
minister from the cabinet set in train a series of changes
and it was in this context that Edward Heath, in a move
that was accompanied by 'virtually no comment in the press',[42]
became, as lord privy seal, number two to the Earl of Home
in the latter's new capacity as foreign secretary. Duncan
Sandys, who was something of a progressive with regard
to Europe,[43] was moved from Aviation to the CRO and
Christopher Soames (whose attitude to the issue is reflected
in the fact that he was later to become the first British vice-
president of the European Commission) replaced John Hare
at the MAG – a move occasioned by Hare's move to the
Ministry of Labour. Peter Thorneycroft, a steady advocate
for a pragmatic approach to Europe, was brought back into
the cabinet as minister of aviation and Heathcoat Amory
was replaced at the Treasury by Macmillan's trusted adviser,
Selwyn Lloyd. Viscount Hailsham, having lost his position
as privy seal to Edward Heath was moved to the Ministry of
Science, from where any damage arising out of his opposition to British overtures to the EEC would be more easily
contained.

Although evidently not contrived solely for the purpose
of facilitating a more easy passage for 'Europeanist' ideas,
the timing and nature of these cabinet changes certainly
did no harm to the cause of those who advocated a radical
change of direction for Britain. The appointment of
Edward Heath, who was to combine his duties as privy seal,

with special responsibility for European affairs, with those of a Foreign Office minister, was to prove a particularly effective one. As Camps points out, 'as a newcomer to the Cabinet Heath was untainted by the previous abortive free trade area negotiations'.[44] There is some irony in the fact that, in the same week that parliament was told of the reasons why Britain could not apply for membership of the EEC, a cabinet reshuffle took place, which was to make realizable the adoption of just such a policy.

While it is evident that the views of leading civil service officials were broadly accepted by the PM, the evidence shows, too, that these same officials were unable – largely because of the PM's uncharacteristic impulsiveness – to avert the rejection of their views by the cabinet. After the care that had been taken in drafting replies to the PM's questions, the outcome of the July cabinet meeting would have been, for them, particularly disappointing.

It was clear by now that the views of Reginald Maudling – who had the manifest authority to speak on behalf of the British government on matters relating to Commonwealth and European trade – would pose particular difficulties for Lee and his colleagues in the months to come. For the time being though, through exploiting to the full his central role, Lee had succeeded in ensuring that the foreign secretary's speech to parliament left the door open for the further development of Britain's European policy. The events of early summer 1960 serve to illustrate that the balance between the formal power of minister of the Crown and the facility accorded to civil servants, by virtue of their essential role in government, for influencing policy development was a very fine one indeed.

9 At Home and Abroad

The events following the July cabinet meeting show how the development of British policy was constrained not only by the conflicting views of government ministers and officials but also by the influence of external forces, which operated in a sphere that was even more outside the PM's control. It was in the context of less than favourable external conditions that ministers and officials were now obliged to reconstruct a viable policy. Here, as with internal exchanges, subtlety, perspicacity and sound political judgement were the prerequisites of success. But here, as before, progress was susceptible to over-frequent recourse by the opponents of change to prevarication or self-delusion.

Far from putting an end to the debate, the cabinet decision of 13 July, and the subsequent cabinet reshuffle, signalled a new round of activity with regard to the European issue that took place at many discrete though interlocking levels. At the international level, Britain's EFTA partners retained some confidence in the Trade Committee. British ministers and officials, though, having identified an unholy and an unhelpful alliance between France, America and the EEC Commission, had come to believe that little would be achieved there. At a more direct high politics level, during the parliamentary summer recess, the PM, the foreign secretary and the privy seal would venture (quietly) into the heart of Europe for some face-to-face discussions. Even less conspicuously, a new round of discussions was set in train between British and German officials, while at home Lee and his colleagues continued in their attempt to build a constructive approach from the mass of conflicting information emanating from a multifarious array of internal and international meetings.

Also at home, the president of the Board of Trade and the privy seal were set to embark upon low-key and primarily tactical confrontation. While Maudling had the advantage of a direct line, through the BOT representative (Betty Ackroyd), to the official discussions with the Germans, the privy seal had the advantage of sharing the objective of Lee's influential steering committee. Maulding's aims were well known. As for the privy seal, according to Sir Michael Wilford (his private secretary), he was intent, from the outset, upon taking Britain into the EEC. Sir Michael suggests that Heath 'came in with the mandate to go into Europe'.[1] In this regard he suggests that it was also appreciated from 'early on' that such a move would 'mean the end of Commonwealth preference as it existed'. Even allowing for the difficulty – over thirty years after the event – of placing an exact timing on ministers' feelings and objectives, Sir Michael's recollections suggest, at the very least, that the privy seal embarked upon his duties of seeking a solution to Britain's trading problems, with considerable zeal.

Lacking the resolution of the privy seal, the PM nevertheless felt that some high-level discussion would be beneficial. Less than a month after the cabinet meeting that had rejected the idea of British membership of the EEC, and with the study group bogged down in formalities, the PM set off with the Earl of Home to Bonn for talks with Dr Adenauer.[2] On his return the PM communicated to the chancellor of the exchequer his confidence that the German chancellor was now of a mind to address the problem of the economic division of Europe. 'A quiet exchange of views' between the British, the Germans and the French had been proposed for October.[3] The PM told Selwyn Lloyd that while it had been made clear to the Germans that Britain could not join the EEC 'as it now is' (because of the problems of the Commonwealth, agriculture and EFTA), 'we did, however, indicate that we would be prepared to consider any solutions which took account of these difficulties.' Numbered among these possible solutions was British membership of the EEC – subject to certain conditions. Macmillan wrote to his confidante, Lady Waverley: 'We had a very interesting trip to Bonn and on the whole much more successful than we expected.'[4]

In fact, though, the German government, for all its appearance of acting in good faith, posed almost as many riddles for the British as did the attitude of the French. While the official negotiators appeared to be fairly consistent in their approach, Adenauer was prone to vacillate between suspicion of de Gaulle and of Macmillan.[5] By now well into his eighties, the German chancellor could not be relied upon to define a particular policy line and stick to it. The assurances given by the German ambassador to Roderick Barclay, that Adenauer had given instructions to German officials to do everything possible to make progress on the issue, provided only limited comfort to those who were aware of the German chancellor's unreliable disposition.[6]

British confusion was not relieved either by the activities of Ludwig Erhard, the German deputy chancellor, who took a consistently over-optimistic line with regard to achieving a settlement. This was partly due to Adenauer's failure to confide in his deputy.[7] But the lack of confidence from his chancellor did not prevent Erhard from putting forward his own assessment of the situation. In May he had suggested that if the Seven could stay together for another two years or so, it was likely that the Six would be 'sufficiently coherent' to consider joining EFTA.[8] Pronouncements of this sort, from a senior member of the German administration who enjoyed the personal esteem of the prime minister,[9] did little to encourage the adoption of a more realistic view in London even though, by the beginning of June, it was recognized in the FO that Dr Erhard was regarded as 'a sort of antichrist in Paris' and was, as a consequence, 'singularly ineffective' in dealing with the French.[10]

Maudling found that 'while he [Erhard] was bulging with geniality and confidence he did not appear to have much of a grasp on the facts of the situation'. Indeed, in a meeting with the president of the Board of Trade, he 'had to start off rather pathetically', Maudling told the PM, 'by asking what happened at your meeting in Bonn'.[11] Maudling did, however, glean from his meeting with Erhard that there was 'some argument going on between the [German] Foreign Office and the Economics Ministry as to whether the objective should be a minimum solution or a maximum solution'.[12] This competitiveness between German government departments was confirmed by Betty Ackroyd, who detected in a meeting with Meyer-Cording a growing concern that his Economics Ministry was being side-lined in the formulation of German policy.[13] On the other side of the argument, Harkort later told a British Embassy official in Bonn that he was 'determined for the time being to keep representation on the German side confined to the Foreign Ministry'. He feared that if the Economics Ministry became involved, 'it would be impossible to avoid leaks'.[14] The combination of the frail chancellorship of Adenauer, the unreliability of his deputy and the destructive rivalry of the two key government departments offered hope to the embattled PM only because there seemed nowhere else left to put it.

In spite of these impediments, the PM's visit to Bonn and the privy seal's trip to Italy (see below) set in train a series of discussions where Britain effectively 'sold out' its EFTA partners through seeking a solution with little regard for their partners' difficulties – this, despite the regular reassurances given to them by government ministers. By now rumour about British intentions had become rife among EFTA ministers who, for their part, remained lamentably unperturbed. The Swedish ambassador to Bonn went so far as to welcome a report that the UK was seeking a deal with the Six since he believed that 'any agreement the United Kingdom reached could obviously be extended to the other countries of the Seven'.[15] His confidence seemed well enough placed when the foreign secretary said on Austrian television, the following month, that the reconciliation that HMG sought between the Six and the Seven was 'very different from suggesting that the United Kingdom would ever contemplate a solution in isolation from her E.F.T.A. partners'.[16] Duncan Sandys, on a visit to Sweden, further reassured his hosts by saying that the UK was thinking 'solely in terms of an agreement between the Six and the Seven and not a separate agreement between the Six and the United Kingdom'.[17]

At home, the ministerial European Economic Association committee now reflected the results of the PM's cabinet reshuffle. The most notable addition to their number was Edward Heath. At the first meeting of the reconstituted committee, the PM told his colleagues of the optimistic conclusions that he had drawn from his meeting with Dr Adenauer.[18] Heath then told the committee of the outcome of his own meeting with Mr Fanfani, the Italian prime minister, where the latter had expressed alarm at talk among

EEC ministers of extending cooperation to include military matters. Mr Fanfani had intimated, Heath said, that it was for this reason, among others, that he was keen to bring the UK into closer involvement with the Six. According to Heath, the Italian prime minister made it clear that the Italians were ready to see changes in the Treaty of Rome to accommodate the Seven.

In the light of these optimistic indicators, the committee gave consideration to the best way to handle the French. They decided, on the whole, that it would be best to allow the Germans and Italians to bring pressure to bear here especially since their leaders now appeared to favour a British association with the Six. The diminishing hope that the Six might agree to join EFTA, had been given new life, not only by Erhard, but by the PM himself, who had persuaded the German chancellor to concede that such an idea remained a possibility. While the committee agreed that the Six as a whole would be unlikely to accept it, the persistence of this happy prospect, in the minds of some ministers, together with the notion that the Seven might yet find accommodation in a new version of the Treaty of Rome, undoubtedly affected their judgement as to the concessions that they would be prepared to make in the pursuance of a more demanding solution. The committee concluded that while the plan for the EEC joining EFTA was preferred, the acceptance of a customs union with the Six should not be ruled out.

Ministers, including the PM himself, were evidently still ready to grasp any opportunity that would afford them a solution that did not involve unpalatable choices and political risk. Despite the best efforts of their officials to promote a realistic and constructive outlook, it is evident that ministers were still disposed to bouts of unwarranted optimism – in this case, based on little more than the eagerness of German and Italian statesmen to retain British goodwill. This was an example of groupthink on a grand scale since French agreement to EEC membership of EFTA had long been dismissed as unthinkable and British involvement in a customs union amounted to a half-way solution about which the PM had earlier expressed severe doubts. The self-deception was accompanied by the deception of Britain's EFTA partners, who were consistently assured that 'it would be an essential condition of any arrangement' that it would have to be acceptable to the other members of E.F.T.A.'.[19] In this regard even British officials serving on the small EFTA secretariat in Geneva, or indeed, in EFTA countries themselves, were not made privy to all the relevant information.[20]

The meeting with Adenauer had given rise – largely unjustifiably – to a new air of optimism among ministers and officials alike. Relations with America, though, were still strained. If anything, the new confidence led to the perpetuation rather than the amelioration of Anglo-American misunderstanding. From now on, ministers and officials would be circumspect in the amount of information that they (intentionally, at least) would allow the US administration to share. When Sir Harold Caccia wrote from Washington asking for any new information on the UK's position that he could offer to Herter, the US secretary of state, and Dillon, his under-secretary, Jackling suggested that HMG 'should not be forthcoming about the nature of possible solutions just yet'.[21] 'Their attitude over the past year', he said, 'has not been helpful, and we don't want to give them the ammunition to lobby against any of our tentative ideas.'

While ministers were once again assailed by the tendency to translate hope too easily into confidence, Lee's committee remained under no illusion about Britain's position. In a paper entitled *Next Steps After Bonn*,[22] ministers were told that 'it is difficult to see how we could achieve any economic association unless it were accompanied in some degree by harmonization of policies and common acceptance of appropriate institutions.'[23] The committee cited Selwyn Lloyd's express willingness (in his House of Commons speech) to see the UK accept the Treaty of Rome 'if changes could be made to meet our difficulties'. The committee concluded that 'in further discussions with the Germans we should be prepared to reaffirm our readiness to consider joining a modified Treaty of Rome which would provide appropriate safeguards for our basic interests and for E.F.T.A.'. In this though, the possibility of maintaining free entry on anything like the existing basis was clearly ruled out.

In the light of subsequent government pronouncements,

it is worthwhile to note the extent to which ministers were apprised of the necessity for the virtual abandonment of the principle of Commonwealth free entry if Britain were to join the EEC. Officials under Lee's leadership went on to recommend that, at the forthcoming meeting of the Commonwealth Economic Consultative Council, the situation should be explained to Commonwealth ministers 'with complete frankness'.[24] Commonwealth ministers should be told, Lee's committee advised, that 'we would do all in our power to preserve intact Commonwealth free entry, but we should warn them that we do not think we could secure a settlement *without substantial departures from that principle.*'[25] The committee urged a low-key approach, which would involve taking soundings from the Germans – about their opinion of French attitudes – and from EFTA and Commonwealth partners. On no account, though, officials warned, should ministers enter into negotiations.[26]

In some concluding remarks, Lee referred to annexes attached to the report which included a pessimistic submission from the BOT.[27] 'These annexes are for the most part factual', the committee advised, 'but they contain a number of departmental opinions which have not yet been discussed by the Economic Steering (Europe) Committee and the Committee does not necessarily agree with them.'[28] The consignment of the BOT's submission to an annex was a particularly effective means of ensuring that it would attract the least possible amount of ministerial attention while at the same time fulfilling the committee's obligation to furnish ministers with the full facts as seen from the point of view of the BOT. Providing for the eventuality of ministers actually reading the annexes, a disclaimer as to their validity had been placed in the main text.

A further blow to the traditionalists' cause came in the form of a message to Commonwealth ministers. Prepared by Lee, it outlined the proposal to discuss with Commonwealth ministers 'what the difficulties would be if we were obliged to consider the acceptance of a common tariff over part of the field as a *sine qua non* of a solution'.[29] The message was formulated and dispatched while the president of the Board of Trade was away. Lee wrote an apologetic note, trusting that Maudling would be happy with its contents.

Maudling, though, had been at work at a different level. Despite the misgivings of his permanent secretary, he had despatched Betty Ackroyd to Germany in order 'to educate the Germans gradually about the technical problems [i.e. Commonwealth free entry] involved in any rapprochement'.[30]

With little of consequence (despite the optimism it engendered) having arisen out of the PM's trip to Bonn, ministers and officials had been thrown back, once again, upon their own resources for finding a solution. These resources would now be addressed to winning over influential opinion at home rather than overseas. It had become clear to all but the most incurable optimists that a move towards the EEC must amount to a move away from the Commonwealth. The question of which way Britain would move now hung on the issue of Commonwealth free entry.

Freddie Bishop, concerned as ever with tactical considerations, suggested to the PM that because the meeting of Commonwealth finance ministers would be 'something of a landmark' – in so far as they would be asked to consider the possibility of giving up free entry and accepting a tariff on some of their products – the privy seal should mention this to the cabinet.[31] In fact, the subject of broaching 'closer association of the UK with European countries', with Commonwealth finance ministers was the third point for debate of the third item on the cabinet agenda entitled: *Commonwealth Economic Consultative Council*.[32]

The privy seal told the cabinet that he would explain to Commonwealth ministers that there were two possibilities: the first – that the EEC would join EFTA – was not likely to be acceptable; the 'broad alternative' he described was 'some form of closer association' between the UK, other EFTA countries and the Six that would involve 'to some degree' the acceptance of a common external tariff. Heath told his colleagues that it would be difficult to establish 'how much derogation from the principle of free entry would be tolerable without unduly alarming them' and he emphasized again that it would be made clear that the UK was not, at this stage, conducting negotiations with the EEC. Cabinet minutes record that 'discussion showed that the cabinet were in general agreement with the way in which it was proposed to explore the European problem at the meeting of the

Commonwealth Economic Consultative Council'.

There are several points arising out of the conduct of this meeting that are particularly worthy of note. The first is that the privy seal was working on the assumption that British policy was now based upon seeking agreement on a common external tariff that would involve undermining the system of Commonwealth free entry – a policy that had never been endorsed by the cabinet. The presentation of this assumption as fact made it particularly difficult to oppose. Moreover, the fact that the matter was being discussed in the context of its presentation to third parties, gave the impression that the policy itself was not up for discussion.

The tactic of appearing to offer a choice of options where none realistically existed was once again deployed. In this regard, it was important for cabinet members to feel that they were not being presented with a *fait accompli*. In theory, the cabinet was fulfilling its role at the heart of the decision-making process. In practice, though, no substantial contribution was sought or made by any minister not directly involved with the development of policy.

The language, as before, had been carefully chosen. The chancellor of the exchequer spoke of obtaining a *settlement* by means of effecting an *association* with the Six involving the acceptance *to some degree* (according to the privy seal) of a common external tariff. Heath also spoke of the *broad alternative* as if there were a wide spectrum of choices open to the UK arising out of British acceptance of a common external tariff. No reference was made to the political ramifications of such a policy nor to the PM's ambitions in this regard. The privy seal also spoke of *derogations* from the principle of free entry, when it had already been made clear by Lee's committee that the Six would not be happy with anything less than the virtual end of the free entry arrangement while allowing, themselves, for a small number of derogations.

By giving its approval for the pursuance of policy along the lines set out by the chancellor and the privy seal, the cabinet furnished those ministers with the authority to allow, in future policy, for the erosion of Commonwealth free entry. In this respect the cabinet meeting of 15 September, where Britain's relationship with the EEC did not even appear on the main agenda, marked another material development in the formulation of British European policy. The matter was not raised for full cabinet discussion again until 20 April the following year, when it again appeared on the agenda as a sub-heading under the main subject entitled, 'Washington Talks'.

Once the hurdle of gaining cabinet approval had been overcome, responsibility for drafting a speech to be made by the privy seal (who was to replace the chancellor as opening speaker) at the Commonwealth Economic Consultative Council was given to Lee's steering group. As might have been expected, officials did not waste this opportunity to advance the cause of a British application to join the EEC. Though never actually alluding to this possibility, they set out the rationale for this course of action in terms most likely to appeal to Commonwealth ministers. References to British *participation* and *association* and to the seeking of an *accommodation* and *closer contact* were given at various junctures throughout the draft speech. Perhaps the most telling observation, though, was that 'there can be no question of our being ready to go into the Common Market irrespective of the terms we can get. That would be completely irresponsible and we would not contemplate it.'[33] This amounted to as bold a statement of intent as Lee's committee dared to make. For, since no government would be likely to enter into a treaty 'irrespective of the terms', the intention to do so if the terms were right was all but spelled out.

Only at the end of the draft speech did Lee and his colleagues allude to British participation in a customs union with the Six and the possible ramifications of such a policy for other Commonwealth countries. On this point it was stated that 'while it would certainly be our aim to work out arrangements with the Six which would enable us to maintain free entry in full, we must recognise that this is most unlikely to be fully acceptable'.[34] Before the speech was to be delivered, minor adjustments were made at the *ad hoc* meeting of ministers nominated the previous week by the PM.[35]

When he finally met the Commonwealth finance ministers, the privy seal, following the recommendations that had been made to him, gave the broadest possible hint about his true intentions for Britain.[36] He said that 'we, who are members of the Commonwealth, but who feel ourselves to be part of Europe as well are anxious that this should develop on lines which permit us to take our part in it.' We can only do this', he declared, 'if we are on the inside.' Then, using precisely the form of words prescribed by Lee's committee, Heath stated that, in line with the foreign secretary's speech in July, 'there can be no question of our being ready to go into the Common Market irrespective of the terms we can get.' He added that it was now a question of whether a balance could be achieved between 'changes we may be able to make and any requirements on which the Six may insist'.[37]

By way of attempting to assuage the mounting concern of Commonwealth ministers, Selwyn Lloyd then insisted that 'it was important to keep recent developments in perspective'.[38] He assured them that 'it was the United Kingdom's present purpose to give the Commonwealth an opportunity to express views on this matter before her ideas crystallised'. But, despite the chancellor's attempt to paint the best possible picture, Commonwealth ministers remained sceptical. A number of them said that they feared 'serious damage to their economic interests and thus indirectly to the structure of Commonwealth trade and possibly more broadly the Commonwealth itself'.[39]

On 22 September, the chancellor of the exchequer made a short statement to the cabinet informing ministers that, with the exception of New Zealand and Australia – who were said to have feared the effects of an association between EFTA and the EEC – Commonwealth finance ministers 'had shown themselves to be more sympathetic than had been expected to the United Kingdom's difficulties'.[40] The foreign secretary displayed similar optimism by drawing the conclusion that there was 'a greater realisation than before of the long-term political importance of our being closely associated with Europe'.[41]

After the decision of the July cabinet meeting and Selwyn Lloyd's subsequent speech to the House of Commons, ministers would have been forgiven for believing that the European issue had been shelved for the foreseeable future. This, as the evidence shows, was not however the case. Four factors

– the persistence of Sir Frank Lee and his colleagues on
the steering committee, the ever-growing interest in the issue by Treasury and FO officials (see Chapter 10), the burgeoning ambition of the PM, and the appointment of a master
tactician in the person of Edward Heath – combined to ensure
that the European question remained firmly on the
government's agenda. As for the prime minister, the fact
that he showed particular interest in a proposal by the chairman of the German industrial federation for seeking a solution through a tariff quota deal between the EEC and the
UK[42] indicates that, in the autumn of 1960, Macmillan still
viewed the problem in terms of economic rather than political exigency.

By September 1960, some progress had been made at home
towards a realistic approach to the problem of Commonwealth free entry. At the same time, though, relations between the British and US administrations – on the European
question at least – remained strained. Britain's relations with
its EFTA partners had become uneasy and progress towards
formulating a workable understanding with the Germans
remained elusive. The attitude of the French to British discomfiture was, as ever, impenetrable. Britain's external relationships, it seems, posed as many difficulties for the PM
and his colleagues as did the growing dichotomy of opinion on the issue in government circles at home.

10 In the Departments

Sir Frank Lee's move to the Treasury in January 1960, though the most consequential for Britain's relationship with Europe, was not the only significant move among officials to take place during those crucial months and years. Sir Richard Powell, previously at the Ministry of Defence, was appointed (unexpectedly, he recalls) to replace Sir Frank Lee as permanent secretary to the BOT.[1] Sir Richard's appointment presented Maudling with a permanent secretary whose views on Europe were considerably at odds with his own. In the FO at the same time, Edward Tomkins, on his return from Paris to Whitehall, set about establishing the Western Organizations Department to deal with the *political* aspects of Britain's relationship with the various defence and economic institutions – a task that had, until then, been spread thinly across various FO departments. These changes represented an important development in the management of British policy. It would seem appropriate, at this juncture, to put them into the context of the attitudes and ideas that lay behind policy formulation from the perspective of the three departments most involved in the issue: the Treasury, the BOT and the FO.

As far as the Treasury as a whole was concerned, Europe was not an issue that commanded a great deal of attention. As always, claims on the energies of Treasury officials were many and various. The matter of Britain's relationship with the EEC was largely left to the cabinet committees, in the secure knowledge that both the key committees were chaired by Treasury officials.

In April 1960, a request by the PM for a note from the Treasury about the difficulties involved in reconciling the UK position as a food importer with the position of EEC countries who were self-supporting, created little in the way of interest or excitement. In passing the matter on to the MAG, Robert Workman, a Treasury assistant secretary, proffered the suggestion that the information was needed only in case the PM was pressed again to consider the possibility of the UK joining the EEC.[2]

In May, news of Lee's proposals resulted in a muted flurry of activity as colleagues debated the possible ramifications of an adjustment of Britain's trade arrangements with the Six.[3] During the summer of 1960, in response to the PM's questions, various reports were compiled, though they offered little in the way of policy proposals.[4] By that time, though, where recommendations were made, they generally reflected Sir Frank Lee's views about Britain's future role in Europe. For example, at the beginning of July, J.G. Owen wrote that changes in the pattern of industry were taking place all the time and the UK would have to face them sooner or later.[5] Remaining outside the EEC, he declared, would mean that the UK would not be forced to face industrial adjustment in the short term, 'but neither will U.K. industry have the tonic of competition from the Six, and this may lead to stagnation and a reduced standard of living'. Sir Robert Hall wrote that 'economic association with the Community offers potential advantages to the strong and energetic and adaptable, and probably potential disadvantages to those lacking these qualities'.[6] For the most part, though, while closely monitoring press reaction and public opinion in European and Commonwealth countries, the Treasury was content to provide the necessary information and leave Lee and his colleagues to make the appropriate recommendations.

Opinion in the Bank of England, where officials were keeping a close eye on developments, was divided along much the same lines as it was in Whitehall. Lucius Thompson-McCausland, adviser to the governor, noted at the beginning of April 1960 that 'officials see the need for a change while ministers are, apparently, unconscious of it'.[7] At the same time, reluctance to dismiss the idea of an Atlantic preferential area[8] was balanced by uncertainty about Britain becoming involved in a discriminatory bloc at all, especially in the light of convertibility which, taken with the lack of 'balance of payments reasons' for retaining restrictions on imports, seemed to many in the Bank to make trade discrimination illogical.[9] While it was agreed that companies should be encouraged to invest in the Six to avoid losing the UK share of an expanding market, the question posed in the Bank of England (as elsewhere) in April 1960 was 'should the UK snipe at or flirt with the Common Market?'

After an uneasy month of prevarication and argument, the Overseas Office of the Bank of England came out broadly in support of Lee's initiative towards the end of May 1960,[10] though the lack of total unanimity on the issue was indicated by the submission of three separate reports in response to the PM's questions.[11] However, developments during the summer and early autumn resulted, in November, in both the General Office and the Overseas Office expressing the firm opinion that, subject to particular waivers, the UK should accede to the Treaty of Rome.[12]

In the BOT, the division of opinion went considerably deeper and lasted a lot longer than it did elsewhere. Nowhere was disappointment at the failure of the FTA talks more keenly felt than in the department responsible for British trade. A bitter (unsigned) memorandum declared that 'the present situation in Europe is the result entirely of the procrastination of the Six. . . . They repeatedly and explicitly accepted the objective of an F.T.A. . . . They have a duty and a moral obligation to us and the others to do everything possible to minimise the damage.'[13] Throughout 1959, perhaps as a result of a strong sense of having been betrayed by the Six, the attention of BOT officials was focused almost exclusively on dealing with the details of the EFTA agreement. William Hughes confirms that there was very little discussion in the BOT about the ramifications for the UK of the Treaty of Rome until 1960.[14]

By the spring of 1960, though, despite the well-known and often expressed views of its president, opinion in the BOT was moving – albeit at times grudgingly – towards accepting the inevitability of a British application to join the EEC. Sir Richard Powell, who became permanent secretary in 1960, recalls that, by that time, 'on the whole, official opinion in the Board of Trade was in favour of joining the Treaty of Rome'.[15] He says that 'it was the politicians who wished to get the benefits of free trade within the Community without paying any price in terms of closer political collaboration'. Sir Peter Carey concurs with this view saying that 'the senior officials of the time would have seen the EEC as the inevitable partner for Great Britain'.[16] Commonwealth preference was already being viewed by some as a double-edged sword. William Hughes recalls that many in the BOT agreed with their erstwhile permanent secretary, Sir Frank Lee, that preferences, though useful, provided a market cushioned from real competition that often led manufacturers to neglect markets that would be of greater long-term importance.[17]

There were, however, some significant and influential exceptions to this general line. Betty Ackroyd, serving first in the Industries and Manufactures department, and later in the Commercial Relations and Exports (CRE) department, was immovable in her opposition to any shift away from the free entry of Commonwealth manufactures. Ackroyd was the BOT's representative in Roderick Barclay's negotiating group, which began discussions with the Germans in autumn 1960, and from this position she was able to ensure that little progress was made with regard to achieving a compromise over manufactures. Ackroyd had an influential ally in Cyril Sanders who was BOT adviser on commercial policy. Ranged against Ackroyd and Sanders, though, were second secretary, Herbert Andrew, under-secretary in the CRE, William Hughes,[18] the president's private secretary, Peter Carey, and, most significantly of all, Sir Richard Powell, the new permanent secretary.

It was the attitude of the permanent secretary that ensured that Maudling was unable to mobilize the official machinery of his department to advance his own policy preferences. Sir Richard Powell had always taken an interest in the activities of the Six. In the early 1950s, while serving as deputy secretary at the Ministry of Defence, he had been in favour of British membership of the ECSC and, later, of Euratom. He also served as the British observer at the ill-fated EDC discussions. Even at this stage, Sir Richard recalls, 'it was evident, to me at least, that the Commonwealth was of declining value as a trading partnership and that the future lay elsewhere'.[19] By the time he moved to the BOT, Sir Richard was already convinced 'of the need for this country to participate fully in developments in Europe, including membership of the EEC'. In May 1960, he wrote that 'our right and only course is . . . to link ourselves with Europe and particularly with the Six, in some way acceptable to them for which we shall have to pay the price'.[20]

Because of the lack of consensus among officials, Cyril Sanders was forced to tell the president, in June 1960, that

'there is no agreement among Board of Trade officials' on
the question of the desirability of maintaining full or, indeed, any Commonwealth free entry. However, Sanders'
position as adviser on commercial matters provided him with
the opportunity of outlining his own views to the president,
which would undoubtedly have been well received. In a note
to Maudling, Sanders said: 'Some of us too would feel that
the more closely we committed ourselves to Europe the more
we should be committing ourselves to traditions in economic
and social attitude which are in certain fundamental ways
alien to our own.'[21] In October, he provided a useful contact in London for Betty Ackroyd on the negotiating team
in Germany[22] although Ackroyd was, in any case, in direct
communication with the president.[23]

As a result of the intractable differences of opinion between the president and his senior staff (and between officials themselves), no particular BOT line emerged on the
European issue during the years in question. While each
party exploited the formal and informal power available to
them in order to secure piecemeal advantage for their point
of view, no overall position was taken up and promoted. In
common with the majority of their colleagues at the Treasury, BOT officials felt no pressing need to launch or to
overtly back particular initiatives. Sir Richard Powell and
his fellow 'Europeanists' were content to allow Sir Frank
Lee's committee (of which Sir Richard was, in any case, a
member) to take the lead in putting suggestions forward to
ministers. Significantly, William Hughes recalls that BOT
officials and their president seemed, at that time, to be
working in 'different compartments'.[24] Certainly, Maudling
appeared to relish the opportunity that his position accorded
him for 'getting about'. Despite considerable ability, he had
no great appetite for desk work.[25] Macmillan himself described Maudling as 'very clever, a little lazy; and a trifle
vain'.[26] By spring 1960, in any case, it was proposed that
Maudling was, 'in the eyes of nearly everyone in the Six –
"brûlé"'.[27] But while the president of the Board of Trade
was busy abroad, talking to Commonwealth, EFTA and EEC
ministers, his officials in London wrote the reports required
of them. Their emphasis would vary according to which
official's pen they sprang from. But, in common with the

CRO the CO and the MAG, the BOT *responded* to rather than promoted European initiatives.

It is easy to understand why Sir Richard Powell and his colleagues remained, on the whole, untroubled by the stance of their president. By spring 1960, the matter was, after all, being very capably advanced by Sir Frank Lee's committee with the general support of the FO. Sir Richard Powell suggests that the FO was, in fact, in advance of the Treasury on the issue until Sir Frank Lee moved to the Treasury in January 1960.[28] This was almost certainly the case, though it does not say much for the FO view since the Treasury – until Lee arrived – hardly had one. Sir Richard says that Lee's views 'were very significant in forming official opinion and in wearing down the more or less instinctive opposition of politicians' and he adds that, as a member of Lee's committee, he 'fully supported Sir Frank'. But the early lack of FO interest in the issue, at least at ministerial level, is borne out by a comment of Lee himself. He said that the conduct of the UK's affairs with regard to Europe had suffered, 'by reason of the comparative indifference with which Foreign Office ministers have tended in the past to regard the economic issues involved in the problem of the Six and the Seven'.[29]

The conclusion reached in the FO in November 1958 that it was now up to the Six to make proposals to avoid discrimination[30] gives added weight to Lee's complaint that the FO showed too little interest in the European issue at this time. This indifference could not be blamed on a lack of information. Regular communications were sent in from every European capital and, as time went by, more information was procured through the contacts of the British delegation to the OEEC in Paris and at the EEC Commission in Brussels. The fact that much of the information was conflicting reflects the fact that, as in Britain, opinions on the question in France, Germany and the rest (with the possible exception of the Netherlands) varied among their own government departments.

Within the FO itself the many elements of the European issue – until January 1960 – were dealt with, variously, by the Mutual Aid Department, the Economic Department and the Western Department. As a result, there was no means of developing an overall coordinated policy. Perhaps more significantly, there was no appreciation of the need, at this stage, to acquire one. The reluctance of any government department to take responsibility for the European issue during 1959 is suggested in the way a parliamentary question addressed, initially, to the chancellor of the exchequer, was handled. Frederick Bellenger, a Labour MP, asked about progress in the inter-governmental negotiations concerning trade relations. The chancellor passed the question to the BOT, and the BOT passed it on to the FO where a response was drafted. The reply, though, was given in the House by the president of the Board of Trade, Sir David Eccles.[31] This tendency to 'pass the parcel' arose out of the fact that there was no machinery within the departments at this time for formulating policy; it rather evolved out of a triangular correspondence between the CRE Department of the BOT, the British Embassy in Paris and the various departments of the FO. While FO officials advised on the broad approach – such as it was – BOT officials filled in the commercial details. With the inter-departmental committees now directing their attention to the fine details of an EFTA agreement – which the FO always disliked[32] – British policy lacked both commitment and direction.

It was at the GATT discussions on the Treaty of Rome, in July 1959, that there was the first intimation of impatience on the part of FO officials with their colleagues in the CRO and the Colonial Office. An FO delegate to the GATT reported that 'the extent of Commonwealth solidarity was in fact rather embarrassing since it gave a clear impression that this was a struggle between the Commonwealth and the Six in which we were really being a little unreasonable'.[33] And, from the FO perspective, the BOT suffered under the same delusions about Britain's trading difficulties with Europe as did the CO. An FO official noted that the suggestion made to the BOT and the CO that Britain's partners in the Stockholm negotiations should be kept informed of British intentions in the GATT discussions 'came as a novel idea to both Departments'.[34]

FO irritation finally boiled over as the CO continued to press in the GATT for mitigation for colonial produce in the terms of the Treaty of Rome. An FO counsellor wrote:

'This exercise becomes steadily further removed from reality and it is idle to expect the Six to be sympathetic to our requests for mitigation to the effects of their imperfect F.T.A. with the overseas territories when we are about to crave indulgence for our own imperfect F.T.A.'[35]

Unencumbered with the responsibility for securing a particular commercial objective, FO officials were able to recognize, more easily than their colleagues, the necessity for the UK to make some sacrifices in the interests of achieving trade harmony in Europe. Nevertheless, it was concluded in the autumn of 1959 that the FO case should not be overstated since not only did active pursuit of mitigation ensure Commonwealth goodwill but, if the pressure were kept up, it would constitute a 'worthwhile concession' for use later on. It was this heightened awareness of the UK's position that set the FO marginally apart from other government departments during 1959.

Against the consequential appointments of Sir Frank Lee and Sir Richard Powell in January 1960, the return to London at the end of 1959 of Edward Tomkins, an FO counsellor serving in Paris, would seem of far lesser significance. But Sir Edward's return triggered a reorganization at the FO, which was to have important repercussions in the way that department was to handle the European issue in the coming years. In January 1960, the FO European Economic Organizations Department was set up. It was complemented, largely at the behest of Tomkins and his close associates, by the Western Organizations (WO) Department. Sir Edward recalls that he and his colleagues had recognized that there was a glaring need for a department specifically designated to deal with the *political* aspect of western international organizations.[36]

From 1959, Sir Edward remembers, there was a very real (though rarely iterated) sense of fear and foreboding that permeated the FO about the threat of the USSR. The WEU and NATO were at that time 'floating free' in the FO. Tomkins seized them, and together with the EEC, they formed the core of the work of the WO Department. Since, at the time of writing, WO Department papers are not available for scrutiny, it is difficult to assess the amount of work done by that Department and how it fitted in with the work of the

European Economic Organizations Department. It seems likely, though, that it was responsible for informing the PM's approach to the issue which developed throughout 1960 and early 1961. It would also have provided Edward Heath with a secretariat whose views were largely compatible with his own.

Despite these changes, at the beginning of 1960, the uncertainty of ministers on the European issue was still matched by the confusion that pervaded the FO. David Ormsby-Gore, minister of state for Foreign Affairs, summed up the general feeling when, on being asked in January 1960 to 'reintroduce our own ideas', enquired, 'what are they?'[37] L.G. Holliday, an FO counsellor, reported gloomily that an FTA between the Six and the Seven remained the only answer as far as ministers were concerned, 'however irrealisable this objective may now appear'.[38] Sir Paul Gore-Booth, deputy under-secretary, suggested that a Treaty of Association could be launched gradually.[39] Holliday, though, envisaging no other content for such a treaty, said: 'If we mean that we are now prepared to consider a customs union . . . it would be to our advantage to say so.'[40]

Throughout these early months, the European Economic Organizations Department was swamped with the business of OEEC reorganization, leaving officials little time or inclination to address the troublesome question of Six/Seven relations. Like the cabinet committees during 1959 – which turned their attention away from the overall problem and towards securing the EFTA agreement – it is evident that the FO was deflected now from considering the wider question of the UK's trade arrangements with the Six, by concentrating its energies instead on an equally demanding but potentially less contentious issue.

The shift in outlook in the FO during the spring of 1960 was boosted by the secondment of Sir Paul Gore-Booth to serve as the UK representative on the Group of Four – a select international committee which was looking into ways of reorganizing the OEEC. His assignment proved to be an instructive experience. Reporting at the end of April, he said that after two months away, he had formed a more objective view of the UK's position and policy. He suggested that 'our proceedings since January have looked from the outside sterile and inconsequent', and he hinted that ministers would do well 'to re-examine some of the concepts which we rejected at a time when there was a prospect of achieving a pure Free Trade Area'.[41] Just three days later, J.A. Robinson came to the conclusion that an interim solution to the Six/Seven question – even if one were available – would remove the imperative from 'a radical reappraisal of our policy', which he now judged to be necessary. He warned against the advisability of 'opening safety valves of this kind'.[42]

By May 1960, even Lee's initiative was considered by some FO officials not to go far enough. Robinson's response was that, while it signified 'a welcome improvement on the whitewashing of the United Kingdom's prospects that was going on in the Treasury at the end of last year', it was still 'dangerously unrealistic'.[43] Referring to Lee's memorandum, he said: 'We simply cannot afford to conclude that there is "no prospect of successful negotiations in the near future".' His colleague, L.G. Holliday, was more in tune with Lee's tactical approach. He argued that 'if it were to be presented as the basis of an immediate initiative by the United Kingdom it would have no hope at all of surviving in recognisable form'.[44] It would be destroyed by the cumulative opposition of the CRO, the MAG and the BOT, he argued. Edward Tomkins, with a few reservations, went along with Holliday. His main concern was that the matter should not be approached purely from the trade angle but from the point of view of Britain's overall relationship with Europe. He said: 'I am all in favour of Sir F. Lee's idea, but I think that everything depends on how it is presented to ministers and the Six.'[45] Even at this stage, it had become apparent in the FO that any initiative would have to be presented in broader political terms for it to have any chance of being accepted by politicians.

The change of perspective that ran through the FO during the early months of 1960 came from below rather than from above. The FO permanent secretary, Sir Frederick Hoyer-Millar, was not a policy-*maker*; he merely dealt with questions as they arose.[46] Nor was great inspiration forthcoming from the foreign secretary: Selwyn Lloyd was not possessed of any great European vision.

The cabinet decision of 13 July 1960 was greeted in the FO with consternation. Charles Le Quesne wrote a long memorandum saying that the decision and indecision that the cabinet conclusions had implied was damaging to the UK's interest.[47] He supported the proposition that the UK 'should seek to come by a political path to an economic unity, rather than vice versa', adding trenchantly that 'it hardly seems conceivable that we should find it impossible to go as far along the road to political union as General de Gaulle'. Barclay was more sanguine, commenting that he was not surprised that the cabinet rejected an idea that needed a great deal more thought – and preparation of opinion.[48] Jackling, like Barclay, agreed with Le Quesne's promotion of the political path, though he warned that 'until we are prepared to say that we will join the EEC provided that we are given tolerable terms we shall make no progress'. Sir Paul Gore-Booth pointed out that, in any case, there was little to be done while ministers were 'uncertain in their minds and indeed not wholly agreed among themselves' other than ensuring that no available doors were slammed.[49]

In fact, though, by seizing the opportunity to brief the PM before his visit to Germany in August, the FO was instrumental in deepening still further the political emphasis now favoured by Macmillan. The aim, FO officials said, was 'to convince him [Adenauer] that the problem of Seven/Six relations is basically a *political* one; failure to solve it could affect the solidarity of NATO and the strength of the Western position *vis-à-vis* the Soviet Union'.[50] By now FO officials were openly referring to 'our new approach to Europe'.[51] It did not take them long to appreciate that it was unnecessary for them to spend too much time briefing the new privy seal.[52]

As the year drew to a close, tensions between the FO and other government departments grew. Briefs prepared by BOT and MAG officials for the British delegation at the Anglo-German talks gave the impression, Robinson complained, that the UK was still working for an FTA.[53] The Germans should be told, he urged, that this was not all the UK had to offer. Jackling agreed that the Whitehall departments would not 'face up to the price of an agreement'.[54] As a result of Robinson's complaint, a draft message was prepared for the PM to deliver to Adenauer emphasizing Britain's desire for a political as well as a commercial relationship with the Six.

Unbowed by the FO attitude, H.A.F. Rumbold of the CRO wrote to Glaves-Smith in the cabinet office pointing out that any concessions affecting the Commonwealth would have to be discussed with the Commonwealth first.[55] Jackling was given the unenviable task of preparing a list of the assurances that the UK had given to the Commonwealth over the previous three years.[56] It did not make for agreeable reading.

By the end of 1960, with the Treasury and the FO now broadly in favour of compromise over free entry and with Eric Roll (from the MAG) already talking with his German counterpart, the traditionalist wing of the BOT was appearing increasingly isolated. As if opposition from these two senior departments was not enough, the position of Maudling and his supporters was undermined further, not only by dissension inside the BOT itself, but also by the lack of ministerial support from the CO and the CRO where the political presence of Lord Perth and Duncan Sandys, respectively, engendered a climate of compromise, which ensured respect for 'Europeanist' sentiments.

By this time, too, the question of European – and even Western – security had become the mainspring of the FO's approach to the European trade issue. Barclay wrote to Sir Harold Caccia in Washington: 'If we are ever going to solve this Six/Seven problem we shall need at the very least the benevolent neutrality of the U.S. Government and if possible their active support.'[57] To this end, Caccia recommended emphasizing the need for a 'properly organized and united front in the Cold War', together with a commitment by HMG to encourage the expansion of world trade.

In the course of policy development throughout 1960 and into 1961, the FO provided the government with a continuous and an important source of information with regard to the nuances of opinion across the Channel. Many valuable insights were gained over lunch or dinner – more often by less high-profile officials than by senior diplomats. That these reports were not always attended to with the seriousness that they warranted was due largely to the *amount* of information that flowed into the FO from the various embassies and delegations in Europe. The UK Delegation to the OEEC in Paris and the UK Delegation to the European Commission both provided useful – if unwelcome – news of the latest French and German thinking. Formal communication from the British embassies in Paris and Bonn was too often coloured with the perspective of the sender – marked, on Gladwyn Jebb's side, with a rather incautious optimism and on Sir Christopher Steel's, with a failure to appreciate his own government's gradually shifting position. British representatives in EFTA countries suffered from a lack of proper information about the development of British policy which resulted, inevitably, in a good deal of resentment on the part of their hosts when British objectives were finally unveiled.

The advancement of official thinking in the FO through the early part of 1960 followed, in July, by the appointment of Edward Heath were, after Lee's initiative, the main factors that led to a new government outlook. It was the appointment of the privy seal that established a proper line of communication on the issue between the FO and Number 10. The development of opinion in the FO is summed up by Sir Edward Tomkins, who says that by 1959, the FO knew that something needed to be done; by 1960, they knew *what* needed to be done.[58]

The overall impact of the views of civil service officials from the various government departments depended upon the extent and quality of their contact with their political masters and upon whether or not they were appointed to serve on one of the inter-departmental committees. In this respect, those officials who served on Lee's committee, which was the chief advisory body to the ministerial committee and to the PM himself, enjoyed a particularly influential position. Since they included such men as Arnold France (Treasury), Sir Richard Powell (BOT), Sir Paul Gore-Booth (FO) and Eric Roll (MAG), support for Lee's own progressive view on Britain's European role was assured.

11 Exercises in Power Broking

The autumn of 1960 found British policy on Europe still in a state of flux. At home a stiff rearguard action could now be expected from the opponents of change while the uncertainty about British intentions abroad provided opportunities for ministers to advance their domestic position through the exploitation of their formal role on the international stage. During the last few months of 1960 Britain's future European policy would be moulded out of the impact of Britain's fluid international relationships upon an increasingly pliable domestic constituency. Commonwealth free entry and Britain's international role were to be the two key issues.

The substance of the meeting of Commonwealth finance ministers, held at the end of September 1960, had represented a huge advance in the development of government policy for not only had Commonwealth ministers been apprised of the new situation, but this had been accomplished, nominally at least, with the blessing of the whole cabinet. But as always, the path for the Europeanists did not run smoothly. Reporting from Paris, the following month, Heath told the foreign secretary that, while the French position was not 'wholly negative', there was not much sign either of a belief that it would be possible 'for us to come in'[1] – this, despite a suggestion from Couve de Murville that Britain's best course would be to abandon its EFTA partners and join the Common Market.[2]

Gladwyn Jebb had, meanwhile, been replaced as ambassador in Paris, by Sir Pierson Dixon, who now reported on his introductory meeting with de Gaulle.[3] Still uncompromising, de Gaulle told him that 'the reality was that Britain had her Commonwealth and France her Community'. 'It was obvious', he said, 'that Great Britain, which was an island with connexions through the Commonwealth over the world could not come into Europe.' With the retirement of

Gladwyn Jebb, communiqués from Paris referring to the conditions under which de Gaulle would be prepared to allow Britain to join the EEC were replaced by reports that described the French president's consistent and obstinate opposition to any such idea.

It was becoming evident that advances made in respect of domestic and Commonwealth difficulties were now being offset by difficulties in Europe – which had never been properly addressed. Gladwyn Jebb's assessments, which had assumed French acquiescence to British membership of the EEC, as long as Britain was prepared to pay the proper price, were now seen to have been over-optimistic. This misunderstanding had not arisen out of a lack of information. Officials communicated frequently among themselves their recognition of the intransigence of de Gaulle. For example, in September 1960, Rumbold, who was serving as British representative at the WEU, wrote from the embassy in Paris to Evelyn Shuckburgh at the FO about a speech made by Couve de Murville who, he said, went 'as far as he could, within the limits of the General's intention to keep us out for the time being'.[4] Having spoken with Wormser, Rumbold's warning was even clearer. He wrote: 'in no part of the French administration is there now to be found any desire to hasten our entry into the counsels of the Six for quite a long time to come.'[5] But the fact remains that, even in the light of the most unequivocal statement by de Gaulle, no allowance was yet made for the potential failure of a British application to join the EEC arising out of the General's attitude.

Various explanations have been advanced for this ultimately devastating defect in policy management. Sir Arnold France believes that both ministers and officials believed that they would be able to persuade the French president by diplomatic means.[6] This view is shared by Sir Douglas Wass, who points out that 'in international diplomacy in the post-war world it was very rare for people to say no and not give good reasons'.[7] He believes that it was the fact that de Gaulle's power base was not in question that made him prepared to veto Britain's application. Sir Peter Carey ventures that the General's attitude might have been seen by the British government as 'a negotiating position',[8] while Sir Michael Wilford feels that it was widely believed that the General would draw back at the last moment from taking such a drastic step.[9] Sir Roderick Barclay, who was closely involved in the negotiations, says that he and his colleagues believed that the other five EEC members would put enough pressure on de Gaulle to prevent him from rejecting the British application.[10] He adds, though, that he felt that the influential M. Wormser 'was personally against having us in' from the outset.

Because of apparently intractable problems at home, the attitude of the French president had not seemed to warrant much attention before the autumn of 1960. After this time though, the very fact that advances were being made on other fronts contributed towards the tendency for key ministers and officials to persuade themselves – and each other – that all would be well in the end as long as the Commonwealth problem was solved. Ministers relied, to a large extent, upon the information provided by their officials. With regard to the attitude of de Gaulle, the very fact that officials were content to persevere with discussions was taken by ministers to mean that a satisfactory outcome was achievable. At the same time, though, officials were acting in line with the preferences expressed by their ministers. In any event, the potential problem of the attitude of de Gaulle was not properly addressed because, underneath all other explanations, there was a fundamental – and understandable – lack of will to confront the unpalatable possibility that it portended.

There were other problems, too, for the growing band of British 'Europeanists', which had their origin closer to home. It was not until the middle of October that the news filtered through to the steering committee that the president of the BOT had told Commonwealth finance ministers at their September meeting that, in the coming talks with the Germans 'our first objective would be to retain full Commonwealth entry'.[11] This statement (given without the agreed supplementary warning that such an objective would be unlikely to meet with success) might have been indicative of Maudling's eagerness to reassure Commonwealth ministers. It is more likely, though, that it was a calculated attempt to stem the flood of opinion, which was, in Maudling's eyes, in danger of overwhelming the whole basis of the free entry arrangement, leaving the way open for the UK to abandon its EFTA partners and seek unilateral membership of the EEC. Whichever was the case, Lee's committee was forced to agree that the Germans would have to be told that 'the only satisfactory solution would be to retain free entry in full'.[12]

As a senior member of government who was nominally responsible for Britain's trade policy, Maudling was supremely well placed to thwart the aspirations of his colleagues (and those of some of his own officials). His assurance to Commonwealth ministers could not easily be set aside since he had, after all, stated agreed government policy (though not all of it).[13] Sir Arnold France suggests that Maudling might have 'rather jumped the gun when he gave that assurance'. Certainly, he recalls, 'it caused us trouble later on'.[14] Though not prepared to say for certain that the statement was deliberately calculated to stall progress, Sir Arnold points out that as the minister responsible for EFTA, Maudling was 'quite glad to get us committed [to the Commonwealth] as much as possible – particularly when he saw that some ministers were wavering.' Neither was it only at Commonwealth ministers that Maudling aimed his personal crusade. In the course of an address to an FBI banquet in October, he told businessmen: 'the fact that the terms of the [Rome] Treaty would bring Commonwealth free entry to an end is one of the main reasons why its terms are impossible for us to accept.'[15]

Maudling's capacity to continue swimming against the tide, though, was to be short-lived. For he had a formidable and determined opponent in the privy seal. Within a few weeks of Maudling making his commitment, Heath was at work in the president of the Board of Trade's own cherished territory. At the Council of EFTA meeting in Berne, Heath explained to Britain's EFTA partners that at a meeting between the German Chancellor and the PM, it was Adenauer who had emphasized the importance of 'political considerations', which, he said, 'made it essential to find a way through the economic difficulties which existed between the two groups'.[16] The UK, he said, 'had begun to re-examine the possibilities although without reaching any conclusion as yet'. Heath was already, in fact, rehearsing Britain's apologia for what was to come.

By the end of October, Heath evidently felt that a respect-
able enough time had elapsed since Maudling's statement
to Commonwealth ministers for him to propose an adjustment to Britain's negotiating stance. He began by warning
the ministerial committee that if Britain insisted on nothing less than the full retention of free entry, the Germans
'may well be inclined to say that if that is our last word
there is not much point in continuing these exchanges'.[17]
Neither the PM nor the foreign secretary were at the meeting, even though two months had elapsed since the last time
the committee had met.[18]

His absence from the meeting and the fact that there was
no further meeting of the ministerial European Economic
Association Committee until March 1961, indicates the lack
of importance that the PM now attached to the committee
as a forum for policy-making. The fact is that while he was
unable to exclude the president of the Board of Trade from
the committee, he was at liberty to conduct *ad hoc* meetings
between ministers of his own choosing as and when he felt
it necessary to do so. Three developments now combined
to undermine the role of the ministerial committee. They
were: the gradual (though still uneven) strengthening of
the PM's own resolve; the need, in the face of new potential for dissent, for more sensitive and centralized policy
management; and the appointment of Edward Heath to take
responsibility for the finer points of policy development.

It was in November 1960 that Heath was informed of a
disquieting conversation that had taken place between Sir
Frank Lee, Sir Richard Powell and Sir Norman Kipping
(president-designate of the FBI). Over dinner Kipping had
told the two senior officials that the views of most UK industrialists had considerably changed over the previous nine
months. Whereas they *had* considered a 'bridge' between
the Six and the Seven essential, 'they now felt that this would
be impossible, that we could survive without it, and that it
would be much better during the next two or three years
to put this problem aside as an immediate preoccupation'.[19]
Kipping suggested that from the industrialists' point of view,
the best policy over the next few years would be to build
up EFTA 'and keep temperatures down'. Personally, he was
convinced that the French, preoccupied with Algeria and

still protectionist, 'were not disposed to consider any closer association at this time'. Lee felt obliged to comment that, in his experience, Kipping reflected 'pretty faithfully what the average intelligent industrialist/trader is thinking'. British industrialists, from a purely utilitarian point of view, were able to see what the government – perhaps because it had become so inextricably entwined in the issue – could not, that the French would not have Britain in and that it was pointless to pursue the point under present circumstances.

The immediacy of Heath's response to Lee's news betrayed his disquiet. He claimed that Kipping's view did not seem to him to be typical and in any case, that the question of whether or not Britain could get an agreement remained 'a matter of judgment'.[20] For himself, he was determined 'to use all the resources we have with patience and persistence in an endeavour to find a solution'.

In the furtherance of that aim the PM held a meeting with the chancellor of the exchequer, the president of the Board of Trade and the privy seal in his room at the House of Commons in order to settle the question as to who would take responsibility for answering parliamentary questions on Britain's relations with the EEC. The PM proposed that responsibility should be divided between each of the ministers present. Questions relating to trade would normally be dealt with in the House of Commons by the president of the Board of Trade. The PM's intervention suggests that he was particularly concerned that Maudling should not be allowed a free hand to commit the government to a position of irretrievable intransigence with regard to Britain's relations with the EEC. He also took the opportunity of advising his colleagues – no doubt, mainly for Maudling's benefit – 'that he did not propose that any public statement should be made about this'.[21] A week later, by way of 'cutting his losses', the president of the Board of Trade agreed with the PM that the FO should handle the European question for the present, but that his department would have the major input once negotiations were underway.[22] This way, at least, Maudling would secure a platform from which he could advance his own position at a later date.

But, while various means were being employed to contain opposition to the new thinking from *within* government, all was not proceeding smoothly in terms of external relations. At a meeting between Heath and Hallstein, for example, the latter stated his commitment to plans for a federal Europe. The privy seal reported that it was not a very productive meeting since Hallstein also commented that he saw no problem with two low-tariff 'clubs' in Europe.[23] Neither was he very hopeful about the effect on de Gaulle of 'German good offices'. He rather substantiated Kipping's assertion that de Gaulle's preoccupation with Algeria made him 'more rather than less intractable on other issues'.[24] Hallstein was not a man with whom Heath enjoyed doing business. The privy seal found Hallstein arrogant, with 'all the self-confidence of an international official who carries great responsibilities without being answerable to any Government'.[25]

At a further meeting in Brussels the following month, Heath tried again to alert Hallstein to 'the political and strategic dangers' of allowing the current situation to persist.[26] This time, he complemented the security argument which he had emphasized at their previous meeting, with an economic one. He spoke of the wasteful duplication of investment in EFTA and EEC countries. But the president of the European Commission would not be drawn. He told the privy seal that he saw no serious security problem in Europe 'so long as defence was co-ordinated by NATO'. Disquieted by Hallstein's lack of response, Heath retorted that the will of some countries to make sacrifices to defend those who were discriminating against them should not be depended upon. He wrote afterwards that 'the Commission's thinking does not appear to have undergone any basic changes'. Opposition to a British application to join the EEC existed now, it seemed, in the highest reaches of the European Commission. Notwithstanding his lack of success, the regularity with which Heath met Hallstein during these difficult months (despite his obvious lack of rapport with the head of the EEC Commission) indicates that the privy seal – almost certainly alone among his ministerial colleagues – appreciated the need, in the interests of achieving a satisfactory settlement with the Six, to cultivate the goodwill of the Commission. Hallstein's close relationship with Adenauer was an additional – and by no means unimportant – consideration.[27]

Throughout November discussions continued with the Dutch and the Italians involving, variously, the PM, the foreign secretary and the privy seal.[28] In the course of these meetings the Dutch pressed for British involvement in the forthcoming political consultations of the Six, and the Italians suggested more secret talks about agricultural problems to parallel the talks with the Germans over industrial questions. The Italians were always eager for information about the Anglo-German talks,[29] betraying, perhaps, that communication between the EEC partners themselves was less than effective. The enthusiasm of the Dutch and the Italians, together with the (occasional) readiness of the Germans to seek a compromise, had the effect of overshadowing in the minds of British ministers, the unbending opposition of the French president and the reservations of his unlikely confrère on the European Commission.

In the light of ministers' preoccupation with courting the goodwill of the smaller EEC countries, Britain's EFTA partners were in grave danger of becoming the Cinderellas at the European ball. It is evident from the nature of the discussion of the EQ committee that it was now an unambiguously British rather than an EFTA settlement that was being sought.[30] On this count, it would have been hard for officials to miss the poignancy of a message from Berne. Schaffner, the Swiss commercial counsellor, still determinedly unsuspicious of British intentions, wrote that he was 'glad to know that the Germans were not insisting on a solution on the lines of a full scale customs union entailing acceptance by Switzerland of a common tariff'.[31]

Only two days later, though, Schaffner was disabused of his thankfulness. At a meeting of heads of EFTA delegations in Geneva he received a further report of the Anglo-German talks.[32] Its contents caused him to complain that it was unwise for the UK to have gone so far as to say that, provided conditions with regard to the Commonwealth could be met, the UK would be willing to consider a common or harmonized tariff. Sommerfelt of Norway supported Schaffner's claim that if all the partners said as much 'the whole basis of the present E.F.T.A. policy would break up'. Hereafter the Norwegians would become consistently suspicious of Britain's conduct of the Anglo-German talks.[33]

But, by the end of November, despite the protests of EFTA ministers and the best efforts of the president of the Board of Trade, government priorities were drifting inexorably away from both full commitment to the EFTA relationship and the maintenance of Commonwealth free entry. Excluded from ministerial discussions with members of the Six and warned against making unauthorized statements in public, Maudling found himself effectively outmanoeuvred by the formidable alliance of the PM, the chancellor of the exchequer, the foreign secretary and the privy seal. Since there was no overt intention on the part of Britain's senior ministers to work towards British membership of the EEC, the president of the Board of Trade had no effective channel for his objections. From this position, on the margins, he had few opportunities to express his disquiet as the case for compromise gained ground. Though the commitment to full Commonwealth free entry remained British policy, key ministers were becoming increasingly aware, as a result, largely, of the joint efforts of the privy seal and Lee's committee, that they would eventually have to face and deal with the contradiction that such a commitment presented.

French involvement had now become a prerequisite for any further progress. This was noted by both the Anglo-German negotiators[34] and Heath himself.[35] At the same time demands were made by the EQ committee[36] and by the FO[37] for a revised line to be adopted with regard to Britain's EFTA and Commonwealth commitments. But the nature of such a revision itself depended upon the likely response of the French. In order to break out of this apparent impasse, proper channels for negotiations would have to be opened with the French, authorized by de Gaulle himself.

A meeting between French and German officials in December proved Hallstein right in his assessment of the danger of Britain relying upon the good offices of the Germans. Dr van Scherpenberg, the German foreign minister, told Sir Christopher Steel, Britain's ambassador to Bonn, that, at their meeting, Wormser had been very negative.[38] He said that the meeting had not been helped by Erhard, who had apparently 'blundered in with a lot of half-baked ideas and had put French backs up'. Van Scherpenberg, who was 'plainly furious and exasperated by the daily arrest of German ships in the Mediterranean' (occasioned by the French Algerian crisis), was, in any case, 'not wholehearted' in his discussions with the French.

Despite or perhaps because of the lack of progress, the European question was, by now, taking up a good deal more of the PM's time and attention. Curiously, though, in the light of the progressive nature of his most recent pronouncements, the more the PM pondered on the question, the more he tended to revert to the old idea of finding a solution through exploiting the tensions of the bipolar international system. Before Christmas he commented to the foreign secretary that, at their meeting with President Kennedy set for the following spring, the Americans should be asked to support 'a wider economic unity in Europe' to ensure the stability and strength of the Atlantic Community.[39] The new president, he hoped, would be a little more convinced of the strategic necessity for a united Europe than his predecessor had been.

Over the new year Macmillan set out, in a 32-page memorandum, his thoughts about the many and various difficulties facing Britain.[40] Even now unconvinced of the inefficacy of the argument, he wrote that 'we may have to contemplate isolation in order to force through co-operation'. Britain's difficulties, he believed, had a variety of causes. Among these, he numbered the 'monolithic strength of the Kremlin', the lack of unity in the West, the uncertain economic and political relations with Europe, the 'uncertainties of American policies' and 'the difficult task of changing Empire into Commonwealth'. Calculating that the UK was 'in danger of drift', he reasoned that 'if we are to influence events, we must not shrink from strong, and sometimes dramatic, action'.[41]

Referring directly to the question of *Sixes and Sevens,* the PM reflected that, while it was clear that an accommodation *could* be reached 'it is equally pretty clear that it *will not* be reached'. He was forced to the conclusion that 'however bold a face it may suit us to put on the situation, exclusion from the strongest economic group in the civilized world *must* injure us'. 'It must also injure the world', he continued, 'because economic exclusion must in the long run force us into military isolationism and political neutralism.' In the light of this dire prospect – albeit of his own construction – he determined that a settlement between the Six and the Seven must be achieved while de Gaulle was still in power and the federalists were held at bay.[42] He then went on to surmise how Britain might be able to exploit the 'love/hate' relationship between France and Germany to bring about an agreement.[43] But perhaps realizing that the chances of success for this idea would be slim, he returned once again to his Cold War rhetoric, suggesting that if the French refused to cooperate in bringing about a Six/ Seven settlement, 'we should have to denounce our liabilities under W.E.U.'.[44]

He considered next the light in which de Gaulle viewed Britain's position – as a junior partner to America rather than as a European. But out of this apparently unfortunate state of affairs whereby 'Britain wants to join the European concern; France wants to join the Anglo-American concern', the PM saw the 'basis for a deal'.[45] He went on to conjecture how much he would be able to draw out of the Americans with regard to a genuine tripartite agreement involving nuclear weapons. The possibilities here, though, he had to conclude, were limited by Britain's existing non-proliferation agreement with the US. But he determined to suggest to the new US president that 'only if he can help me to do a deal with de Gaulle, can we keep Britain in Europe and relieve the United States of some of their burden'. He now defined his political objective for the UK as 'the general association of the British, with other Governments, in a Confederal system'.[46]

In attempting, not for the first time, to define 'what we want', he suggested the need for 'a plan which we can accept from the point of view of the Commonwealth and British agriculture or which they can be *made* to accept'. But for all his vagueness and uncertainty about what he wanted and how it could be achieved, the PM showed unmatched percipience in his assessment of the power of de Gaulle. 'If he gave the word', he wrote, 'all the Wormsers would turn at once.'[47]

Summing up, the PM reviewed the purpose of his memorandum. He wrote that it was necessary 'to call attention

to the need to organize the great forces of the Free World
– U.S.A., Britain, and Europe – economically, politically, and
militarily in a coherent effort to withstand the Communist
tide all over the world'.[48] The memorandum was to be circulated only among the PM's closest colleagues and advisers.

Though evidently intended to clarify in his own mind the
difficulties facing Britain and their potential solutions, the
PM's new year reflections served mainly to highlight the confusion that still existed with regard to the European question, over *what* he wanted to achieve, *why* he wanted to achieve
it and *how* he should set about it. His broad and ill-defined
aim was to put an end to the period of 'drift' and to bring
about some form of economic and political settlement with
the Six, which would be in keeping with the UK's world
role. The reasoning behind this objective was even less clear
since his concern for Britain's loss of influence if it remained
apart from the Six was tempered by his stated preference
for a confederal arrangement and his perception of Britain
as one of the 'great forces of the Free World' *beside* Europe
and America. And the fact that he signalled a willingness to
exploit Britain's strategic position in the interests of achieving a favourable settlement suggests that his expressed concern for European – and Western – security amounted, still,
to more of a tactical ploy than a genuine preoccupation.

For all its candour, the PM's memorandum sheds little
light upon his views with regard to the detailed nature of
Britain's relationship with the EEC. This is probably because
Macmillan remained not totally convinced, even at this stage,
as to what was desirable as well as what was possible. Even
while it raised the option of finding an answer through international power broking, the memorandum represented
for the most part a summary of his frustrations rather than
a blueprint for a solution. His readiness, now, to admit the
potential political difficulties of Britain's exclusion from the
Six did not amount to an unreserved resolve to promote
British membership of the EEC. Though not ruling out a
'drastic step', his objective was a workable political relationship, together with a satisfactory economic arrangement. That
full membership of the EEC was the only practical way of
achieving this – though probably by now suspected – was
not fully acknowledged.

While promoting no answers in itself, save his very own 'Grand Design' linking French cooperation with tripartite (US/UK/French) negotiations, the PM's memorandum triggered a new series of activity – this time involving an even more select group of ministers and officials with whom Macmillan was keen to share his ideas. On 11 January, after meeting the foreign secretary and the chancellor of the exchequer, the PM arranged a meeting at Chequers to include these ministers, together with Sir Frederick Hoyer Millar from the FO, Sir Frank Lee and Freddie Bishop.[49] In the meantime, he set in train a series of studies to look into the economic and political possibilities and the wider question of Britain's role in the international political economy.

The Chequers meeting, which, on the advice of Sir Norman Brook, also included the minister of defence,[50] appears at first sight to have been far from conclusive in respect of formulating a way forward. This was due in no little degree to the absence of the privy seal who was on an official visit to the Persian Gulf.[51] While Lee expressed the view that it was desirable on economic grounds 'to reach a settlement between the Six and the Seven', the chancellor speculated that 'the absence of a settlement would not be as damaging as had been suggested'.[52] By way of countering this lapse into irresolution, it was ventured that the EEC might either break up because of external rivalries or else 'move towards a tighter form of federation': in either eventuality, it was argued (most likely by Lee) that Britain ought to be in a position to bring influence to bear. The PM – all too mindful still of the unpleasant prospect of having to deal not only with a hostile reaction from Commonwealth ministers but also with the effects of their dissatisfaction in the domestic political arena – concluded that 'the problem was to find some means of inducing a political will, especially on the part of the French, to accept a settlement of the sort which we would regard as tolerable'.

This new bout of wavering had, at its roots, a final attempt to avoid admitting to the fact that an economic settlement with the Six could only be achieved through the sacrifice of a substantial proportion, at least, of Commonwealth free entry. That reality had become apparent during two rounds of discussions with the Germans. Hitherto, lip-service had been paid by senior ministers to the necessity for contemplating the need for real sacrifice. Key ministers, with the exception of Edward Heath, had evidently never fully faced up to the ramifications of such a policy. A belief had persisted, despite the countless warnings made by officials, that a way would be found, through skilful bargaining and diplomacy, of avoiding the need for a choice between the EEC and the Commonwealth. Faced, in the absence of the persuasive privy seal, with the ineluctable moment of decision, ministers retreated into a renewed wave of uncertainty, calling once again upon already refuted arguments and already discredited proposals.

Out of the results of the Chequers discussions, though, the foreign secretary, writing to Sir Pierson Dixon in Paris, identified a new urgency to settle the matter of Britain's relationship with the EEC.[53] One of the reasons he gave (already alluded to in the PM's new year reflections) was that France was becoming a nuclear power and there was little that the UK could do about it.

The issue of nuclear proliferation and the problem that France would present as a nuclear power had now arrived at the very heart of a decision, which had hitherto been concerned almost solely with Britain's trading relationship with the Six. To what extent, though, was this a *real* concern? Certainly, for the PM and his foreign secretary, it had carried the issue onto a whole new level of urgency. But this urgency was, in truth, merely a manufacture of opportunism. For it was only in casting around for a means of persuading de Gaulle to make a favourable trading settlement (which would not involve sacrificing Commonwealth free entry) that the PM stumbled upon a diplomatic lever with which he hoped to bring pressure to bear upon both the Americans and the French. It will be seen as particularly ironic that it was through his exploitation of this very issue that the French president was eventually able, in January 1963, to thwart British aspirations for EEC membership.

Though the Chequers meeting was, of itself, inconclusive, it did serve to highlight in ministers' minds, once and for all, the real lack of a credible alternative to British membership of the EEC. An inevitable adjunct to this realization was that ministers came to appreciate the lack of an alternative to seeking a compromise with regard to the issue of Commonwealth free entry. The large question that remained still unresolved, though, was that of the probable intransigence of the French.

Macmillan put his confidence in his own skill in power broking not least because – as all the other doors to a European settlement appeared to be closed or closing – there seemed nowhere else to put it. The fact that his plan (to find a solution through connecting Britain's trading interests with the question of France's role in the Western Alliance) failed so dismally, would be well compensated for and considerably disguised by the increased strategic emphasis that he was able to place on the issue following his meeting with Kennedy.

The marginalization of Maudling and the confidence that the PM now displayed in the privy seal were important developments in the closing months of 1960. During these months, though, several warnings about the likely attitude of the French went, for the most part, unheeded. It was evident as the year came to a close that the momentum for change set in train by the initiative of Sir Frank Lee and boosted by the appointment of Edward Heath could still be derailed by indecisiveness at home or intransigence abroad.

12 Back to the Cabinet

The new year brought with it little in the way of new resolve. It was now over two years since the FTA talks had broken down; the EEC was established and hopes in Europe for its success were high. EFTA too enjoyed support though, as nothing more than an industrial trading agreement between Britain and some peripheral European states, its achievements were necessarily limited by its own parameters. It had become clear, even before the Stockholm Convention was signed, that it would provide no long-term solution to Britain's trading difficulties.

In Whitehall, the European issue still inspired little interest except among those directly concerned. The same was true of the cabinet itself. Having been largely shielded from the ups and downs of policy development, ministers were, for the most part, uncommitted to a European ideal. Busy with their respective briefs, they awaited a convincing argument that would tip the balance in favour of a positive move towards Europe. They had not yet heard one.

In some ways, though, the quietude was illusory. For management of the European issue was becoming considerably complicated by the discussions now being undertaken and proposed with members of the Six. The task ahead for both politicians and officials was to develop a firm line upon which all key ministers could consistently agree while continuing to indicate to the Germans a readiness to make concessions. As well as this, officials saw the need to convince the PM to take a softer line with the Americans, while allowing him to attempt to convince the new US administration that Western security depended upon their intervention on Britain's behalf. Ministers and officials also needed to determine the likelihood of de Gaulle accepting British overtures (without actually making any) while ensuring, in the light of the delicate position *vis-à-vis* Commonwealth free entry, that the issue received as little public attention as possible.

Government activity continued at three levels. On the international plane, officials were busy preparing a brief for the PM for his forthcoming visit to General de Gaulle. Shortly after this trip he was due in Washington to meet the new US president. On the home front, the question of cabinet involvement would sooner or later have to be addressed while at the official level discussions continued between departmental representatives and their German counterparts. Of these three distinct areas of activity, the matter of cabinet 'management' – especially in the light of previous experience – was to be by far the most consequential. The excursions of the PM were significant (for the European issue at least) only in so far as they firmed up Macmillan's own ideas on how he would approach the cabinet.

For these final few months leading up to the cabinet decision of 26 April, the prime minister's own papers indicate clearly that the most significant obstacle to the advancement of policy was seen both by the PM and by the privy seal to be the cabinet itself. The objections of the French and the opinion of the US president were secondary, in the PM's mind, to securing cabinet agreement. Strategy was no longer directed towards obtaining the goodwill and support of Germany and the rest, nor even towards gaining approval for derogations with regard to Commonwealth free entry – though this had yet to be achieved. It was directed instead at finding a means of convincing cabinet colleagues of the need for a radical departure from a free trade policy and world outlook that had stood Britain in good stead for nearly a century and a half. For this task, Edward Heath, the grammar school boy from Broadstairs, was far better suited than the prime minister, an old Etonian, who, in spite of many years in politics, still had the air – and some of the scruples – of an Edwardian gentleman.

The meeting at Rambouillet provided the PM with little in the way of encouragement to present to his colleagues. De Gaulle opened the discussions by stating that he did not see how an arrangement between the Six and the Seven could be made.[1] In the course of their subsequent wide-ranging conversation (which was by no means restricted to the European question), as often as Macmillan referred to the Six/Seven problem, de Gaulle spoke of the difficulties caused by the Commonwealth and of the need for a joint Anglo-French policy in dealing with the Americans. The PM's

very thinly veiled threat about the difficulty of defending a
Europe in two parts drew no response at all from the French
General. De Gaulle conceded that in three years' time, perhaps, there might be advantage in having one economic
system for Europe. But he was reluctant to set French experts to examine the possibility of finding a settlement since,
he pointed out, they had enough to do already in dealing
with the Common Market. He finally conceded the point,
though his reluctance to do so signalled clearly his own
negative attitude to the outcome.

The following day, in an attempt to draw a more positive
response from the French president, Macmillan spoke of
the great renaissance in France and Germany and went on
to suggest that 'close relations between the United Kingdom and the United States were perhaps no longer enough
in these changed circumstances'.[2] He proposed that a joint
Anglo-French policy in Europe would be beneficial. But de
Gaulle would not be drawn. He advised that the UK should
'take her time and move little by little'. 'France had had to
move faster because she was more afraid of Germany than
was the United Kingdom,' he pointed out. Assuring the PM
that the position of Britain would be discussed at the three-
monthly meetings of the heads of governments of the Six,
he wondered, 'how long it would be possible for the United
Kingdom to pursue both a European and an American policy
simultaneously'. Macmillan's response was to point out that
the UK was now prepared to consider a common tariff with
the Six as long as it provided for 'suitable protocols of exception', but de Gaulle was far from convinced that a satisfactory
system could be worked out while 'imperial preference' still
existed. He added that, in any case, Britain did not do much
trade with Europe. He suggested, too, that Britain could not
come closer to the Six without endangering the Commonwealth
– an eventuality which France would not wish to see.

Returning to London, Macmillan put the best possible
construction on the outcome of his meeting. In cabinet on
31 January, he simply made a statement on the promising
nature of his talks with de Gaulle with regard to seeking a
'settlement' of Britain's 'economic and political relations
with Europe.'[3] He said that it would be preferable to seek a
settlement while de Gaulle was still in power in France since

the General was opposed to federalism. Mindful of the potential for cabinet disagreement, though, the PM took the matter no further, recommending instead that his colleagues should give further consideration to the matter 'at an early date'. Again, it was the necessity to work out tactics for dealing with colleagues *at home* that appears to have overshadowed the very real problem of the attitude of the French president.

The PM wrote to Philip de Zulueta, on 6 February, to ask him how the privy seal intended to proceed.[4] His own proposal was that agreement among ministers should be sought with regard to how far they would be prepared to allow British experts to go in their discussions with the French. For example, he asked, 'can we accept the Common Tariff with reservations, and if so what reservations?' Sir Norman Brook urged the PM to hold a 'limited meeting' of ministers – which would include the privy seal, the chancellor of the exchequer and possibly the foreign secretary – to discuss instructions for British officials.

Heath agreed that it would be 'a mistake' to bring the matter before the cabinet since, he advised, it would not be wise to raise 'fundamental questions such as foreign policy, national sovereignty and the problem of association with or membership of the Common Market' before the forthcoming Anglo-French talks.[5] Referring to the discussion paper that the PM had already had prepared for the cabinet (which contained, at various junctures, references to an *association*, a *settlement*, an *accommodation*, a *partnership*, an *arrangement* and an *agreement* before finally and tentatively recommending *joining* the EEC), Heath asserted that it would 'lead to a resurgence of opposition on the grounds of principle rather than of practice'. 'The detailed technical exposition of the sort of solution we would wish to see', he went on, 'will provide much room for argument about what is or is not desirable or possible.' He suggested that 'we should try to carry our colleagues with us at this stage' by informing them of the proposals that had already been put to the Germans. This would show, he believed, the efforts that had been made and the difficulties that the UK faced. Such a paper, he proposed, would provide 'a factual basis for discussion on which we can ask for authority to carry on the future talks with the French'.[6]

The privy seal was evidently anxious to obtain understanding and approval from the cabinet without putting at risk the progress that had been achieved so far. His tactic was to present the details of the issue to the cabinet for discussion, but not the principle itself. He knew that it would be hard for any cabinet minister to propose back-tracking on a nego-tiating stance that was already in position. Objections of ministers not closely involved would be even less likely, he judged, in the light of the apparent unity of purpose which would be shown to exist between the PM, the foreign secretary and the chancellor of the exchequer. At the same time, though, the privy seal was anxious to avoid the danger of a position being taken up before the precariousness of Britain's economic and political situation was revealed by the lack of progress that he expected from talks with the French. His intention, when the time was ripe, was to present the cabi-net with no real alternative other than a British application to join the EEC.

Well aware, himself, of the likely intransigence of the French in any non-specific bilateral talks with the UK, Heath told the PM that if such talks were to prove 'unproductive', then the choice was between abandoning the idea of arriving at a satisfactory outcome for some years or taking 'a bold step towards a closer economic relationship with Europe'.[7] He expressed the view that if the cabinet was to be persuaded that a major decision was necessary, it would have to be demonstrated to them that everything had been done to achieve British objectives in line with current thinking, that the price of the next step would be worth paying and that it would be politically manageable. 'This will require con-siderable preparation with our colleagues', he warned, 'a lot of work with our Party and thereafter a major educational campaign in the country.' At this crucial time, it is signifi-cant that the cabinet was shown to be not so much a forum for decision-making as an *object* of the tactical machinations of a few key ministers advised and supported by their con-scientious officials.

The appointment of Edward Heath had provided Macmillan with a colleague who, while complementing his own dedi-cation to settling the European issue, brought with him from the Chief Whip's Office an aptitude and an appetite for tactical manoeuvring. The PM had prepared a paper to present to the cabinet. Without Heath's guidance, he would almost certainly have delivered it, and might well – even at this late stage – have been defeated. While it was the PM himself who would eventually come up with a successful new approach to the cabinet, it was the privy seal who ensured that he would be allowed the opportunity to do so.

Never fully comfortable with deploying a conspicuously tactical approach in handling his cabinet, and still not wholly convinced that the presentation of his own paper to cabinet colleagues would not be the safer course, the PM turned once again to his trusted adviser, Freddie Bishop. Responding to the PM's fears, the deputy secretary of the cabinet warned him that 'bearing in mind that you have dropped a hint to General de Gaulle which goes a little further than officials were previously authorised to go by the ministerial committee' it would be dangerous to 'leave far behind' the home secretary, the president of the Board of Trade or the minister of agriculture.[8] But he advised the PM that, if these ministers were to be included in discussions between himself, the chancellor of the exchequer and the privy seal, then his draft paper should be 'put in more tentative terms'.

A few days later, aware of the PM's obvious disquiet, Sir Norman Brook wrote to the PM on the same subject. Summing up the PM's dilemma, he affirmed that 'the cabinet may well be reluctant to face the major issues while they remain, in a sense hypothetical'. 'On the other hand', he said, 'you may feel that you ought not to go further in your personal exploration of these possibilities without knowing that you will be able, when the time comes, to carry your cabinet colleagues with you.' In the light of this he suggested that the next step would be for the PM to 'discuss this question of tactics' with the privy seal.[9] Sir Norman advised that either the chancellor or the exchequer or Sir Frank Lee should be invited to the meeting and assumed that he, personally, should also attend.

In the event, the foreign secretary intimated his own desire to attend the meeting and it was found that Sir Frank Lee was away. Sir Richard Powell confirmed that the president of the Board of Trade would be satisfied at not attending provided that he would be able to speak to the PM about the question before it was brought to cabinet.[10] Not unexpectedly, the views of the privy seal, who had now made the issue his own, dominated the meeting. It was decided that he would give 'an oral report' on the present position to the cabinet after the forthcoming ministerial meeting of EFTA and before the Anglo-French talks.[11] There would be full discussion in cabinet, he promised, after the talks with the French and before the PM met the new US president. Heath was well aware that an 'oral report' to the cabinet would avoid the more concentrated and directed discussion that might arise out of the presentation of a paper. He was also confident that he would be able to present his case far more effectively in the wake of an unsatisfactory outcome to the Anglo-French talks now set for the end of February.

At a cabinet meeting on 21 February, the privy seal reported, as promised, on the tariff arrangements agreed by EFTA countries.[12] He also noted the 'approval' of EFTA members for the discussions being held by the British government with certain member governments of the EEC. Heath told the cabinet that these 'exploratory talks' were directed towards establishing 'the possibility of a settlement of the economic and political divisions in Europe'. He stressed that the talks had been undertaken 'entirely without commitment'. In order to dispel any lingering doubts, he told his colleagues that, after the meeting of UK and French officials set for the following week, 'it would be convenient if the cabinet could review the whole question of our relations with Europe'.

The PM met Maudling, as promised. There is no record of the meeting but a note that the PM wrote to Maudling afterwards indicates that it was made plain that he expected loyalty from the president of the Board of Trade. He wrote: 'We have very difficult problems ahead and I was glad to be able to tell you the way in which I am trying to approach them.'[13] Shortly afterwards Maudling's private secretary, Peter Carey, wrote to Freddie Bishop suggesting that the president of the Board of Trade 'would be grateful if, in view of the vital trade interests and principles involved in this subject, he could in future be included in any discussions such as that held by the PM'.[14] If Maudling knew, by now, that he was losing the hard-fought battle for the FTA principle, he wanted at least to ensure that he was present at the obsequies.

Maudling's rehabilitation was partially secured by his invitation to a meeting of senior ministers and officials with Chancellor Adenauer and his staff at Admiralty House on 22 February.[15] On the subject of Western European unity, Adenauer told of how he had resisted de Gaulle's attempts to set up Six-power political institutions and ensured, instead, that political relations between the Six were advanced through meetings of heads of states on an *ad hoc* basis without the aid of a permanent secretariat. He told British ministers that he would like to see British involvement with the Six, though he would not wish to undermine Germany's relationship with France. Despite the best efforts of the privy seal to impress upon the German chancellor Britain's new attitude toward the Six, the issue soon became blurred by the many other considerations that concerned Adenauer at the time. The PM, though, was encouraged by the German chancellor's comments and afterwards reviewed with his colleagues all the reasons why they should press on with their efforts to find a solution, which, he now unequivocally admitted, would ideally be British membership of the EEC.

Care was still needed, though, to ensure that the issue retained its low salience status. A report of the meeting to be distributed by the FO to British ambassadors in Europe indicated that the main point discussed at the meeting with the German chancellor was the need for political consultation in Europe and the state of NATO. 'The question of Sixes and Sevens' the report said, 'was only touched upon.'[16]

Heath spoke again at a cabinet meeting the following week. As before, his strategy was to secure the consent of his colleagues to the development of policy through an indirect approach. This time he utilized the rebuttal of 'misleading accounts' in the press – concerning a statement that he had made to the Council of Ministers of the WEU (see below) – to advance the parameters of his cause a little further. He told the cabinet that no move involving tariff changes affecting Commonwealth trade would be acceptable to the United Kingdom *'except in principle as part of a comprehensive settlement with the Community which we would regard as satisfactory'.*[17] Turning what should have been a defensive position to his own advantage, Heath planted in the minds of his colleagues the idea of compromise and the notion that the sacrifice of

Commonwealth preference was an inevitable price to pay for a European settlement. Setting aside his commitment, made the previous week, the privy seal gave no intimation of when a full cabinet discussion was likely to take place.

The ministerial Economic Association Committee met on 2 March, a full four months since the previous meeting. Once again, in the PM's absence, his place was taken in the chair by the chancellor of the exchequer. The meeting had been called primarily to discuss the ramifications of the privy seal's statement to the WEU Council of Ministers on 27 February (already referred to in cabinet) where he had intimated a British intention to form closer political ties with the Six through joining or forming some association with the European communities. He had also indicated a British willingness to sacrifice some Commonwealth preference in favour of securing an agreement with the Six on a common or harmonized tariff. His most revealing remark, though, had been in response to a proposal from the WEU Assembly that the UK should accede to the Treaty of Rome. Heath told the Council of Ministers that the British government, while not wishing to express a view, kept an open mind on this proposal. In this regard, he said that the British government recognized the need for common institutions to control either a common or a harmonized tariff, and that such institutions held no fear for them. He added that his government would not be satisfied with a purely economic arrangement.[18]

So tight, by now, was the privy seal's grip on Britain's European policy that senior ministers on the ministerial committee, including Selwyn Lloyd, Duncan Sandys, Reginald Maudling, Christopher Soames and Lord Perth, were left to decide only whether the privy seal's speech 'represented a move forward in United Kingdom policy towards Europe and, if it did, how any enquiries arising from it should be dealt with'.[19] The particular part of Heath's speech that caused the greatest concern was his suggestion that Commonwealth preference was now negotiable. In this, though, he found perhaps unexpected support from the Commonwealth secretary, who commented that, while the statement would doubtless attract attention, 'it was only a recognition of the inevitable'. As a gesture of acknowledgement towards the irregularity of Heath's behaviour, though, ministers – including ironically the privy seal himself – set themselves to consider 'whether any improvements should be made in the arrangements for co-ordinating ministerial speeches on relations with Europe'. In truth, though, Heath had played Maudling at his own game – and had got away with it. By publicly announcing his version of the government's position at the WEU, Heath's position *had become* the government's position.

By way of setting the fox to guard the hen-house, the committee then decided to charge Sir Frank Lee with responsibility for coordinating the content of ministerial speeches. It was also proposed that 'ministers would find it valuable to receive regular bulletins, perhaps on the lines of the Foreign Office guidance telegrams, explaining current United Kingdom policy towards Europe'.[20] Ministers had evidently come to recognize that, with the PM (in the company of a few trusted advisers) setting his own course, those not in the PM's confidence could find themselves vulnerable to questions about a policy that appeared to be susceptible to regular and alarming shifts of emphasis. The fact that the making of policy had been taken out of their hands disturbed them less than the prospect of being left uninformed of the latest position taken by the PM and his advisers.[21]

Much as Heath had expected, the official Anglo-French discussion proved to be unproductive. This was ensured not only by the refusal of Sir Roderick Barclay to be drawn on the exact terms that the UK would be prepared to accept (mainly because there was no agreement yet among ministers about what they should be), but also by the satisfaction of the French, as expressed by M. Wormser, with the existing arrangements.[22] Reporting on the progress of the talks, Lee's steering committee concluded: 'it is doubtful if anything concrete or worthwhile will emerge from them.'[23] After reviewing all the alternatives, the steering committee concluded that the implications of Britain expressing a willingness to join the Six 'and then seeking to negotiate derogations from the full application of the Rome Treaty' should be carefully examined.[24] They recommended that there should be a full study of the implications of taking such a course 'drawing particular attention to the points on which we have stood out hitherto which we shall certainly have to concede and those on which concessions *might* prove to be necessary'.[25]

While a solution to the problem of how to handle the cabinet was yet to be found, Selwyn Lloyd reported to the PM on his successful meeting with Erhard and his advisers in Germany. At this meeting Lloyd had confirmed with the Germans that it would be possible for Britain to accede to the Treaty of Rome. It is worth noting here that while the chancellor of the exchequer was now talking openly to the German delegation about British acceptance of the Treaty of Rome, the cabinet was still unaware that such a policy existed. This was an untenable situation which could not be allowed to persist for very much longer.

Still with no full cabinet discussion, despite separate undertakings made by the privy seal to the PM, to close colleagues and to the cabinet, the PM set off for Washington. The groundwork for the PM's visit had been meticulously prepared by the FO and by the PM himself. A policy statement for delivery to Washington had been drafted by the FO in January and approved by the foreign secretary before being amended by the PM himself. The changes introduced by Macmillan were mainly in connection with putting the European question in its 'proper context', namely the strength of the Western Alliance. He composed the opening sentence of the message himself: 'The policy of the United Kingdom Government is to strengthen the Western Alliance as a whole, and for this purpose to work for greater unity in Europe – politically, economically and commercially.'[26] To underpin the PM's statement, the British ambassador, Sir Harold Caccia, was advised by the FO to emphasize to the Americans British fears about the outcome of allowing the Six to develop 'more or less on their own'.[27] On this count, Sir Harold Caccia reminded the new US administration that there were large Communist parties in both France and Italy and that the stability of these countries was not therefore assured. Sir Frank Lee had visited Washington in February. His talks with US under-secretary of state, George Ball, while not particularly encouraging, left plenty of room for further advancement.[28]

George Ball and Sir Frank Lee met again in March – this time in London – in the (occasional) presence of the privy seal.[29] At this meeting Ball expressed his regret that the UK 'had not yet felt able to accept the Rome Treaty commitments', to which Lee responded that the US government should not underestimate the extent to which opinion in the UK had altered. Greatly encouraged by his comments, Ball declared that 'there was no question but that a British decision to join the E.E.C. would have full American support'.[30] He had no doubt that 'so long as the number of derogations requested from the Rome Treaty was kept to a minimum, the French Government would agree to United Kingdom membership'. Ball concluded the meeting by saying that while the US would not approve of a UK *association* with the EEC, they would applaud UK *membership*, 'which they would regard as a great contribution to the cohesion of the free world'.[31] Only Mr Vine of the US state department remained unconvinced by the Western allies' newly discovered security imperative.[32]

With the groundwork so well prepared, Macmillan was more or less assured of a successful outcome to his meeting with the new US president. As anticipated, Kennedy indicated that he favoured British membership of the EEC so that, as Macmillan noted, 'we should be able to steer them, and influence them, whatever might be the political personalities'.[33] But Kennedy balked at Macmillan's tripartism idea. He proposed, instead, discussions about the feasibility of offering de Gaulle a small independent nuclear force with the hope that he would be persuaded 'to put it back in [NATO] trusteeship'. Macmillan recorded in his diary: 'How far he will be able to go with de Gaulle to help me, I do not know . . . but he will try.'[34]

It is likely that this endorsement by the US president of Macmillan's own inclinations removed any last remaining doubt from the PM's mind about the advisability of proceeding with a policy to bring the UK into the EEC. Horne comments that the meeting with Kennedy 'was to lend powerful impetus to Macmillan's campaign to galvanise British initiatives on his return'.[35] This was, perhaps, to overstate Macmillan's personal commitment to EEC membership thus far. What the Washington talks did achieve, though, was to put an end to the PM's occasional lapses into a surrealist world where Britain would renounce the WEU Treaty and look to a future of isolationism. On his return, Macmillan put his talks with the US president to immediate use. He instructed that a telegram should be sent to the UK High Commissioners in Commonwealth countries telling them that the US president would not support a purely economic association of the UK with the EEC.[36] Kennedy's attitude had provided him with a useful diplomatic lever for advancing the case for a political relationship with the Six whose realization would only be found in British membership of the EEC.

The task of relaying the gist of these talks to Britain's EFTA partners was described as 'a pretty tricky one'.[37] In the end, the blame for what might justifiably have been considered British duplicity was placed on the broad shoulders of the US president. A statement was prepared for delivery to EFTA representatives in London saying that the Americans 'would like to see the U.K. and as many of the Seven as possible, sign the Treaty of Rome'.[38] EFTA representatives were urged to 'consider the position of the new United States Administration, which seems to be somewhat changed from that of its predecessor'. In reply to questions from EFTA representatives, the FO said: 'We have not ourselves had time to consider the implications of the Americans' views; but it looked as though a purely economic solution to the Six/Seven problem would now be more difficult to achieve.'[39]

The cabinet was finally brought in on the decision to apply for British membership of the EEC on 20 April 1961. Under the heading of *Washington Talks*, the PM told his colleagues that his discussions with Kennedy 'had strengthened his view that far-reaching decisions would have to be taken soon about the United Kingdom's relations with Europe'.[40] Effectively completing the transfiguration of the European question from an economic issue – which would leave him open to well-rehearsed objections – to a political/strategic issue – which would not – the PM cited the threat of communist expansionism and pointed to the need 'for the leading countries of the world . . . to draw more closely together'. He went on to point up the potential threat to the 'Atlantic Community' that would be posed by divisions in Europe arising out of a close political relationship of EEC countries under French leadership. Choosing his words carefully, he told his colleagues that 'this might be averted if the United Kingdom together with some of the Seven, could join the political association of the Six'.

Then, instead of detailing the economic advantages that would accrue to Britain, he proceeded, with characteristic cunning, to associate the economic interests of the UK with those of the rest of the Commonwealth. It had to be recognized, he declared, that difficult economic adjustments would have to be made both by Britain and by other Commonwealth countries, though 'it was arguable', he went on, 'that both we and the other Commonwealth countries would in the long run gain greater economic advantage from access to a wider market in Europe.' Gone now was the economic exigency that had fired the whole issue from the outset. Here in its place was a strategic predicament that would demand Britain taking as much economic risk as that demanded of other Commonwealth countries. If the cabinet considered that it was right for the UK to draw nearer to Europe, he said, 'they would have to consider what economic price might have to be paid and what were the tactics by which this objective could be attained.' Paradoxically, where he could get no agreement from his cabinet colleagues for a policy that would result in economic gains at the expense of the Commonwealth, he was hopeful of getting their consent, instead, for the same proposition on the ground that it would demand an 'economic *price*'.

The president of the Board of Trade, sensing that opposition would now be fruitless, lined up behind the PM. Unlike Macmillan, though, Maudling was not shy about the potential economic advantages. 'The Common Market was now firmly established', he said, 'and, as it developed, our economic interests would be gravely prejudiced if we remained outside it.'[41] As for Britain's EFTA partners, Maudling expressed the hope that an agreement could be formulated that would allow them some form of economic participation in the EEC.

The Commonwealth secretary then spoke of the difficulties, but came out in favour of the proposition overall. It was Duncan Sandys who proposed making a decision to apply

182   *The Macmillan Government and Europe*

in principle so that the subsequent negotiations would reveal the difficulties and costs involved. In spite of all the
promises made to Commonwealth ministers, the Commonwealth secretary suggested that 'it would be a mistake to
get into further consultation with them before a decision
of principle had been taken'.[42] The minister of agriculture
then pointed out that current developments indicated that
the UK should, in any case, be thinking along the lines of
the arrangements proposed by the Six and, this being the
case, 'it would make it easier for us to join the Six'. Like
Sandys, he stressed the need for speedy action but he drew
attention, too, to the political difficulties with regard to
promises already made to farmers.

In general discussion it was noted that, with regard to
the loss of sovereignty, 'a major effort of presentation would
be needed'.[43] Concern was also expressed about the effects
of such a decision on the public sentiment about the Commonwealth that existed in Britain as well as the difficulties
of handling the objections of Commonwealth countries themselves. Taking up the lead given by the PM, it was suggested
that the presentation of the move as 'a necessary measure
to draw the countries of the Western world more closely
together', perhaps as 'a first step towards a wider assimila-
tion of trading areas on both sides of the Atlantic', would
mitigate some of the domestic and Commonwealth objections. The advantages that British industry would derive from
'the wider market opened to it by our association with the
Six'[44] was finally affirmed, almost as an afterthought. After
this, ministers agreed to resume their discussion the following week.[45]

Summing up after the next meeting, the PM insisted that
the 'question must be viewed in the wider context of the
East–West struggle'. 'In this', he declared, 'the Communist
bloc were gaining ground and the Western countries were
in some disarray.' He told his colleagues that 'there was a
real risk of a growing economic weakness in the Western
world unless its countries could find means of drawing more
closely together'.[46] Once into his stride, Macmillan spoke
of the historic role that Britain could now play 'as the bridge
between Europe and North America'.[47] He went on to claim
that there was strong pressure on EFTA countries to join

the EEC,[48] which could result in Britain becoming economically isolated. If this should happen, he warned, the older Commonwealth members would be obliged to turn toward the US 'and new world groupings would arise, as a result of which the United Kingdom would lose much of her influence in world affairs'. He finally concluded that 'on balance of advantage, it was in our interest to join the political and economic association of the Six if we could gain admission on terms which would be tolerable to us'.

In the conclusions of the cabinet meeting, it was recorded that, subject to being able to secure special arrangements 'to preserve the main trading interest of the Commonwealth', satisfactory arrangements with the other EFTA countries and special provisions for British agriculture, 'there seemed to be no reason of principle why the United Kingdom should not accede to the Treaty of Rome, including its political institutions'. It was agreed that, 'if President Kennedy's approach elicited a favourable response from General de Gaulle', negotiations should begin.[49] In the event, President Kennedy reported to the PM that he was forced to conclude from his meeting with de Gaulle that the General 'had no particular wish to see the United Kingdom join the Six'.[50] But by the time this information was received, the direction of policy was set and the appropriate machinery had been set in motion.

The PM's tactics – of appearing to allow himself to be convinced by the arguments rather than leading them, and of presenting the issue as a question of western security and the maintenance of Britain's influence in the world – proved, in the end, to be successful. But the rationale upon which the cabinet agreed that the UK should seek membership of the EEC was essentially flawed.

First, it could well have been argued that the Western Alliance would be weakened rather than strengthened by the emergence of a powerful European trading bloc capable of challenging American hegemony. As it was the 'West' consisted in a diffusion of interests that found their resolution in American leadership. The emergence of a new balance of economic and political power at this crucial time might well have militated against western unity instead of promoting it. Secondly, long-standing American indifference (except with regard to their commercial interests) to the whole European issue indicates that Washington did not view a solution to the Six/Seven split as a strategic imperative. Thirdly, it is evident that the PM and his advisers were concerned about the inclusion of Britain's EFTA partners in the new arrangements only in so far as they felt themselves obliged to honour their existing commitment. The fact that Macmillan would have been prepared to take Britain into the EEC without any other member of EFTA – provided that satisfactory arrangements had been made – serves to undermine the legitimacy of the fear that he expressed about the dangers of a divided Europe.

Many of the men closely involved in the development of policy at the time believe that the strategic factor was not crucial. In the opinion of Sir Douglas Wass, security arrangements, with NATO in place, were never seen as being under threat. As far as he remembers, it was not an argument put forward by officials.[51] Sir Michael Wilford, while viewing the decision as essentially political, is quite sure that there was nothing in the strategic argument. 'The thing was settled; NATO was grand – it was going well,' he recalls.[52] The chairman of the European Questions Committee, Sir Arnold France, believes that the deciding factor was undoubtedly related to trade discrimination – that Britain could not afford to be left outside a discriminatory bloc operating on its doorstep. The presentation of the strategic argument, he agreed, would have let ministers off their departmental briefs and allowed them to think more broadly.[53] Geoffrey Baker, a member of the UK Delegation to EFTA, also believes that the decision was based upon commercial considerations.[54] He, like Sir Douglas Wass and Sir Arnold France, believes that, had satisfactory commercial arrangements been negotiated in the summer of 1961, the government would not have recommended British membership of the EEC. A slightly more circumspect view is taken by Sir Roderick Barclay, the key British negotiator. He believes that, by the summer of 1961, the government was interested in something more than a tariff and quota arrangement.[55] All the same, though, he comments that if the EEC had not existed, Britain would not have invented it. As for the main reason for seeking membership, he believes that it was partly economic and partly political. With regard to the strategic argument advanced by the PM, he believes that it was probably deployed for tactical reasons.

Indeed, Macmillan's concern that Britain's exclusion from the European club posed strategic dangers for Western Europe had certainly not existed eight months earlier. In August 1960, the PM had agreed that the best possible solution to Britain's problems was for the Six to join EFTA[56] – an organization which, because of Swiss and Swedish neutrality, eschewed political institutions. Leaving aside the fact that there was not the slightest possibility of the scheme coming to fruition, the fact that Macmillan lent his support to the idea indicates that three months after the failure of the summit, the PM's commitment to establishing a closer political association with the Six for the sake of unifying Western Europe against the threat from the Eastern bloc was less than wholehearted.

The final evidence, perhaps, is that there is no appreciable reason why the Western Alliance should have been deemed to be under more threat of disunity in April 1961 than it had been when the government took the decision to sign the Stockholm Convention in November 1959. What *was* different was that it had gradually become clear in the intervening period that no solution was available with regard to Britain's disadvantageous trading position with the expanding continental economies other than Britain's accession to the Treaty of Rome. Furthermore, after the failure of two British applications to join the EEC, the Western Alliance, despite French 'separatism', was to remain firmly intact. It seems then, that after all the arguments and deliberations, the machinations and manoeuvring, it was an essentially 'manufactured' rationale that set Britain on the long road to full membership of the EEC.

For all this, though, in the opinion of the PM (and no doubt of the privy seal), it was a necessary dissimulation. The structure of cabinet government presented Macmillan with a team of politicians who looked instinctively to preserving their own position both in terms of their departmental responsibilities and their party. Only by presenting them with a cause that would override or at least not conflict with their departmental brief (and that they, in turn, would be able to defend to colleagues and in their constituencies) would the PM be able to secure their support. By lighting on the strategic imperative, Macmillan was assured of the success that had eluded him when, in July 1960, he had concealed his real concern for Britain's industrial future under the all too transparent veil of an unspecified political exigency.

After the approval of the cabinet had been secured, the machinery was swiftly set in motion to ensure that the proposal was put to parliament before the summer recess. In early July all major Commonwealth countries were visited by a senior cabinet minister to allow their representatives to voice their views. Once this had been accomplished, it was considered that the necessary consultations had been held. Macmillan put his government's proposal to parliament on 31 July 1961 – slightly more than one year after Edward Heath had been invited to join the cabinet. It was passed with a substantial majority, which would have come as something of a pleasant surprise to the PM. Only two days before, he had indicated to Heath that, even taking account of the attitude of de Gaulle, 'our chief difficulty at the moment is to carry the House with us'.[57]

But even after the decision had been made by the cabinet, doubts about French attitudes, though largely suppressed, lingered on. Heath dissuaded the PM from contacting de Gaulle again until after the round of Commonwealth visits.[58] In any case, reports were still tantalizingly contradictory. Lord Perth pointed to Jean Monnet's conviction that de Gaulle 'wouldn't and couldn't object' to British membership of the EEC.[59] Assuring Lord Perth that de Gaulle was intent on securing himself a place in history as a European leader who supported European unity, Monnet suggested that the General was 'strongly in favour of our joining the Six'. Maudling, though, drew very different conclusions from a memorandum from M. Wormser. The president of the Board of Trade maintained that on the accumulated evidence, 'it seems to me to be pointless to be talking about any negotiations'.[60] He said to the PM – with more than a little justification – that the French had 'rejected in advance any proposals on the points of vital interest to us'. Even at this late hour he proposed that 'in the light of this wholly negative French attitude' a complete change of tactics should be considered. But Maudling's well-known distaste for the whole EEC venture militated against his advice being seriously considered. At the subsequent meeting of ministers and officials, the agenda formulated by Freddie Bishop allowed no place for Maudling's reservations.[61]

It was on the recommendation of Edward Heath that the French were not told of the government's decision until three days before the PM's announcement to the House of Commons. Heath's private secretary, Michael Wilford, wrote to the PM that 'the statement will come as an unpleasant surprise to the French'.[62] The timing had been chosen, on the grounds that it 'would be consistent with the need for reasonable notice but late enough to prevent the French from raising serious last-minute objections'. Ominously, de Gaulle's immediate reaction to the information was to assert that the achievement of the British government's aims 'would take a long time'.[63] In hindsight, the delay in informing the French of British intentions might have been an unwise decision. If the information had, indeed, come as an unpleasant surprise to de Gaulle, it would have done little to soften his attitude with regard to the British application. The General was known to have a long memory – especially with regard to injuries to his pride and to the pride of France.

Claiming, in the light of the Nassau agreement, that the UK was not ready for membership of the EEC, de Gaulle effectively vetoed the British application at a press conference on 14 January 1963. Negotiations were formally called off on 29 January.[64]

Conclusion

Britain's trade relations with Europe, during the middle years of the Macmillan premiership, became a depressing and a vexing business. Cut adrift from old certainties, ministers struggled to steer a steady course in the wake of unprecedented cooperation between the continental European states. On this matter, far from setting an agenda of policies formulated to appeal to the party and the electorate, the government was forced into devising an acceptable response to the agenda of foreign powers. But this was no wartime situation when a beleaguered nation could be expected to rally behind its leadership; this was a time of peace and relative prosperity when expectations were high and electorates unforgiving. In the light of this, the difficulty that the government faced of reconciling the maintenance of Britain's position as leader of the Commonwealth and player on the world stage with the more mundane demands of securing an economic accommodation with the Six was a well-nigh intractable one. Macmillan's goal when he came to power was to arrive at an agreement with the EEC countries that fell well short of British accession to the Treaty of Rome. In so far as he was forced to revise that objective, his European policy could be said to have failed.

Policy development, throughout the period, was marked by surges of (usually ill-founded) confidence followed by troughs of disillusion and depression. At the end of 1958, thrown into confusion by the failure of the FTA negotiations – upon which the future of Britain's trading relationship with Europe had been staked – the government drifted into an EFTA agreement that provided no answer to either long-term or short-term problems. The inadequacy of the Stockholm Convention was never properly addressed as ministers covered their uncertainty with a veneer of optimism, convincing themselves, as well as each other, that EFTA would provide a bridge between the UK and the EEC.

A year was wasted as ministers and officials gratefully turned their attention away from the wider issue toward the EFTA negotiations. But by Christmas 1959, ministers began again to acknowledge that the underlying question of Britain's relationship with the Six remained unresolved. The key constraints on British European policy – the aspirations of the French, the Commonwealth relationship and the requirements of British industry – were themselves contradictory. Lee's April 1960 initiative caught Macmillan's imagination but the PM's poor handling of the cabinet in July allowed a rare opportunity to slip by. Heath's appointment triggered a fresh round of activity and soon Maudling was effectively side-lined as the new privy seal, with the able assistance of Sir Frank Lee and his colleagues, skilfully engineered a route down which he directed a largely nescient cabinet. Macmillan's visit to Washington in April 1961, though failing to furnish him with the sort of deal for which he had hoped, provided him nevertheless with a rationale for British membership of the EEC which would be hard for his cabinet colleagues to resist. One of the consequences of ministerial preoccupation with squaring the domestic constituency, especially in the latter months, was that no proper consideration was given to the possibility that de Gaulle would be prepared to veto Britain's application for membership of the EEC – this, despite regular insightful reports from Brussels and Paris, and unequivocal statements from the French president himself.

The factors that informed the process of policy development were many and various. They can be roughly divided into five main categories or sources of policy: developments in the international sphere, the domestic response to those external developments, the limitations of the machinery of government, the opportunities for influence arising out of the machinery of government and the aptitude of those charged with the task of policy-making.

The need for a review of existing policy was first instigated by external pressure – notably the activities of the European Six and the attitude of the US administration. Internal pressure, aside perhaps from unofficial contacts between Treasury officials and industrialists, was minimal. With regard to British industry as a whole, while individual directors (especially of the larger companies) recommended British participation in the Common Market, the membership

of the leading association of industrialists – the Federation
of British Industry – was by no means united on the issue.
Indeed, in spite of an initial flurry of activity in 1958–9 which
strengthened the government's own inclination to enter into
the Stockholm Convention, the FBI gave little in the way of
concerted encouragement to the government to take Britain into the EEC. Ministers, then, did not respond to the
pressure of industrialists so much as to a spontaneous *recognition* that the interests of industry were synonymous, in an
advanced industrial economy, with the national interest. The
prime minister did not need industrialists to point out the
difficulties that would lie ahead for Britain if it were to become commercially isolated in Europe.

Demand for action certainly did not emanate either from
the Conservative Party, where the voices of a few eager pro-
ponents of British membership of the EEC were drowned
out by the thundering silence on the issue from the vast
majority. The farming community, who saw much to lose in
the proposition, were unlikely Euro-enthusiasts and the influence of other pressure groups was virtually non-existent.

The weakness of public opinion on the issue is hinted at
by the dearth of opinion polls taken on the question during this crucial period. Such was the lack of interest among
the electorate that, even by 1961, more than half were unsure
whether Britain belonged to EFTA, the EEC or neither.[1] The
reasons for this were three-fold. First, the question was a
complex one – a fact that allowed ministers to imbue the
issue with a 'mystical' quality. It became commonly held that
only the government was competent to tackle it. On this
count, polls indicate that, for the most part, the people were
content to let the government decide, bearing out Douglas
Ashford's observation that 'the British see nothing strange
in leaving the early stages of policy formation and the later
stages of policy implementation almost entirely to a very
few politicians backed up by the Civil Service.'[2] Secondly,
the issue was not (yet) 'emotive' – that is to say, it did not
arouse strong feelings as, for example, would the deployment of British troops abroad. And thirdly, the issue was
managed by the government in such a way as to minimize
public debate.

Outside Downing St and Whitehall, therefore, it appears

that the only sustained encouragement for a British application to join the EEC came from a number of directors from the larger firms and a handful of high-profile journalists; but even their support for a radical initiative was more often than not hedged around with conditions and limitations. In the end, the decision to enter into negotiations with the Six marked the culmination of a series of negotiations and deliberations that had taken place, largely unremarked (outside government circles, at least), over a number of years.

With regard to the policy-making process itself, an important factor in the early period – from the end of 1958 until April 1960 – was the phenomenon of 'groupthink' (referred to in Chapter 5) where like-minded decision-makers became trapped within a circle of ideas that precluded a proper assessment of the situation. Too often during this time the 'psychological environment' of ministers and officials was at odds with the 'operational environment'. Decisions were coloured by wishful thinking rather than by objective assessments. There was an understandable lack of will to confront the problem; the tendency, instead, was to seek ways round it in the vain hope that it would eventually go away. In this respect, there was no interest in the matter as a challenging 'ideal'. The whole European issue, as far as the British administration was concerned, boiled down to one of trade. Perhaps the British were, after all, 'a nation of shopkeepers'; or perhaps, as the evidence suggests, their idealism was inhibited by the repercussions of a glorious past.

From April 1960 onwards, the analytical emphasis changes from the passive to the active. Whereas before this time a major factor in the process of policy development was ministerial susceptibility to groupthink and cognitive dissonance, after Lee's memorandum, government activity was marked much more by the exploitation of the various devices of formal and informal power.

The organizational devices of informal power were effectively utilized by the PM when he took the issue out of the hands of the cabinet and even of the ministerial committee. Here he was resorting to a measure of secrecy and exclusivity allowed for by tradition and precedent. Edward Heath too took advantage of organizational devices by cleverly exploiting his opportunity to speak to the WEU Council of Ministers. Maudling's earlier attempt to exploit his own position as government trade spokesman, at the meeting of Commonwealth finance ministers in September 1960, met with more temporary success.

In this regard too, Sir Frank Lee made the most of his association with Freddie Bishop and his position as chairman of the steering committee (and joint permanent secretary to the Treasury) in order to bring influence to bear on the uppermost echelons of the political administration. Lee also had the advantage of access to relevant information – an important source of power – which he utilized to impressive effect. As a general rule, ministers depended upon officials to provide them with all relevant information. Though Lee and his committee were scrupulous in this regard, they were able through the way they handled that information to direct their political masters down a particular route. Ministers' decisions were necessarily made, for the most part, on the basis of what officials believed was relevant. This circumstance, though, by no means represented a novel departure. As Schumpeter wrote in 1943, 'it is not enough that the bureaucracy should be efficient. . . . It must also be strong enough to guide and, if need be, to instruct the politicians who head the ministries.' 'In order to be able to do this', he argued, 'it must be in a position to evolve principles of its own.'[3]

Presentational devices of informal power were exploited, too, by ministers and officials alike. Ministers used ambiguity in their statements to parliament and the press. The most notable example of this was the foreign secretary's statement to parliament on 25 July 1960. Lloyd's speech was carefully drafted in order to give the impression that it outlined clearly the government's position. In fact, though, it left unanswered most of the questions that the European issue posed. Lee too was particularly skilful at using ambiguity in order to open the way for the implementation of his own objective. He did this more than once with regard to the question of Commonwealth free entry, both when drafting speeches for ministers and, on his own account, in the reports he compiled in his capacity as chairman of the steering committee.

Agenda-setting was another presentational device that the government exploited productively. With regard to the European issue, though, the object was to keep it off the political agenda. The fact that the matter was barely alluded to during the 1959 election and that no organized opposition to the government's stance was initiated until after the PM's statement to parliament in July 1961 is a measure of the government's success. Macmillan's presentation of the issue to the cabinet and to parliament as one of high international politics was another instance of agenda-setting which had important ramifications for policy development.

In respect of the various constraints on the government such as the Commonwealth, British agriculture, British sovereignty and later membership of EFTA, ministers gave the impression – through the very vagueness of their language – that those interests would be protected. The purported safeguards were eventually whittled away, however, through gradual and barely discernible shifts of emphasis and adjustments to the policy agenda. With regard to the key question of Commonwealth preference, the process began with a refusal to contemplate any change to existing arrangements. This was followed by acknowledgement that changes might be necessary, but only if the essence of the arrangement was maintained. When it was found that no further progress was yet being made, the value of the arrangement itself began to be questioned. With this, the preparation of Commonwealth ministers for the abrogation of some Commonwealth preference began. Finally, during the early summer of 1961, Commonwealth ministers were made aware that Commonwealth preference was no longer a priority for the British government. Though even now, public statements were drafted to give the impression that no substantial change of policy had taken place with regard to the Commonwealth relationship.

Perhaps one of the most remarkable examples of the exploitation of informal power was in the fact that there was no discussion of substance in the cabinet on the European issue between 13 July 1960 and 20 April 1961 – a time when British policy with regard to Europe underwent its most material modification. Where the issue was referred to at all in cabinet during this time, it was done under an

apparently unrelated heading on the agenda and usually
took the form of a statement by the privy seal to which no
response – other than acknowledgement – was required.
Heath was exceptionally astute in managing the cabinet
agenda to his own advantage. He prepared his colleagues
for what was to come by making occasional allusions to the
progress he was making, postponing time and again the promised debate until he was sure that all alternatives to his own
plan could be ruled out. This was as much a matter of the
careful use of timing as it was agenda-setting.

Government papers show that informal power which is
made available to ministers and officials through their formal roles, provided a range of devices that were utilized
more or less effectively throughout the period under discussion. It is equally evident, though, that the effective exploitation of this source of power depended wholly upon
the capacity and the willingness of the key players to take
advantage of the opportunities that it accorded them.

In all this, did the decision to apply for membership of
the EEC entail the deliberate frustration of the democratic
process? The ingenuity of ministers and officials was, indeed,
severely tested, but the evidence shows that they employed
no other means to achieve their aims than those made avail
able to them by the British system of democracy. By the
end of 1960, it had become clear to a number of ministers
and officials that Britain was left with no viable option other
than to seek membership of the European trading club. But
agreement to open negotiations was achieved not by instigating a national debate – where it was (rightly) felt that
appeals to sentiment and short-term self-interest would most
likely win the day – but through recourse to political stealth.
The cabinet, as well as parliament, was seen by those closely
involved with the issue as part of the problem. Ministers
were advised on how to handle their colleagues by civil service officials, including the deputy secretary to the cabinet
himself. As the PM and the privy seal, together with (occasionally) the chancellor of the exchequer and the foreign
secretary, firmed up their policy objective, even the ministerial committee that had been appointed to deal with the
issue was not taken into the confidence of the inner grouping. Finally, as already noted, the privy seal, with his speech

to the WEU Council of Ministers, virtually single-handedly set a new course for government policy without any regard to the views of his cabinet colleagues.

The tendency of ministers and officials to exploit their role in the official policy-making machinery for the purposes of their own agenda was inevitable given the nature of the British system of democracy. Ministers were forced, for reasons both of efficiency and political self-preservation, to resort to a variety of 'informal' means to achieve their goals. A problem for ministers, arising out of the adversarial democratic process, was the unvoiced and sometimes subconscious expectation on the part of a largely apathetic electorate that the government would be able to deliver national advantage out of the most unpromising circumstances. With regard to Britain's trading relationships, though, ministers were conscious that there was no prospect of achieving a best-of-all-worlds solution. The aim of ministers least involved was to remain so. The response of those unable to 'let the chalice pass' was to take the European issue behind closed doors and there mull over such possibilities as still existed, away from the public gaze.

The way that the European issue was addressed by the Macmillan government points up the imperfections of the British system of democratic government. It shows too, though, that democratic government cannot be other than an imperfect machine. It was, after all, the very machinery of democracy that made proper debate difficult. The adversarial system and the accountability of politicians to a partially informed electorate, together with the complexity and potentially emotive nature of the issue, militated against openness.

In this respect, policy-making by the Macmillan government was conducted along the lines proposed by Edmund Burke, who argued that the institutions, rules and practices of government should be developed out of circumstances rather than preceding them. Rousseau's notion of a social contract that would require such decisions to be made subject to the general will in order to determine the common good is challenged not only by Schumpeter's doubts as to whether a 'common good' can exist in a capitalist society[4] but also by Rousseau's own admission that 'our will is always for our own good, but we do not always see what that is'.[5]

Macmillan and his colleagues were faced with a problem that had no perfect solution. The evidence shows that they were conscientious in their resolve to develop a European policy that would at the same time serve the national interest and be approved by the majority of the people. That they found it necessary on occasions to employ less than forthright means to achieve their aims reflects the difficulty of reconciling those two goals. It is only necessary to consider the difficulty that the prime minister experienced in presenting the complexities of the issue to his own colleagues to appreciate the reasons why he ruled out promoting a party – let alone a national – debate.

In terms of public involvement in the decision-making process, the way the government handled the European issue – by presenting the people with the answer rather than with the question – was not unusual. In keeping with the British tradition, most of the important decisions that had a foreign policy element were dealt with in a similar manner. British membership of NATO was not the subject of prior popular debate; neither was Britain's role in the WEU. Discussion about the 'British' nuclear deterrent only took place after it had been acquired, and the people's involvement in the Suez debate occurred mainly after the event. Even the 1975 referendum on Europe took place after the commitment to British membership of the EEC had been made.

Whether or not the conduct of policy-making by officials and ministers fell short of the democratic ideal, democracy in its broadest sense was never under threat. The acceptance by parliament of the government's proposal to begin negotiations with the Six would have been followed in due course (had de Gaulle not intervened) by a parliamentary vote on whether or not the UK should accede to the Treaty of Rome. Though it is true that a very few ministers and officials were able to manage the policy-making machinery in order to make their own views prevail, government policy would still have to be tested in parliament before it could be put into effect.[6] So, while it could not be said that the decision to begin negotiations with the Six was reached 'in spite' of the democratic process, it could be said that the decision was reached *in spite of* rather than *through* the utilization of the provisions of cabinet government. The nature and timing of policy development was determined in the end by the conjunction of the machinery of government with the capabilities of the particular officials and politicians who administered it.

The coming together of particular personalities and particular circumstances has provided historians with an endless source of conjecture and controversy. All but the most fervent determinist would agree, though, that it is impossible to tell whether or not the outcome would have been the same had the personalities involved been different. Insight may be gained only by pointing up the contributions and errors of particular individuals or groups of individuals while avoiding, where possible, the temptation to speculate on how it might have been otherwise.

It is of some consequence that, at this potentially epochmaking moment of British history, the government was not fortunate in the personalities with which it was fated to deal. Dr Adenauer was sick and, according to some reports, tending towards feeblemindedness. The motives of de Gaulle, who remained for the most part detached and aloof, were not always easy to gauge, while M. Wormser was clever, manipulative and teasingly inconsistent. Professor Hallstein remained defensive and, for the most part, unyielding. Even the friendship and goodwill of Professor Erhard was a mixed blessing. His enthusiasm, far from engendering an atmosphere of confidence and understanding, gave rise more often to ill-will and confusion. And where, in happier times, Britain might have been able to rely upon the goodwill of the US State Department, Douglas Dillon had no particular sympathy for or empathy with post-Suez Britain, and as a result was apt to be uncompromising and insensitive with regard to Britain's problems.

At home, in the government departments, it is evident that while officials in the FO were, on the whole, in advance of the rest on the European question, Sir Frank Lee, in the Treasury was better placed, in the spring of 1960, to influence policy development. The key committees were dominated by Treasury officials. The role of the BOT is less certain. Opinion in that department was split and the result was that BOT reports reflected more the opinion of the particular contributor(s) than that of the department as a whole. The upshot of the lack of unity in the BOT was that no initiatives were forthcoming from the government department that should, perhaps, have led opinion in respect of Britain's trading relationships. After July 1960 the dissent that might have been expected from departments such as the MAG and the CRO was muted, to some extent, by the appointment of ministers who were broadly in favour of a radical solution with regard to Europe.

Despite differences within and between the departments, the evidence points to the fact that it was officials rather than politicians who instigated the change of orientation, which found its eventual fulfilment in British membership of the EEC. The extent to which officials such as Sir Frank Lee and Freddie Bishop were able, through the exploitation of their respective roles, to initiate changes in the broad sweep rather than, as might have been expected, in the finer details of British policy is particularly worthy of note.

It has already been suggested that Edward Heath played a pivotal role. When, in July 1960, he was given special responsibility for Britain's relationship with Europe, Heath began to tip the balance in favour of a new outlook almost at once. But his contribution should not be viewed in isolation from that of Lee. Without Lee's initial courage and clarity of vision, Heath would have had no foundation upon which to build.

Macmillan's conversion to 'Europe' is difficult to pin down. He was undoubtedly influenced by Lee's April 1960 memorandum, though the failure of the May summit did not (as might have been expected in the light of his later pronouncements) nudge him any further toward British participation in the integration of Western Europe. On the contrary, his immediate response was to look for ways of exploiting the new international uncertainty to obtain a satisfactory compromise from the Six that fell some way short of that objective. Nevertheless, by now Macmillan's mind was no longer closed to the idea of British membership of the EEC.

The setback of the July 1960 cabinet meeting, though, plunged him, once again, into indecision. He commented later that 'it was, after all, asking a great deal of the Conservative Party, so long and so intimately linked with the ideal of Empire, to accept the changed situation'.[7] Three months later he was looking favourably on a proposal (which never had the slightest chance of success) that the Six should join EFTA. Macmillan certainly did not feel strongly enough about British membership of the EEC to risk his own position by openly promoting the idea himself (not, that is, until he judged in April 1961 that he would be able to carry his colleagues with him).

By Christmas 1960, Macmillan's reflections indicated that he was still not wholly convinced that membership of the EEC was the only answer to Britain's problems. As might have been expected of a true pragmatist, Macmillan's enthusiasm for the idea grew and declined in almost exact proportion to the possibility of the proposal finding acceptance. Once he had lighted upon the strategic rationale (to buttress the economic imperative) though, Macmillan was confident of carrying the cabinet in the direction that he had, by then, come to regard as the least bad option.

Macmillan, then, was no driving force on Europe. In this regard, it is worth noting that his policy from the very outset was coloured more by necessity than by enthusiasm. Britain, under Macmillan's leadership, did not stride purposefully towards Europe, it was rather driven in that direction by an ever-worsening economic chill. Whereas the EEC was instituted by France, Germany and the rest primarily for political/strategic reasons, Britain's application to join was predicated mainly upon commercial considerations. It is this dichotomy of purpose between Britain and the rest that set Britain apart from the prime movers of European unity and which goes some way towards explaining British difficulties in coming to terms with the idea of political union in Europe even today.

On 16 September 1960 Macmillan wrote to his private secretary: 'we are a country to whom nothing else matters except our export trade. . . . Our only hope of an agreement on Sixes and Sevens . . . is by a political situation arising which brings about the economic solution.'[8] Though his political ambitions developed in line with economic exigency during the winter of 1960/1, this memorandum summarizes, more accurately than any of his public pronouncements, Macmillan's true priority in seeking a solution to the European problem. Although the issue became *politicized* over time – and even took on political/strategic overtones – the exigency, as far as Macmillan was concerned, was always an economic one.

His failure to bring government policy to fruition, however devastating, was not absolute. As Horne points out, 'Macmillan had pointed the way; he set Britain on a new course from which there could now be no turning back, and he had placed a foot in the European door which even Gaullist France could not keep closed for ever.'[9]

Could the whole process have been done better? Given the constraints of human fallibility, the British system of government, the prevailing external circumstances and the intractable contradiction between the government's political and commercial goals, it is doubtful that it could. The decision not to participate in the plans of the Six had been made in the context of French and German agreement to enter into negotiations for an all-Europe FTA. In previous post-war negotiations with the continental states, the British line had consistently been validated by subsequent events. For example, there was little regret about the decision not to join the ECSC and British reservations about the EDC plan had proved well founded. Moreover, British confidence that its interests would be attended to by the Six was boosted by the widespread acknowledgement of its leadership of the OEEC. Under those circumstances, the government's confidence in the likelihood of achieving its objective in 1958 could hardly be considered unfounded.

The delay in arriving at the most viable solution was, indeed, costly. Had the government not gone down the road to EFTA, it would have saved a good deal of time which could then have been spent negotiating acceptable terms before the EEC had 'bedded down'. Had the PM handled the cabinet debate in July 1960 more skilfully, he might again have saved a year of prevarication – a year that was crucial to de Gaulle's ability, in January 1963, to withstand the censure of France's EEC partners. But both events occurred in the context of entrenched party and cabinet opinion which would not easily be overcome. These, in any case, are the imponderables of history and it has not been the intention here to dwell on the might-have-beens.

At the time of writing, more than thirty years after these

events took place, a Conservative government remains a long way from achieving party consensus on Europe. In the light of what must, by now, be considered inherent party disunity on the European question, Macmillan's greatest achievement, perhaps, was in holding the Conservative Party together – a feat achieved largely by keeping the issue off the political agenda while working out policy behind closed doors. But that victory was won at a high price. The Conservative Party had avoided a proper debate on an issue that was to remain of central importance to government and of increasing interest to the people over the years to come. The split in the Conservative Party over Europe that was plastered over in 1960 began to be fully exposed only in 1975, by which time it had become deeper and potentially more damaging. Twenty years later it persists.

Afterword

Because the decision to enter into negotiations with the Six effectively drew a line under policy development on the European issue – at least as far as the Macmillan government was concerned – my inquiry too ends there. The negotiators' strenuous efforts – that were complicated not only by the need to balance a number of interests, but also by the opposition of the Labour leadership and by the gradual hardening of public opinion – in the end came to nothing. The twists and turns of the negotiating process are well documented by Miriam Camps and, for those interested in the detail, by copious records housed at the Public Record Office.

A finer point of interest that has emerged from this work – the role played by the European issue in Conservative disunity – has a special relevance for the 1990s. In September 1961, Macmillan identified a divergence of opinion in the Conservative Party between the old Whig, Liberal, tradition and modern Tory paternalism. It is of some significance for the future of the Conservative Party, though, that he did not associate that divergence with the European policy that his government had set in train. Although, in hindsight, the alignment of the Liberal wing of the Conservative Party with Euroscepticism would seem a logical development, there was nothing in the ideological perspective of the early Eurosceptics that would hint at such an association. It is particularly striking that, as one of Edward Heath's keenest opponents over Europe, Maudling was nevertheless a practitioner of consensus politics who came to be regarded as a 'Wet' in Margaret Thatcher's shadow cabinet. The career of Rab Butler – another early Eurosceptic – was also marked more by consensus than by rightist or liberal conviction.

When Macmillan directed Britain towards Europe, his prime objective was to secure Britain's economic future. Confident of a buttress against supranationalism in the person of de Gaulle and still unfamiliar with the already burgeoning

202

ambition of the European Commission, Macmillan had no fears for British sovereignty and no apprehension of the political ramifications of a single European market. The problem for Macmillan's Conservative successors, in developing a broadly acceptable response to European unity, has hinged upon the related questions of British sovereignty and Conservative ideology. Whether this change of emphasis has its roots in the ineluctable development of the European ideal or in the amplification of Whig–Tory divergence of opinion in the Conservative Party, which Macmillan himself identified, or in a combination of the two, must be regarded (as he would say) as a 'matter of judgement'.

Appendix I Some Cabinet Ministers, 1958–61

Agriculture	John Hare	until July 1960
	Christopher Soames	July 1960 onwards
Aviation	Duncan Sandys	from October 1959
	Peter Thorneycroft	July 1960 onwards
Board of Trade	David Eccles	until October 1959
	Reginald Maudling	October 1959 (–Oct. 1961)
Chancellor of Exchequer	Derick Heathcoat Amory	until July 1960
	Selwyn Lloyd	July 1960 onwards
Colonies	A. Lennox-Boyd	until October 1959
	Iain Macleod	October 1959 (–Oct. 1961)
Commonwealth	The Earl of Home	until July 1960
	Duncan Sandys	July 1960 onwards
Defence	Duncan Sandys	until October 1959
	Harold Watkinson	October 1959 onwards
Foreign Secretary	Selwyn Lloyd	until July 1960
	The Earl of Home	July 1960 onwards
Home Secretary	R.A. Butler	throughout
Labour	Iain Macleod	until October 1959
	Edward Heath	October 1959–July 1960
	John Hare	July 1960 onwards
Lord Chancellor	Viscount Kilmuir	throughout
Paymaster General	Reginald Maudling	until October 1959
	Lord Mills	October 1959 (–Oct. 1961)
Privy Seal	R.A. Butler	until October 1959
	Viscount Hailsham	October 1959–July 1960
	Edward Heath	July 1960 onwards
Science	Viscount Hailsham	July 1960 onwards

Appendix II Some Senior Civil Servants, 1958–61

G.H. Baker	Assistant secretary (Cabinet office) until 1960
	UK Delegation to EFTA (1960 onwards)
Sir R.E. Barclay	British ambassador to Denmark (until 1960)
	Adviser on European trade questions and under-secretary of state, FO (1960 onwards)
(Sir) F.A. Bishop	Principal private secretary to PM (until 1959)
	Deputy secretary of the cabinet (1959 onwards)
Sir N. Brook (Lord Normanbrook)	Joint permanent secretary, Treasury (throughout)
Sir H.A. Caccia	British ambassador to Washington (throughout)
(Sir) P. Carey	BOT (until 1960)
	Principal private secretary to president BOT (1960 onwards)
(Sir) K. Christofas	Diplomatic Service, Rome (until 1959)
	Deputy head, British delegation to EEC (1959–61)
Sir A.H. Clarke	British ambassador to Italy (throughout)
(Sir) R.W.B. Clarke	Third secretary, Treasury (throughout)
Sir J. Coulson	Assistant to paymaster general (until 1960)
	British ambassador to Sweden (1960 onwards)
Sir H. Ellis-Rees	Official chairman, OEEC (until 1960, retired)
(Sir) A. France	Third secretary, Treasury (throughout)
F.W. Glaves-Smith	Assistant secretary, Treasury (until 1960)
	Assistant secretary, Cabinet office (1960 onwards)
Sir P.H. Gore-Booth	Deputy under-secretary, FO (until 1960)
	British High Commissioner, India (1960 onwards)
W. Hughes	Under-secretary, BOT (throughout)
(Sir) R.W. Jackling	Assistant under-secretary, FO (throughout)
Sir G. Jebb (Lord Gladwyn)	British ambassador to France (until 1960, retired)
Sir F. Lee	Permanent secretary, BOT (1958–60)
	Joint permanent secretary, Treasury (1960 onwards)
Sir R.M. Makins (Lord Sherfield)	Joint permanent secretary, Treasury (until 1959)
	Chairman, UK Atomic Energy Authority (1960 onwards)
Sir R.R. Powell	Secretary, MOD (until 1960)
	Permanent secretary, BOT (1960 onwards)
J.A. Robinson	First secretary, FO (throughout)

Sir H.A. Rumbold	Assistant under-secretary of state, FO (until 1960) UK representative on Permanent Council of WEU (1960 onwards)
Sir C.E. Steel	British ambassador to Bonn (throughout)
(Sir) E.E. Tomkins	British embassy, Paris (until 1960) Counsellor, FO (1960 onwards)
(Sir) D. Wass	Private secretary to chancellor of the exchequer (1959–61)
(Sir) M. Wilford	Assistant private secretary to Foreign Secretary (1959) Private secretary to the lord privy seal (1960 onwards)
(Sir) P.F. de Zulueta	Private secretary to PM (Overseas Affairs) throughout

Appendix III Cabinet Committees Concerned with Britain's Trading Relationship with Europe

OFFICIALS

	Chairman
EUROPEAN FREE TRADE AREA STEERING GROUP October 1957–December 1959	R.W.B. Clarke
*SUB-COMMITTEE ON CLOSER ECONOMIC ASSOCIATION WITH EUROPE January 1957–March 1960 *became:	A.W. France
EUROPEAN ECONOMIC QUESTIONS (OFFICIAL) COMMITTEE March 1960–September 1961	A.W. France
**EUROPEAN ECONOMIC QUESTIONS OFFICIAL STEERING GROUP December 1958–March 1960 **became:	Sir Roger Makins (Sir Frank Lee from January 1960)
ECONOMIC STEERING (EUROPE) COMMITTEE March 1960–June 1961	Sir Frank Lee

MINISTERS

AD HOC MINISTERIAL COMMITTEE ON EUROPEAN ECONOMIC QUESTIONS December 1958–January 1959	Chancellor of the Exchequer
FREE TRADE AREA COMMITTEE March 1957–October 1959	Prime Minister
COMMITTEE ON EUROPEAN ECONOMIC ASSOCIATION October 1959–August 1961	Prime Minister

Notes

INTRODUCTION

1. For a detailed exploration of the issue of world order in the context of the state system, see H. Bull, *The Anarchical Society* (London: Macmillan, 1985).
2. There were no women in Macmillan's cabinet and only a very few in the higher echelons of the civil service.
3. H. Macmillan, *At the End of the Day, 1961–1963* (London: Macmillan, 1973), p. 37. In this respect, Macmillan saw a division that was to become more marked twenty years later when it made itself felt through a contest for the heart of the party between *Thatcherites* and *Wets*. In the 1990s, the same conflict of ideology has been manifested in the disharmony between so-called *Eurosceptics* and *Europhiles*.
4. See M. Brecher, *The Foreign Policy System of Israel* (London: Oxford University Press, 1972), p. 4.
5. The slowness of the response by the democratic powers to the rise of Nazism and the belated withdrawal of US forces from Vietnam are two notable examples, in the twentieth century, of the apparent inability of democratic governments to react swiftly to events. Schumpeter sums up one of the key problems for the leader of a democracy in directing the affairs of state. He says: 'The prime minister in a democracy might be likened to a horseman who is so fully engrossed in trying to keep in the saddle that he cannot plan his ride.' J.A. Schumpeter, *Capitalism, Socialism and Democracy* (London: Unwin, 1987; first published 1943), p. 287.
6. For a particularly insightful study of the concept of power that has great relevance for this work, see S. Lukes, *Power: A Radical View* (London: Macmillan, 1974).
7. See Sir Ivor Jennings, *Cabinet Government* (London: Cambridge University Press, 1961), particularly chapters V, VIII, IX and XV, for a contemporary account of the distribution of power and the division of responsibility in the British system of government.
8. It could well be argued that the delay in setting up a department in the Foreign Office to deal exclusively with European economic organization is illustrative of the British attitude towards the question of Britain's role in Europe right up to the year before the first application to join the EEC was made.

1 NO EASY SOLUTION

1. Jean Monnet, *Memoirs* (London: Collins, 1978), p. 306.
2. Barzini, *The Impossible Europeans* (London: Weidenfeld & Nicolson, 1983), pp. 58–9.
3. CAB 130/118 Gen 535, 22.6.56.
4. Ibid.
5. See A. Horne, *Macmillan Vol. I, 1894–1965* (London: Macmillan, 1988), p. 314.
6. R.R. James' keynote address at Conference: *'Staying in the Game': Macmillan and Britain's World Role* (Centre for International Studies, University of Cambridge), 7.7.93.
7. Interview with Sir Peter Carey, 6.4.93.
8. Horne, *Macmillan, Vol. I*, p. 323.
9. J. Colville, *The Fringes of Power* (London: Hodder and Stoughton, 1985), p. 649.
10. D. Carlton, *Anthony Eden* (London: Allen Lane, 1981), p. 395.
11. Jean Monnet played a leading role in promoting the ECSC and the ill-fated EDC. In 1956 he became chairman of the Action Committee for the United States of Europe. Paul Henri Spaak was prime minister of Belgium at the outbreak of the Second World War. During the 1950s and 1960s he served in the Belgian ministry of foreign affairs. He was secretary general of NATO, 1957–61. For more on integration theory including *federalism* and *functionalism*, see R.J. Lieber, *Theory and World Politics* (Cambridge, Mass: Winthrop, 1972); and M. Hodges, 'Integration Theory', in T. Taylor (ed.), *Approaches and Theory in International Relations* (London: Longman, 1978).
12. See CAB 129/50 C(52)56, 29.2.52. This was not altogether a justifiable regret since, as Lord Sherfield recalls, Monnet made it quite clear at a meeting with Edwin (later Lord) Plowden and himself that 'if we were not prepared to accept the objective of a federal system in Europe, they didn't want us in' (interview with Lord Sherfield, June 1992).
13. S. Ball, *Staying in the Game* (CIS Cambridge Conference: 7.7.93).
14. CAB 129/82 CP(56)172, 9.7.56.
15. CAB 129/82 CP(56)191, 27.7.56.
16. PREM 11/2133, 11.2.57. Later musings indicate that Macmillan's (optimistically conceived) alternative FTA would have consisted of the UK, the US and the Commonwealth.
17. PREM 11/2133, 18.4.57.
18. Ibid., 15.7.57.
19. CAB 130/123 Gen 580/2, meeting of the ministerial Free Trade Area Committee, 11.7.57.
20. PREM 11/2531, 21.10.57.
21. Ibid., 23.10.57.
22. Ibid., 23.10.57.
23. See J.A. Schumpeter, *Capitalism, Socialism and Democracy* (London: Unwin, 1987), pp. 260–1.

24. See CAB 133/192, minutes of meeting of Commonwealth officials called to discuss the EEC and the proposed FTA, 9.7.57.
25. PREM 11/2531, 6.12.57.
26. Ibid., 6.1.58.
27. See ibid., report from Sir Hugh Ellis Rees at the UK permanent delegation to OEEC in Paris dated 6.3.58.
28. PREM 11/2531, February 1958.
29. CAB 128/32 14 (6), 4.2.58.
30. PREM 11/2531, 17.3.58.
31. CAB 128/32 27 (3), 27.3.58.
32. These 'features' and this relationship were to become the starting point for the EFTA.
33. PREM 11/2531, 27.5.58.
34. FO 371/137276 (WF1053/13), 25.6.58.
35. PREM 11/2315, 24.6.58.
36. PREM 11/2531, 27.5.58.
37. Ibid., 29.6.58.
38. Ibid., 14.7.58.
39. FO 371/137272 (WF/1051/62), 15.10.58.
40. FO 371/137145 (W1122/5), 22.10.58.
41. PREM 11/2532, 25.10.58. The PM wrote originally about the threat of economic 'disaster' (which was crossed through and replaced with 'discrimination'). The original text indicates better the strength of Macmillan's feeling and the urgency with which he had come to view this problem.
42. PREM 11/2532, 31.10.58.
43. Ibid., 3.11.58.
44. CAB 129/95 C229, 3.11.58.
45. PREM 11/2532, 6.11.58.
46. Ibid., 7.11.58.
47. Ibid., 15.11.58.
48. Ibid., 10.11.58.
49. Ibid., 28.11.58. Cutting taken from the *Financial Times*, which the PM drew – with approval – to the attention of the foreign secretary.
50. CAB 128/32 80 (8), 11.11.58.
51. H. Macmillan, *Pointing the Way 1959–1961* (London: Macmillan, 1972), p. 47.
52. Ibid., p. 68.

2   FINDING A WAY FORWARD

1. See M. Brecher, The Foreign Policy System of Israel (Oxford: Oxford University Press, 1972), pp. 3, 4. The *psychological environment*, according to Brecher, is made up of a combination of ideology, historical legacy and personality predispositions, which contribute to and combine with a particular image of the *external environment*.

2. CAB 130/123 Gen 580/10, 21.11.58.
3. CAB 130/123 Gen 580/11, 25.11.58.
4. FO 371/134516 (M611/990), 14.11.58.
5. FO 371/134515 (M611/950), 19.11.60.
6. FO 371/134516 (M611/986), 24.11.58.
7. CAB 130/123, Gen 580/11, 25.11.58.
8. The Portuguese later requested that they should be present at the meeting and were welcomed.
9. See M. Camps, *Britain and the European Community 1955–1963* (London: Oxford University Press, 1964), p. 178.
10. CAB 130/123 Gen 580/8th meeting, 27.11.58.
11. See PREM 11/2532, Cypher from British Embassy, Bonn 2.12.58, and memo from Maudling to the PM, 2.12.58.
12. PM's report to colleagues on ministerial committee. CAB 130/123 Gen 580/9th meeting, 4.12.58.
13. CAB 130/123 Gen 580/9th meeting, 4.12.58.
14. CAB 130/154 Gen 670/1st meeting, 8.12.58.
15. CAB 130/123 Gen 580/10th meeting, 12.12.58.
16. By recognizing the need to curb the power of protectionist agricultural interests to damage the country's broader commercial concerns, Macmillan was following in the footsteps of Disraeli, who came, eventually, to acknowledge that 'protectionism was not only dead but damned'. See R.C.K. Ensor, 'Some Political and Economic Interactions in Late Victorian England', in *Transactions of the Royal Historical Society*, Fourth Series Vol. XXXI, 1949.
17. PREM 11/2826, 9.12.58.
18. Ibid.
19. Ibid., 16.12.58.
20. See M. Camps, *Britain and the European Community 1955 to 1963* (Oxford: Oxford University Press, 1963), pp. 179–81.
21. Ibid., pp. 9–10, 181–2.
22. Bank of England Archive, OV46/24 27C, 38B, & 47A, January 1959. The suggestion was made by David Pitblado in the Treasury. The Bank of England warned against such a move, fearing a deterioration in relations with the Bank of France.
23. J. Fforde, *The Bank of England and Public Policy 1941–1958* (Cambridge: Cambridge University Press, 1992), p. 585.
24. PREM 11/2826, 28.11.58.
25. CAB 130/154 Gen 670/3rd meeting, 22.12.58.
26. This 'abandonment' by the US was a severe blow and was to be even more deeply felt the following year as HMG attempted unsuccessfully to draw some enthusiasm from the US administration for a Six/ Seven agreement.
27. PREM 11/2826, 20.12.58.
28. Ibid., 8.1.59.
29. Ibid., 30.12.58.
30. Ibid., 20.1.59.
31. CAB 130/154 Gen 670/ 4th meeting, 20.1.59.
32. PREM 11/2826, 8.1.59.

3 EFTA: THE LEAST BAD OPTION

1. CAB 128/32 86 (4) cabinet meeting, 18.12.58.
2. R.J. Lieber, *British Politics and European Unity: Parties, Elites and Pressure Groups* (London: University of California Press, 1970), p. 234.
3. The title of this committee refers to the all-Europe FTA that Britain had hoped to negotiate until talks broke down in November 1958, *not* the organization brought into being by the Stockholm Convention.
4. A. Horne, *Macmillan 1957–1986, Vol. II* (London: Macmillan, 1989), p. 75.
5. Interview with Lord Sherfield, June 1992. Monnet admits in his memoirs that before he consulted his British counterparts 'the essential prize had already been won, irrevocably'. He had, indeed, secured the basis for agreement with the Germans before arriving in London. This timing was deliberately planned in order to prevent the British from reconstituting the terms of reference of the Schuman Plan, which he rightly calculated they would otherwise have attempted to do. See J. Monnet, *Memoirs* (London: Collins, 1978), p. 306.
6. PREM 11/2826, 22.1.59.
7. The liaison group was called the Palmer Working Party after its chairman, Sir William Palmer. See Lieber, *British Politics*, pp. 74–80.
8. CAB 130/123 Gen 580/13th meeting, 9.2.59.
9. Ibid.
10. Ibid.
11. Ibid.
12. See M. Camps, *Britain and the European Community 1955 to 1963* (Oxford: Oxford University Press, 1964), p. 183. The UNISCAN idea did not meet with much enthusiasm but no more constructive proposals were put forward. See *Hansard*, House of Commons, 12.2.59.
13. PREM 11/2827, 17.2.59.
14. Ibid.
15. Ibid.
16. CAB 130/156 Gen 671/4, 25.2.59.
17. CAB 130/156 Gen 671/5, 27.2.59.
18. CAB 130/155 Gen 671/4th meeting, 3.3.59.
19. CAB 130/123 Gen 580/14th Meeting, 5.3.59.
20. See CAB 130/124 Gen 580/22, 16.3.59.
21. CAB 130/123 Gen 580/14th meeting, 5.3.59.
22. Ibid.
23. Ibid.
24. See PREM 11/2827, 3.3.59 and 24.3.59.
25. Ibid., 2.4.59.
26. CAB 130/123 Gen 580/16th meeting, 3.4.59.
27. H. Macmillan, *Pointing the Way 1959–1961* (London: Macmillan, 1972), p. 51.
28. Interview with Sir Peter Carey, 6.4.93.
29. Interview with Lord Sherfield, 28.1.93.
30. Interview with Sir Douglas Wass, 1.11.93.
31. Interview with Sir Arnold France, 20.4.93.
32. CAB 130/123 Gen 580/17th meeting, 5.5.59.

33. Ibid.
34. Bank of England Archive OV46/25 1A and 6, June 1959.
35. PREM 11/2827, 6.5.59.
36. CAB 128/33 30 (6), 7.5.59.
37. CAB 130/156 Gen 671/7, 18.3.59.
38. PREM 11/2827, 14.5.59.
39. Ibid., 22.5.59.
40. CAB 130/155 Gen 671/10th meeting, 25.8.59.
41. *The Times*, 18.6.59, quoted by R.L. Pfaltzgraff in 'Great Britain and the European Economic Community: A Study of the Development of British Support for Common Market Membership between 1956 and 1961' (PhD, published by the University of Pennsylvania, 1964), p. 261.
42. FO 371/145644 (WF 1151/2), 22.2.59.

4 'WHAT IS IT WE WANT?'

1. The measure of their success is indicated by Butler and Rose, whose only reference to the issue in their wide-ranging study of the October 1959 election is that 'Britain's relationship with the European Common Market was neglected'. See D.E. Butler and R. Rose, *The British General Election of 1959* (London: Macmillan, 1960), p. 72.
2. This is borne out by the infrequency with which the matter appeared on the cabinet agenda. It is further illustrated by the fact that the issue is barely even alluded to in the memoirs of Lord Butler, who, though he was serving as home secretary at the time and would not therefore have departmental responsibility, was a key member of Macmillan's government. More telling still is the omission of references either to EFTA or to the EEC in D.R. Thorpe's official biography of Selwyn Lloyd. Lloyd served as foreign secretary from 1955 until July 1960, when he became chancellor of the exchequer. Thorpe had access to Lloyd's papers, so the lack of import attached to the European issue was surely his subject's rather than his own. See D.R. Thorpe, *Selwyn Lloyd* (London: Jonathan Cape, 1989).
3. See A. Horne, *Macmillan Vol. II, 1957–1986* (London: Macmillan, 1989), p. 182.
4. See K. Middlemas, *Power, Competition and the State, Vol. I: Britain in Search of Balance* (Basingstoke: Macmillan Press, 1986), ch. 9.
5. PREM 11/2828, 25.7.59.
6. Lord Gladwyn, *The Memoirs of Lord Gladwyn* (London: Weidenfeld & Nicolson, 1972), p. 288.
7. Ibid., pp. 299–301.
8. Ibid., pp. 325, 303.
9. Ibid., chs. 17 and 18, passim.
10. PREM 11/2828, 28.7.59.
11. At this time, European affairs were dealt with in the FO across a number of departments (see Chapter 10).
12. PREM 11/2828, 18.8.59.

13. See FO 371/150264 (M6114/37), 19.2.60.
14. PREM 11/2828, 22.10.59.
15. Writing for the American Council on Foreign Relations, Herter was unequivocal in describing EFTA as a *rival* organization to the EEC, which goes some way to explaining American antipathy to it. See C.A. Herter, *Toward an Atlantic Community* (New York: Harper & Row, 1963), p. 23.
16. PREM 11/2828, 23.10.59.
17. Ibid., 27.11.59.
18. Interview with Sir Douglas Wass, 1.11.93.
19. CAB 130/155 Gen 671/14th meeting, 29.10.59.
20. CAB 134/1818 EQ (59) 1, 26.10.59 & EQ (59) 2nd meeting, 30.10.59.
21. CAB 130/155 Gen 671/16th meeting, 24.11.59.
22. CAB 130/156 Gen 671/26 (Revise), 4.11.49.
23. Despite his change of designation, Bishop remained palpably a member of the PM's team.
24. PREM 11/2828, 25.11.59.
25. Ibid.
26. PREM 11/3132, 29.11.59.
27. Ibid., 30.11.59.
28. CAB 130/157 Gen 671/49, 9.12.59. It is likely that the chancellor of the exchequer also attended this meeting, though this cannot be confirmed.
29. This was the representative body of EFTA and EEC members proposed by the French in the hope that it would satisfy EFTA countries that a forum existed where grievances could be aired.
30. This article was noted for the PM's attention. See PREM 11/3121, 10.12.59.
31. PREM 11/3121, 10.12.59.
32. Ibid.
33. CAB 128/33 63 (3), cabinet meeting, 15.12.59.
34. CAB 129/99 C(59) 188, December 1959.
35. CAB 128/33 63 (3), cabinet meeting, 15.12.59.
36. PREM 11/3132, 20.12.59.
37. Horne, Vol. II, pp. 140-1.
38. PREM 11/3132, 22.12.59.
39. Ibid., 28.12.59.
40. Ibid., 31.12.59.
41. Ibid., 22.12.59.

5 DISSONANCE AND DRIFT

1. I.L. Janis, *Groupthink* (Boston: Houghton Mifflin, 1982), pp. 175, 242-50, passim.
2. Ibid., p. 175.
3. Ibid.
4. CAB 130/157 Gen 671/52, 1.1.60.
5. CAB 128/34 1 (4), cabinet meeting, 4.1.60. (The New Economic

Committee was to comprise all the EEC countries except Luxembourg, all EFTA members except Norway and Austria, the European Commission, Greece, the US and Canada.)

6. See A. Horne, *Macmillan Vol. II, 1957–1986* (London: Macmillan, 1989), pp. 186–99.
7. CAB 130/157 Gen 671/57, 18.1.60.
8. CAB 128/34 2 (7), cabinet meeting, 18.1.60.
9. CAB 129/100 (60) 6, 9.2.60.
10. FO371/150151 (M611/70), 19.1.60.
11. FO371/150154 (M611/95), 28.1.60.
12. FO371/150151 (M611/82), 20.1.60.
13. Bank of England Archive OV46/26 37, 11.1.60.
14. FO371/150154 (M611/97), 18.1.60. An observant official would have noted that this report of a discussion between Maudling and Merchant consisted almost entirely of what the president of the BOT said to the US under-secretary.
15. T172/2142, 25.1.60.
16. CAB 130/155 Gen 671/22nd meeting, 19.1.60.
17. See CAB 134/1819 EQ (60) 1st meeting, 8.1.60.
18. Bank of England Archive OV47/32 4A, 1.4.60.
19. CAB 130/157 Gen 671/64, 3.2.60.
20. FO 371/150264 (M611/22), 3.2.60.
21. CAB 130/155 Gen 671/24th meeting, 4.2.60.
22. Interview with Sir Douglas Wass, 1.11.93.
23. Interview with Sir Roderick Barclay, 5.8.93.
24. Interview with Sir Arnold France, 20.4.93.
25. Interview with Sir Peter Carey, 6.4.93.
26. Interview with Sir Douglas Wass, 1.11.93.
27. There is no evidence to suggest, as Camps claims, that Lee's steering group concluded 'early in the new year' that Britain should seek to join the EEC. See M. Camps, *Britain and the European Community 1955 to 1963* (Oxford: Oxford University Press, 1964), pp. 280–1.
28. CAB 130/155 Gen 671/24th meeting, 4.2.60.
29. CAB 134/1819 EQ (60) 2nd meeting, 9.2.60.
30. Ibid.
31. CAB 130/157 Gen 671/68, 16.2.60.
32. FO 371/150156 (M611/119), 11.2.60.
33. See memorandum to sub-committee CAB 134/1875 ES (EI) (60) 7th meeting, dated 1.3.60 (emphasis added).
34. American consent to set a date for the Trade Committee was conditional on the UK agreeing not to propose an FTA. See FO371/150154 (M611/107), 15.2.60.
35. FO 371/150156 (M611/121), 17.2.60.
36. FO 371/150267 (M6114/89), 3.3.60.
37. Alistair Horne is convinced that many of Macmillan's problems over Europe emanated from his inability 'to square the Tory Party' (letter from Alistair Horne, 9.2.94).
38. PREM 11/3132, 19.2.60.
39. Ibid., 20, 23 and 27 February, 1960.

40. See Horne Vol. II, pp. 197–8.
41. CAB 130/155 Gen 671/28th meeting, 3.3.60.
42. CAB 134/1819 EQ (60) 3rd meeting, 7.3.60.
43. Ibid.
44. Ibid.
45. CAB 130/155 Gen 671/29th meeting, 10.3.60. Information about the decisions of the European Commission came via the FO's delegation in Brussels. See CAB 134/1877 ES (EI) (60) 55, 10.3.60 and addendum, 18.3.60.
46. CAB 130/155 Gen 671/30th meeting, 16.3.60.
47. Ibid.
48. Ibid.
49. CAB 134/1819 EQ (60) 4th meeting, 18.3.60.
50. Ibid.
51. Ibid.
52. FO 371/150154 (M611/108), January 1960.

6   A MOMENTOUS PLAN

1. There is a parallel to be drawn here with the change of direction implemented by Ramsay MacDonald's coalition government when the Disarmament Committee of 1933 became the Rearmament Committee of 1934.
2. See CAB 128/34 22 (1), 1.4.60; CAB 134/1852 ES (E) (60) 3rd meeting, 13.4.60 and CAB 134/1853 ES (E) (60) 21, 1.9.60, p. 8.
3. See CAB 134/1819 EQ (60) 9th meeting, 30.8.60.
4. The exploitation by ministers of linguistic nuances did not come fully to public attention for another 33 years, when it was eloquently described by a former government minister. Giving evidence to the Scott Inquiry into the 'Arms to Iraq affair', in December 1993, Alan Clark said of government guidelines to arms manufacturers, that they were 'imprecise and ... obviously drafted with the objective of flexibility, of elasticity ... a kind of patching which you could wrap around decisions'. Report in *The Guardian*, 14.12.93.
5. See R.J. Lieber, *British Politics and European Unity* (London: University of California Press, 1970), p. 208.
6. A. Horne, *Macmillan Vol. II, 1957–86* (London: Macmillan, 1989), p. 223.
7. Telephone conversation with Lord Perth, 3.2.94.
8. See Horne, pp. 222–3.
9. PREM 11/3133, 17.3.60.
10. Ministers were, nevertheless, always mindful of public opinion with regard to the Commonwealth. Although no significant polls were undertaken on this issue by Gallup during the period in question (which in itself, may suggest that support for the Commonwealth was assumed), a poll taken as late as 1969 indicated that 34 per cent still believed that the Commonwealth was 'the most important to Britain', while only 26 per cent believed that this was true of Europe.

George H. Gallup (General Editor), *The Gallup International Public Opinion Polls, Great Britain, 1937–1975, Vol. II* (New York: Random House, 1976), p. 1036.
11. CAB 134/1823 EQ (O) (60) 4, 21.3.60.
12. PREM 11/3133, 21.3.60.
13. Ibid., 24.3.60.
14. Ibid., 25.3.60.
15. FO371/150269 (M6114/134), 30.3.60.
16. Ibid., 31.3.60.
17. FO371/150269 (M6114/144), 1.4.60.
18. Ibid., 8.4.60.
19. CAB 134/1852 ES (E) (60) 1st meeting, 31.3.60. Attending this meeting were Sir Robert Hall (Treasury), A.W. France (Treasury), H.A.F. Rumbold (CRO), W.L. Gorell-Barnes (CO), Sir Richard Powell (BOT) and E. Roll (MAG). Later meetings were attended by Sir Denis Rickett (Treasury), Sir John Coulson (FO), Sir Paul Gore-Booth (FO) and Sir Roderick Barclay (FO). Miss D.E. Ackroyd (BOT) was also occasionally present.
20. CAB 134/1852 ES (E) (60) 1st meeting, 31.3.60.
21. Ibid.
22. CAB 134/1852 ES (E) (60) 2nd meeting, 6.4.60.
23. CAB 134/1819 EQ (60) 5th meeting, 8.4.60.
24. PREM 11/3133, 8.4.60.
25. CAB 134/1852 ES (E) (60) 3rd meeting, 13.4.60.
26. Ibid. (emphasis added).
27. Ibid.
28. Private information, cabinet official.
29. PREM 11/3133, the cabinet secretary's memorandum to the PM, 22.4.60.
30. PREM 11/3133, Sir Frank Lee's memorandum to the chancellor of the exchequer, 22.4.60. p. 1.
31. Ibid., p. 2.
32. Ibid., p. 3.
33. Ibid., p. 4.
34. Ibid., p. 5.
35. Ibid.
36. Ibid., p. 7.
37. Ibid., p. 8.
38. Ibid.
39. Ibid., p. 9.
40. Ibid.
41. Ibid., p. 10.
42. Ibid.

7 PRESSURE, POLITICS AND PERSUASION

1. The former trade and industry minister, Alan Clark, offered some personal insight into the relationship between the government and

parliament when he gave evidence to the Scott Inquiry. He said of the Houses of Parliament: 'They are a bit of a nuisance, you have to respond and get the machinery going and ministers have an aversion to this unless they are very exhibitionist.' Reported in *The Guardian*, 14.12.93.

2. In the event, Macmillan sought parliamentary approval only for opening negotiations with the Six. Had these negotiations come to fruition, the question would have to have been brought again to the House of Commons.

3. R.J. Lieber, *British Politics and European Unity* (London: University of California Press, 1970), p. 95.

4. R.L. Pfaltzgraff, 'Great Britain and the European Economic Community' (PhD diss. University of Pennsylvania, 1964), p. 268.

5. *The Times*, 21.7.61, quoted by Lieber, p. 96.

6. 'British Industry in Europe' (FBI, 1961), quoted by Pfaltzgraff, p. 270.

7. Lieber, p. 80.

8. Pfaltzgraff, p. 246.

9. See BT11/5783 CRE 30/pt 1/1961, 2.1.61; and Pfaltzgraff, p. 265. The Export Council for Europe procured statistical and tariff information from BOT sources to assist British industrialists. Its aim was to aid the export drive and especially to direct British exporters to the opportunities that existed in Europe.

10. Lieber, p. 97.

11. Interview with Sir Eric Faulkner, 27.11.92.

12. Ibid.

13. Telephone conversation with Sir Alec Cairncross, 5.12.95.

14. Telephone conversation with Lord Perth, 3.2.94.

15. Lieber, p. 207.

16. Pfaltzgraff, p. 119.

17. Lieber, p. 219.

18. BT11/5563 CRE 161/2/1960, memorandum by Betty Ackroyd, 1.6.60.

19. Lieber, p. 219.

20. Gallup, Vol. I, pp. 497, 585.

21. Ibid., p. 666.

22. Lieber, p. 219.

23. In the correspondence between officials and ministers, any allusion to press comment – reflecting either satisfaction or concern – was very rare. Occasionally, cuttings were drawn to ministers' attention, but these were almost invariably concerned with *events* rather than with *comment*.

24. Lieber, p. 219.

25. See Chapter 10.

26. T230/543, 5.5.60.

27. National Institute Economic Review, 1960, p. 7.

28. Ibid., March 1960, p. 49.

29. T230/543, 7.6.60.

30. PREM 11/3133, 20.5.60.

31. Horne, *Macmillan Vol. II, 1957–86* (London: Macmillan, 1989),

p. 226n. There was much disagreement at the Commonwealth Prime Ministers' Conference over the question of South Africa's remaining within the Commonwealth.

32. BBC 1, 6.6.72, quoted by Horne, Vol. II, p. 231.
33. CAB 128/34 32 (2), cabinet meeting, 20.5.60.
34. Interview with Sir Arnold France, 20.4.93.
35. Interview with Sir Roderick Barclay, 5.8.93.
36. Interview with Sir Douglas Wass, 1.11.93.
37. Interview with Sir Roderick Barclay (see also Chapter 10).
38. CAB 134/1820 EQ (60) 26, 24.5.60.
39. CAB 134/1820 EQ (60) 27, 25.5.60.
40. FO371/150283 (M6114/358), 20.5.60.
41. Ibid., 21.5.60.
42. PREM 11/3133, 26.5.60.
43. CAB 134/1819 EQ (60) 8th meeting, 27.5.60.
44. Ibid., p. 1.
45. Ibid., p. 2.
46. Ibid., p. 3.
47. CAB 134/1819 EQ (60) 8th meeting, 27.5.60.
48. The documentation of this exchange ruffled some feathers when it was received in the FO, since not only had the FO not been informed about the meeting in Switzerland (which was attended by senior French officials), but it was evident that the president of the BOT had discussed the matter with his permanent secretary over an open telephone line. See FO371/150287 (M6614/424/G), 2.6.60.

8 THE CABINET SAYS 'NO'

1. PREM 11/3133, 23.6.60.
2. BT11/5563 CRE 161/2/1960, correspondence between 9.6.60 and 16.6.60.
3. PREM 11/3133, 23.6.60.
4. FO371/150362 (M6136/17), 23.6.60.
5. CAB 134/1853 ES (E) (60) 14, 27.6.60, p. 1.
6. Ibid., p. 2.
7. Ibid., p. 3.
8. T230/502, 27.6.60.
9. CAB 134/1853 ES (E) (60) 14, 27.6.60, p. 4.
10. CAB 134/1853 ES (E) (60) 15, 28.6.60.
11. Ibid., question 3.
12. Ibid., questions 6 and 7.
13. Ibid., question 11.
14. Ibid., question 13.
15. Ibid., questions 16–18.
16. BT/5564 CRE 161/3/1960, 28.6.60. Significantly, Andrew did not advise on which option should be taken.
17. CAB 134/1852 ES (E) (60) 9th Meeting, 30.6.60.
18. T230/502, cypher from Ottawa to CRO, 9.6.60. When Duncan Sandys

visited Ottawa on his 'sounding out' tour of the Old Commonwealth in the summer of 1961, the Canadian representatives refused to enter into serious discussions with him. Interview with William Hughes (who accompanied Douglas Sandys), 24.8.94. Maudling's heavy-handedness at this earlier encounter may go some way to explaining the Canadian attitude to Sandys' visit.

19. CAB 134/1853 ES (E) (60)16, 4.7.60.
20. FO371/150288 (M6114/455), 7.7.60.
21. CAB 128/34 41 (1), cabinet meeting, 13.7.60.
22. CAB 129/102 C (60) 107, 6.7.60.
23. CAB 128/34 41 (1), cabinet meeting, 13.7.60, p. 3.
24. Ibid.
25. Ibid.
26. Ibid., p. 4.
27. Interview with Sir Douglas Wass, 1.11.93.
28. CAB 128/34 41 (1), cabinet meeting, 13.7.60, p. 5.
29. Ibid., pp. 5–6. It is not possible to ascertain who made this proposal.
30. CAB 128/34 41 (1), cabinet meeting, 13.7.60, p. 6.
31. FO371/150289 (M6114/472), 18.7.60.
32. Ibid., 20.7.60.
33. FO371/150289 (M6114/473), 20.7.60.
34. Ibid., 21.7.60.
35. See Hansard, House of Commons, 25.7.60, cols. 1099–218 for the full debate.
36. FO371/150290 (M6114/493), 29.7.60 and (M6114/494), 30.7.60.
37. FO371/150290 (M6114/495), 28.7.60. Much the same complaint could be heard in Maastricht, some thirty years later.
38. Letter from Macmillan to Lady Waverley, 15.7.60. Bodleian Library, MS Eng C 4778, Vol. 4, No. 73. For more about Macmillan's correspondence with Lady Waverley, see A. Horne, *Macmillan Vol. II.* (London: Macmillan, 1989), p. 168.
39. See Horne, p. 432.
40. Ibid., p. 240.
41. Interview with Sir Douglas Wass, 1.11.93.
42. Horne, Vol. II, p. 242.
43. M. Camps, *Britain and the European Community* (Oxford: Oxford University Press, 1964), p. 314.
44. Ibid., p. 315. Heath had, in fact, served as minister of labour since the October 1959 election.

9 AT HOME AND ABROAD

1. Interview with Sir Michael Wilford, 3.3.93.
2. The original invitation had been issued to Heathcoat Amory when he was chancellor of the exchequer. His successor, Selwyn Lloyd, declined to go, pleading the pressure of his new role and a visit to Washington at the end of the month. See FO371/150290 (M6114/483), 27.7.60.

3. PREM 11/3131, 13.8.60.
4. Bodleian, MS Eng C 4778, Vol. 4, No. 76, letter dated 16.8.60.
5. See A. Horne, *Macmillan Vol. II* (London: Macmillan, 1989), pp. 110–12, 217.
6. BT11/5566 CRE 161/7/1960. Record of conversation between Herr von Herwarth and Roderick Barclay, 26.9.60.
7. Steel reported in July that while Erhard and others still supported the idea of an FTA, Adenauer now felt that the scheme would weaken the Franco-German entente. Steel told the foreign secretary that despite the fact that Erhard had the confidence of the Central Bank, 'the Chancellor will do what the French do on the issue'. FO371/150363 (M6136/27), 8.7.60.
8. FO371/150283 (M6114/340), 21.5.60.
9. See H. Macmillan, *Pointing the Way* (London: Macmillan, 1972), p. 46. With 'his large face and small mouth' Macmillan recalled, Erhard reminded him of Henry VIII.
10. FO371/150285 (M6114/394), 2.6.60.
11. BT11/5565 CRE 161/6/1960, 12.9.60.
12. Ibid.
13. BT11/5566 CRE 161/7/1960, 26.9.60.
14. Ibid., 2.10.60.
15. FO371/150283 (M6114/329), 16.5.60.
16. T230/502, cypher from Vienna to FO, 24.6.60.
17. FO371/150286 (M6114/412), 16.6.60.
18. CAB 134/1819 EQ (60) 9th meeting, 30.8.60.
19. FO371/150292 (M6114/516), Sir Richard Powell to the Swiss ambassador, 24.8.60.
20. FO371/150292 (M6114/518). A request by G.H. Baker (in Geneva) for more information about the PM's talks in Bonn received short shrift from the FO, 26.8.60. A similar request was made by Sir John Coulson, British Ambassador to Sweden, who had heard nothing for a month and was anxious for guidance. FO371/150294 (M6114/555), 21.9.60.
21. FO371/150365 (M6136/69), 29.8.60.
22. CAB 134/1853 ES (E) (60) 21, 1.9.60.
23. Ibid., p. 2.
24. Ibid., 1.9.60, p. 8.
25. Emphasis added.
26. CAB 134/1853 ES (E) (60) 21, 1.9.60, p. 9.
27. This submission was most probably prepared by Cyril Sanders, who was sympathetic to Maudling's view (see Chapter 10).
28. CAB 134/1853 ES (E) (60) 21, 1.9.60, p. 5.
29. BT11/5565 CRE 161/6/1960, 1.9.60.
30. BT11/5566 CRE 161/7/1960, 12.9.60–26.9.60.
31. PREM 11/3131, 12.9.60.
32. CAB 128/34 50 (3), cabinet meeting, 15.9.60.
33. CAB 134/1853 ES (E) (60) 22 (third revise), 16.9.60.
34. Ibid.
35. CAB 134/1853 ES (E) (60) 24, 13.9.60. The *ad hoc* meeting was

222 *The Macmillan Government and Europe*

planned by the PM to ensure 'that our line for the Commonwealth was coordinated and agreed by all ministers concerned'. Invited to the meeting were: Selwyn Lloyd, a minister from the CRO, Iain Macleod, Reginald Maudling, Edward Heath and Christopher Soames. Rab Butler, while not formally invited, was offered either the opportunity of attending or a private meeting with the PM who was at pains to ensure that he should not be 'made to feel left out'. See note in PREM 11/3131. 6.9.60.

36. CAB 134/1826 EQ (0) (60) 105, 5.10.60.
37. Ibid.
38. Ibid.
39. See report in PREM 11/3131, 20.9.60.
40. CAB 128/34 51 (3), 22.9.60, cabinet meeting.
41. T172/2143, letter from the foreign secretary to the PM, 22.9.60.
42. See BT11/5566 CRE 161/7/1960, letter from the PM to the privy seal, 30.9.60.

10 IN THE DEPARTMENTS

1. Letter from Sir Richard Powell, 15.8.94.
2. T230/502, letter from R.L. Workman to J.A. Barrah, 21.5.60.
3. See, for example, T230/502, 9.5.60 and 20.9.60.
4. T230/502, May/June 1960.
5. Ibid., 1.7.60.
6. Ibid.
7. Bank of England Archive OV47/32 11D, 7.4.60.
8. Ibid., OV/32 26C and 40B, 21.4.60.
9. Ibid., OV/32 23B, 19.4.60.
10. Ibid., OV/32 65, 20.5.60.
11. Ibid., OV/33 36 and 49, 16.6.60.
12. Ibid., OV/35 l00, 26.10.60 and 32, 14.11.60.
13. BT 11/5650 CRE 1942/3, c.24.11.58.
14. Interview with William Hughes, 24.8.94.
15. Letter from Sir Richard Powell, 15.8.94.
16. Interview with Sir Peter Carey, 6.4.93. Sir Peter, who served as principal private secretary to successive presidents of the BOT between 1960 and 1964, had been in favour of a more positive response to the ideas of the Six since the Messina Conference in 1955.
17. Letter from William Hughes, 22.9.94.
18. Interview with William Hughes, 24.8.94.
19. Letter from Sir Richard Powell, 15.8.94.
20. BT11/5563 CRE 161/2 1960, 11.5.60.
21. BT11/5564 CRE 161/3/1960, 21.6.60.
22. BT11/5567 CRE 161/8/1960, 19.10.60.
23. Ibid., memorandum from Ackroyd to Maudling 7.11.60.
24. Interview with William Hughes, 24.8.94.
25. Private information.
26. A. Horne, *Macmillan, Vol. II* (London: Macmillan, 1989), p. 10. See also, pp. 243 and 536.

27. Conversation between Anthony Meyer (FO) and M. Georges Berthoin (deputy to Dr van Kleffens). FO371/150283 (M6114/318), 12.5.60.
28. Letter from Sir Richard Powell, 15.8.94.
29. BT11/5563 CRE 161/2/1960, memorandum from Sir Frank Lee expressing his qualified approval for the suggestion made by a group of Conservative MPs, for an FO minister with special responsibilities for Europe, 1.6.60.
30. FO 371/134516 (M611/975), 26.11.58.
31. FO 371/145644 (WF 1151/6), 9.4.59.
32. Letter from William Hughes, 22.9.94.
33. FO 371/141138 (UEE 1011/55), 2.7.59.
34. Ibid.
35. FO 371/141138 (UEE 1011/68), 10.9.59.
36. Telephone conversation with Sir Edward Tomkins, 26.7.94.
37. FO 371/150149 (M611/23G), 7.1.60.
38. Ibid.
39. Ibid., 8.1.60.
40. Ibid., 12.1.60.
41. FO371/150275 (M6114/225), 22.4.60. Paul Gore-Booth was soon able to make his new perspective count. At the end of May he excised from a speech to be made in the parliamentary foreign affairs debate the comment that 'joining the Common Market is a theoretically perfect solution, but one which we cannot in practice seriously hope to achieve'. FO 371/150162 (M611/219), 27.5.60.
42. FO371/150276 (M6114/238), 25.4.60.
43. FO371/150279 (M6114/278), 11.5.60.
44. Ibid., 11.5.60.
45. Ibid., 13.5.60.
46. Telephone conversation with Sir Edward Tomkins, 26.7.94. The lack of initiatives on the European issue from the FO permanent secretary or from the foreign secretary himself is evident from the documents.
47. FO 371/150363 (M6136/33), 18.7.60.
48. Ibid., 19.7.60.
49. Ibid., 21.7.60.
50. FO371/150364 (M6136/45), 4.8.60.
51. FO371/150164 (M611/262), memorandum by R.W. Jackling, 23.8.60.
52. See FO371/150297 (M6114/620), 20.11.60.
53. F371/150368 (M6136/110), 23.11.60.
54. FO371/150368 (M6136/110), 24.11.60.
55. FO371/150369 (M6136/135), 15.12.60.
56. FO371/150369 (M6136/138), 21.12.60.
57. FO371/158160 (M614/1), 22.12.60 and 28.12.60.
58. Telephone conversation with Sir Edward Tomkins, 26.7.94.

11 EXERCISES IN POWER BROKING

1. PREM 11/3131, 5.10.60. This gloomy prognosis was borne out by the tone of a meeting between M. Wormser and Sir Denis Rickett of the Treasury, FO371/150224 (M619/105), 27.9.60 and later by a

meeting between Gallagher from the FO and M. Deniau of the European Commission, FO371/150295 (M6114/547), 3.10.60.

2. BT11/5566 CRE 161/7/1960, record of meeting between Edward Heath and Couve de Murville, 3.10.60, p. 4.
3. PREM 11/3131, 19.10.60.
4. BT11/5565 CRE 161/6/1960, 20.9.60.
5. Ibid.
6. Interview with Sir Arnold France, 20.4.93.
7. Sir Douglas was evidently not convinced by the reasons that de Gaulle gave. Interview with Sir Douglas Wass, 1.11.93.
8. Interview with Sir Peter Carey, 6.4.93.
9. Interview with Sir Michael Wilford, 3.3.93.
10. Interview with Sir Roderick Barclay, 5.8.93.
11. CAB 134/1853 ES (E) (60) 26, 19.10.60.
12. Ibid.
13. Maudling's statement is an early example of a practice that later became known as being 'economical with the truth'.
14. Interview with Sir Arnold France, 20.4.93.
15. BT11/5566 CRE 161/7/1960, 4.10.60.
16. BT11/5567 CRE 161/8/1960, report of privy seal's speech to Council of EFTA, 11 and 12 October 1960.
17. CAB 134/1820 EQ (60) 36, 26.10.60.
18. CAB 134/1819 EQ (60) 10th meeting, 31.10.60.
19. BT11/5567 CRE 161/8/1960, report from Sir Frank Lee, 9.11.60.
20. BT11/5567 CRE 161/8/1960, 10.11.60.
21. PREM 11/3131, 15.11.60.
22. BT11/5568 CRE 161/9/1960, 22.11.60.
23. PREM 11/3131, 16.11.60.
24. FO371/150368 (M6136/105), report by A.H. Tandy from the UK delegation to the EEC on his conversation with Hallstein. 9.11.60.
25. FO371/150368 (M6136/105), 16.11.60.
26. FO371/150369 (M6136/139), 10.12.60.
27. See Horne, Vol. II, p. 447.
28. PREM 11/3131, November 1960.
29. See, for example, FO371/150296 (M6114/604), 9.11.60.
30. CAB 134/1822 EQ (0) 60, 16th meeting, 17.11.60.
31. BT11/5567 CRE 161/8/1960, 10.11.60.
32. Ibid., 12.11.60.
33. See FO371/150297 (M6114/622), 28.11.60.
34. CAB 134/1827 EQ (0) (60) 142, 7.12.60.
35. PREM 11/3131, 30.11.60.
36. CAB 134/1827 EQ (0) (60) 144, 8.12.60.
37. CAB 134/1853 ES (E) (60) 31, 12.12.60.
38. FO371/150224 (M619/128), 22.12.60.
39. PREM 11/3325, 22.12.60.
40. Ibid., 29.12.60–3.1.61.
41. Ibid., 29.12.60–3.1.61, pp. 2 and 3.
42. Ibid., 29.12.60–3.1.61, pp. 8 and 9.
43. Ibid., 29.12.60–3.1.61, p. 13.

44. Ibid., 29.12.60–3.1.61, p. 16.
45. Ibid., 29.12.60–3.1.61, pp. 17 and 18.
46. Ibid., 29.12.60–3.1.61, pp. 19–24.
47. Ibid., 29.12.60–3.1.61, p. 25.
48. Ibid., 29.12.60–3.1.61, p. 32.
49. Ibid., 11.1.61, memorandum to Sir Norman Brook.
50. PREM 11/3325, 17.1.61. Note by Harold Watkinson, 25.1.61.
51. See FO 371/156719 (DB 1051/3), 15.1.61. I am indebted to the FO Historical Branch, (Library and Records Department) for this information.
52. PREM 11/3553, 14.1.61.
53. PREM 11/3325, 24.1.61.

12 BACK TO THE CABINET

1. PREM 11/3553, record of the meeting between Macmillan and de Gaulle at Rambouillet, 28.1.61.
2. PREM 11/3553, 29.1.61.
3. CAB 128/35 3 (1) cabinet meeting, 31.1.61.
4. PREM 11/3553, 6.2.61.
5. Ibid., 7.2.61.
6. Ibid.
7. Ibid., 7.2.61.
8. Ibid., 8.2.61.
9. Ibid., 13.2.61.
10. Ibid., 13.2.61.
11. Ibid., 14.2.61.
12. CAB 128/35 9 (3) cabinet meeting, 21.2.61.
13. PREM 11/3553, 21.2.61.
14. Ibid., 28.2.61.
15. Record of a meeting in PREM11/3553, 22.2.61–23.2.61.
16. PREM 11/3345, 23.2.61.
17. CAB 128/35 10 (3), cabinet meeting, 28.2.61 (emphasis added).
18. See M. Camps, *Britain and the European Community 1955 to 1963* (Oxford: Oxford University Press, 1964), pp. 330–3.
19. CAB 134/1821 EQ (61) 1st meeting, 2.3.61.
20. Ibid.
21. In his autobiography, Macmillan records that the privy seal was 'acting with the full authority of the Cabinet'. See H. Macmillan, *At the End of the Day* (London: Macmillan, 1973), p. 5. The fact is, though, cabinet ministers were not given the chance to object until *after* the privy seal had made his announcement.
22. CAB 134/1829 EQ (0) (61) 29, 4.3.61, record of Anglo-French talks in London on 27 and 28 February 1961.
23. CAB 134/1854 ES (E) (61) 29, 13.3.61, para. 9.
24. Ibid., para. 20.
25. Ibid., Conclusion (b).
26. FO371/158160 (M614/14), 30.1.61.

27. FO371/158160 (M614/16), 10.2.61.
28. FO371/158162 (M614/44), 10.2.61.
29. FO371/158162 (M614/45), 30.3.61, pp. 6 and 10. The privy seal had to leave the meeting soon after it began and was unable to return until it was nearly over.
30. FO371/158162 (M614/45), 30.3.61, p. 11.
31. Ibid., p. 13.
32. FO371/158161 (M614/21), 20.2.61.
33. PREM 11/3554, 6.4.61. Secretary of State Christian Herter confirmed later (though before de Gaulle's veto) the long-standing American support for British membership of the EEC. He said, a matter of months before the General's veto, that the failure of Britain's application would mean that America's own position 'would become greatly complicated'. See C.A. Herter, *Toward an Atlantic Community* (New York: Harper & Row for the US Council on Foreign Relations, 1963), p. 26.
34. Harold Macmillan's Diaries, quoted in A. Horne, *Macmillan, Vol. II* (London: Macmillan, 1989), p. 295.
35. Ibid.
36. PREM 11/3554, 15.4.61.
37. FO371/158162 (M614/52), 11.4.61. Comment by D.P. Reilly of the FO.
38. FO371/158162 (M614/52), 11.4.61 and 14.11.61.
39. Ibid., 14.11.61.
40. CAB 128/35 (61) 22 (4), cabinet meeting, 20.4.61, p. 4. The only paper that ministers had before them related to the PM's meeting with the US president. The recently prepared paper by the steering committee was not circulated to the cabinet. (I am particularly indebted to the Historical Records Section of the Cabinet Office for furnishing me with a copy of the relevant part of the *Cabinet Conclusions 20.4.60* which are not available to readers at the PRO at the time of writing.)
41. CAB 128/35 (61) 22 (4), cabinet meeting, 20.4.61, p. 5. There are several possible explanations for Maudling's change of heart. The first is that, realizing his cause was now lost and appreciating too after his meeting with Macmillan how strongly the PM felt about the issue, he decided that it was time to refrain from further damage to his political position. The second is that he had privately concluded that the French would not have Britain in and that there was no point in continuing to stand out against a policy that would not, in any case, come to fruition. (He had suggested more than once in the preceding months and years that the French would be unlikely to approve British membership of the EEC.) The third possibility is that he felt he had a better chance of salvaging something of his own position if he remained involved in the negotiations. The answer lies somewhere between these three positions. Maudling was a career politician who had no great personal wealth. At this stage of his career, he literally could not afford to alienate himself from cabinet colleagues. But he was also an astute politician and loyal to his party. Though he would not have gone so far as to sabotage government policy, he would have done his best – in the context of the constraints

of agreed policy – to promote a settlement that *he* judged to be in the national interest.

42. CAB 128/35 (61) 22 (4), cabinet meeting, 20.4.61, p. 5.
43. Ibid., p. 6.
44. Even at this stage, most ministers still felt more comfortable speaking of British *association* with the Six rather than British *membership* of the EEC.
45. CAB 128/35 22 (4), cabinet meeting, 20.4.61, p. 7.
46. CAB 128/35 24 (3), cabinet meeting, 26.4.61, p. 6.
47. Ibid., p. 7.
48. There is no evidence to support this assertion.
49. CAB 128/35 24 (3), cabinet meeting, 26.4.61, p. 8.
50. CAB 128/35 30 (6), cabinet meeting, 6.6.61.
51. Interview with Sir Douglas Wass, 1.11.93.
52. Interview with Sir Michael Wilford, 3.3.93.
53. Interview with Sir Arnold France, 20.4.93.
54. Interview with Geoffrey Baker, 17.3.93.
55. Interview with Sir Roderick Barclay, 5.8.93.
56. CAB 134/1819 EQ (60) 9th meeting, 30.8.60. Gladwyn Jebb was moved to comment that 'if by any chance the idea did find favour for political reasons with the French it would, whatever the economic results might be, necessarily result in the continued political division of Europe'. With no little justification he remarked that 'I have always understood myself that this is what we were against' (BT11/5565 CRE 161/6/1960, 16.9.60).
57. PREM 11/3559, 29.7.61.
58. PREM 11/3556, 14.6.61.
59. Ibid., 29.5.61.
60. PREM 11/3557, 15.6.61.
61. Ibid., 16.6.61.
62. PREM 11/3559, 25.7.61.
63. Ibid., 28.7.61.
64. See Horne, pp. 444–50; Camps, pp. 468–99.

CONCLUSION

1. See R.L. Pfaltzgraff, 'Great Britain and the European Economic Community: A Study of the Development of British Support for Common Market Membership between 1956 and 1961', (PhD diss., University of Pennsylvania, 1964), p. 375.
2. D.E. Ashford, *Policy and Politics in Britain: the Limits of Consensus* (Oxford: Blackwell, 1981), p. 33.
3. J.A. Schumpeter, *Capitalism, Socialism and Democracy* (London: Unwin, 1987), p. 293.
4. Ibid. p. 250.
5. J.-J. Rousseau, *The Social Contract and Discourses* trans. G.D.H. Cole, rev. J.H. Brumfitt and J.C. Hall (London: Dent, 1973), p. 184.
6. Questions relating to the effect on the democratic process of party

patronage and loyalty, cross-party consensus and the role of referendums must be dealt with elsewhere.

7. Macmillan, *At the End of the Day* (London: Macmillan, 1973), p. 5.
8. Memorandum from Macmillan to Tim Bligh, quoted in A. Horne, *Macmillan Vol. II* (London: Macmillan, 1989), p. 257.
9. Horne, p. 451.

Bibliography

PRIMARY SOURCES

The public archives consulted for this work are listed in the footnotes, using the acronyms given by the Public Record Office. These are as follows:

Cabinet Papers (CAB): Cabinet papers and cabinet and cabinet committee minutes.

Prime Minister (PREM).

Departments of State:
Commonwealth Relations Office (CRO)
Foreign Office (FO)
Board of Trade (BT)
Treasury (T).

Non-government Archives and Correspondence:
Bank of England Archive
Correspondence between the Prime Minister and Lady Waverley (Bodleian Library, MS Eng C 4778)
Letter from Sir Richard Powell, 15.8.94
Letter from Viscount Watkinson, 16.11.92
National Institute Economic Review.

SECONDARY SOURCES

Books were published in London unless otherwise specified.

Ashford, D.E., *Policy and Politics in Britain: the Limits of Consensus* (Oxford: Blackwell, 1981).
Barzini, I., *The Impossible Europeans* (Weidenfeld and Nicolson, 1983).
Bell, C. (ed.), *Europe Without Britain* (Melbourne: F.W. Cheshire Pty, 1963).
Beloff, N., *The General Says 'No'* (Harmondsworth: Penguin, 1963).
Brecher, M., *The Foreign Policy System of Israel* (Oxford University Press, 1972).
Bull, H., *The Anarchical Society* (Macmillan, 1985).
Butler, D.E. and Rose, R., *The British General Election of 1959* (Macmillan, 1960).
Camps, M., *Britain and the European Community 1955 to 1963* (Oxford University Press, 1964).
Carlton, D., *Anthony Eden* (Allen Lane, 1981).
Colville, J., *The Fringes of Power* (Hodder and Stoughton, 1985).
Ensor, R.C.K., 'Some Political and Economic Interactions in Late Victorian

230   *The Macmillan Government and Europe*

England'. *Transactions of the Royal Historical Society.* Vol. XXXI, 1949.
Evans, D., *While Britain Slept: The Selling of the Common Market* (Victor Gollancz, 1975).
Fforde, J., *The Bank of England and Public Policy 1941–1958* (Cambridge: Cambridge University Press, 1992).
Gallup, G.H. (general ed.), *The Gallup International Public Opinion Polls, Great Britain, 1937–1975,* Vol. II (New York: Random House, 1976).
Lord Gladwyn, *The Memoirs of Lord Gladwyn* (Weidenfeld and Nicolson, 1972).
Heath, E., *Old World, New Horizons: Britain, the Common Market and the Atlantic Alliance* (Oxford University Press, 1970).
Herter, C.A., *Toward an Atlantic Community* (New York: Harper & Row, 1963).
Horne, A., *Macmillan Vol. I, 1894–1956* (Macmillan, 1988).
Macmillan Vol. II, 1957–1986 (Macmillan, 1989).
Janis, I.L., *Groupthink* (Boston: Houghton Mifflin, 1982).
Jennings, I., *Cabinet Government* (Cambridge University Press, 1961).
Kitzinger, U., *The Challenge of the Common Market* (Oxford: Blackwell, 1962).
Diplomacy and Persuasion: How Britain Joined the Common Market (Thames and Hudson, 1973).
Lieber, R.J., *British Politics and European Unity: Parties, Elites and Pressure Groups* (University of California Press, 1970).
Theory and World Politics (Cambridge, Mass: Winthrop, 1972).
Lukes, S., *Power: A Radical View* (Macmillan, 1974).
Liggett, E., 'Organization for Negotiation: Britain's first attempt to join the European Economic Community, 1961–1963' (MLitt. thesis, University of Glasgow, 1971).
Macmillan, H., *At the End of the Day 1961–1963* (Macmillan, 1973).
Pointing the Way 1959 –961 (Macmillan, 1972).
Maudling, R., *Memoirs* (Sidgwick and Jackson, 1978).
Middlemas, K., *Power, Competition and the State, Vol. I: Britain in Search of Balance* (Basingstoke: Macmillan Press, 1986).
Monnet, J., *Memoirs* (Collins, 1978).
Pfaltzgraff, R.L., 'Great Britain and the European Economic Community: A Study of the Development of British Support for Common Market Membership between 1956 and 1961' (PhD diss, University of Pennsylvania, 1964).
Rousseau, J.-J. *The Social Contract and Discourses,* trans. G.D.H. Cole, rev. J.H. Brumfitt and J.C. Hall (Dent, 1983).
Schumpeter, J.A., *Capitalism, Socialism and Democracy* (Unwin, 1987).
Sked, A. and Cook, C., *Post-War Britain,* 2nd edn (Harmondsworth: Penguin, 1984).
Taylor, T. (ed.), *Approaches and Theory in International Relations* (Longman, 1978).
Thorpe, D.R., *Selwyn Lloyd* (Jonathan Cape, 1989).

INTERVIEWS AND TELEPHONE CONVERSATIONS

Geoffrey Baker (Southampton), 17.3.93.
Sir Roderick Barclay (Latimer, Bucks), 5.8.93.
Sir Alec Cairncross (telephone conversation), 5.12.95.
Sir Peter Carey (London), 6.4.93.
Sir John Coulson (telephone conversation), February 1993.
Sir Eric Faulkner (Ightham, Kent), 27.11.92.
Sir Arnold France (Lingfield, Surrey), 20.4.93.
William Hughes (London), 24.8.94.
Lord Perth (telephone conversation), 3.2.94.
Lord Sherfield (London), June 1992 and 28.1.93.
Sir Edward Tomkins (telephone conversation), 26.7.94.
Sir Douglas Wass (London), 1.11.93.
Sir Michael Wilford (London), 3.3.93.

Index